Teaching towards Democracy with Postmodern and Popular Culture Texts

IMAGINATION AND PRAXIS: CRITICALITY AND CREATIVITY IN EDUCATION AND EDUCATIONAL RESEARCH

VOLUME 5

SERIES EDITORS

Tricia M. Kress
The University of Massachusetts Boston
100 Morrissey Blvd, W-1-77D
Boston, MA 02125, USA

Robert L. Lake
Georgia Southern University
College of Education, Box 8144
Statesboro, GA 30460, USA

SCOPE

Current educational reform rhetoric around the globe repeatedly invokes the language of 21st century learning and innovative thinking while contrarily re-enforcing, through government policy, high stakes testing and international competition, standardization of education that is exceedingly reminiscent of 19th century Taylorism and scientific management. Yet, as the steam engines of educational "progress" continue down an increasingly narrow, linear, and unified track, it is becoming increasingly apparent that the students in our classrooms are inheriting real world problems of economic instability, ecological damage, social inequality, and human suffering. If young people are to address these social problems, they will need to activate complex, interconnected, empathetic and multiple ways of thinking about the ways in which peoples of the world are interconnected as a global community in the living ecosystem of the world. Seeing the world as simultaneously local, global, political, economic, ecological, cultural and interconnected is far removed from the Enlightenment's objectivist and mechanistic legacy that presently saturates the status quo of contemporary schooling. If we are to derail this positivist educational train and teach our students to see and be in the world differently, the educational community needs a serious dose of imagination. The goal of this book series is to assist students, practitioners, leaders, and researchers in looking beyond what they take for granted, questioning the normal, and amplifying our multiplicities of knowing, seeing, being and feeling to, ultimately, envision and create possibilities for positive social and educational change. The books featured in this series will explore ways of seeing, knowing, being, and learning that are frequently excluded in this global climate of standardized practices in the field of education. In particular, they will illuminate the ways in which imagination permeates every aspect of life and helps develop personal and political awareness. Featured works will be written in forms that range from academic to artistic, including original research in traditional scholarly format that addresses unconventional topics (e.g., play, gaming, ecopedagogy, aesthetics), as well as works that approach traditional and unconventional topics in unconventional formats (e.g., graphic novels, fiction, narrative forms, and multi-genre texts). Inspired by the work of Maxine Greene, this series will showcase works that "break through the limits of the conventional" and provoke readers to continue arousing themselves and their students to "begin again" (Greene, *Releasing the Imagination*, 1995, p. 109).

EDITORIAL ADVISORY BOARD

Peter Appelbaum, Arcadia University, Philadelphia, PA, USA
Roslyn Arnold, University of Sydney, AU, Australia
Patty Bode, Ohio State University, Columbus, OH, USA
Cathrene Connery, Ithaca College, Ithaca, NY, USA
Clyde Coreil, New Jersey City University, Jersey City, NJ, USA
Michelle Fine, CUNY Graduate Center, New York, NY, USA
Sandy Grande, Connecticut College, New London, CT, USA
Awad Ibrihim, University of Ottawa, Ottawa, ON, Canada
Wendy Kohli, Fairfield University, Fairfield, CT, USA
Carl Leggo, University of British Columbia, Vancouver, BC, Canada
Pepi Leistyna, University of Massachusetts Boston, MA, USA
Donaldo Macedo, University of Massachusetts Boston, MA, USA
Martha McKenna, Lesley University, Boston, MA, USA
Ernest Morrell, Columbia University, New York, NY, USA
Pauline Sameshima, Lakehead University in Thunder Bay, ON, Canada
Vera John-Steiner, University of New Mexico, Albuquerque, NM, USA

Teaching towards Democracy with Postmodern and Popular Culture Texts

Edited by

Patricia Paugh
The University of Massachusetts Boston, USA

Tricia Kress
The University of Massachusetts Boston, USA

and

Robert Lake
Georgia Southern University, USA

SENSE PUBLISHERS
ROTTERDAM / BOSTON / TAIPEI

A C.I.P. record for this book is available from the Library of Congress.

ISBN 978-94-6209-873-2 (paperback)
ISBN 978-94-6209-874-9 (hardback)
ISBN 978-94-6209-875-6 (e-book)

Published by: Sense Publishers,
P.O. Box 21858, 3001 AW Rotterdam, The Netherlands
https://www.sensepublishers.com/

Cover figure by Tricia Kress

Printed on acid-free paper

All rights reserved © 2014 Sense Publishers

No part of this work may be reproduced, stored in a retrieval system, or transmitted in any form or by any means, electronic, mechanical, photocopying, microfilming, recording or otherwise, without written permission from the Publisher, with the exception of any material supplied specifically for the purpose of being entered and executed on a computer system, for exclusive use by the purchaser of the work.

TABLE OF CONTENTS

Acknowledgements   vii

Introduction   1
Patricia Paugh

1. Adventures in Adaptation: Confronting Texts in a Time of Standardization   7
   P.L. Thomas

2. Neo-Post-Urban-Noir Graphic Novels and Critical Literacy: The Hard Connection   21
   William M. Reynolds

3. Creating Critical Spaces for Young Activists   37
   Lindy L. Johnson, Tobie Bass & Matt Hicks

4. Teaching Students to Think Critically: Using Young Adult Literature in the 21st Century Classroom – *The Watsons Go to Birmingham – 1963*   59
   Tonya Perry

5. Class on Fire: Using the Hunger Games Trilogy to Encourage Social Action   77
   Amber M. Simmons

6. The Postmodern Picture Book: Reimagining Children's Author "ity" as Readers   97
   Patricia Paugh

7. A Source of Self: Exploring Identity and Discourse in Young Adult Novels as Meaningful Text   117
   Kjersti VanSlyke-Briggs & Heather Matthews

8. What Mainstream Centers Cannot Hold: Growing Critical Literacy with Dystopian Fiction   135
   Megan Marshall

9. Exploring the Tensions between Narrative Imagination and Official Knowledge through the *Life of Pi*   151
   Laura Rychly & Robert Lake

TABLE OF CONTENTS

10. "Clankers," "Darwinists," and Criticality: Encouraging Sociological Imagination vis-à-vis Historicity with the Steampunk Novel *Leviathan* 165
    Tricia M. Kress & Patricia Patrissy

11. Science and Fiction: A Polemic on the Role of Imaginative Fiction in Civics and the Economy of Innovation 179
    Justin Patch

12. Enacting a Critical Pedagogy of Popular Culture at the Intersection of Student Writing, Popular Culture and Critical Literacy 201
    Denise Ives & Cara Crandall

13. Shadows of the Past: Historical Interpretation, Propaganda, and the Story of Ender Wiggin 221
    Christopher Andrew Brkich, Tim Barko & Katie Lynn Brkich

14. Critical Hits & Critical Spaces: Roleplaying Games and Their Potential in Developing Critical Literacy and New Literacy Practices 239
    Kevin Smith

About the Contributors 257

ACKNOWLEDGEMENTS

First of all we want to thank all of the contributors to this book. We are keenly aware that you had to take time away from other projects, deadlines, family responsibilities, and so many other commitments to write for this project. We are especially grateful for the patience and cooperation you showed with the extended timeline for this book. We also want to thank Michel Lokhorst at Sense Publishers for your innovative vision of publishing that makes a project like this possible. We also thank Lisa Roe, a doctoral candidate at the University of Massachusetts-Boston for her marvelous help with proofreading and formatting this book for publication. Finally, we wish to thank our family members for the support and understanding showed us while working on this manuscript for many nights, off days and weekends.

PATRICIA PAUGH

INTRODUCTION

The Critical Literacy pedagogy celebrated by this volume is designed to encourage teachers and their students to identify voices relegated to the margins of society, and through literacy, to creatively negotiate visibility and power for those voices within the social discourse. Why is this an important pedagogy for teachers and teacher educators? First, teachers must have tools to address the powerful messages about the reform of public education that convey its purposes as purely economic. President Obama (2014) recently addressed graduates at an award winning technical high school in my home city – Worcester, MA. The central message of his talk promoted an education focused solely on the imperatives of the labor market. The President's words summarized priorities currently supported by both political parties:

> We live in a culture that so often focuses on conflict and controversy and looks at the glass half empty instead of half full. And you're graduating at a time when you'll no longer be competing just with people across town for good jobs, you're going to be competing with the rest of the world.
>
> But when I meet young people like you I am absolutely certain we are not just going to out-compete the rest of the world, we are going to win because of you. Because we are Americans, that's what we do. We don't settle. We out-work. We out-innovate. We out-hustle the competition. (Applause.) And when we do, nobody can beat us.
>
> And that's why I've challenged high schools all across the country to do what you're doing here – better prepare students for the demands of the global economy.

The discourses of federal education policy visible in Obama's message is one of competition in a free market economy. In this post-industrial, technology dependent global marketplace there is a need for workers who possess a different set of skills than those required by the manufacturing economies of the last century. The words above reflect a strong push for reconfiguring public schooling to expedite the preparation of workers for these times. From the current government/corporate perspective this involves reshaping the classroom to more closely resemble the structures and practices of the business community and standardizing education for public school students to fit this model. There is a clear push for STEM (Science, Technology, Engineering & Math) content, a requisite for workers operating in what have become highly data analytic, technically-demanding environments. Such a push can be observed in arguments related to the

Common Core Standards that demand greater inclusion of informational texts related to STEM in the English Language Arts classroom (see Ravitch, 2012a;2012b). Relatedly, there is a diminished emphasis on the fictional novels and narratives that have been the primary focus for literature study. Educators are also urged to organize curriculum to mirror the flattening of the workplace hierarchy – that is, to provide students with experiences working with a team toward a common goal and to compete against other teams in order to "win."

This volume supports a humanizing dimension to education in this age of "econocracy" (Carr & Porfilio, 2011). It aligns with critical pedagogy advocates who argue that the political spaces of globalization are more than a space of domination (Giroux, 2013) and schooling must be more than the training of "homo economicus" (Luke, 2013) or a society where the production of capital is primary. These chapters demonstrate how education design works to embrace broader imperatives beyond simply the training of workers – where social, ethical moral as well as economic factors are central.

Second, in order to effectively participate in today's globalized society, literate citizens must expand their view of what counts as a text (print and beyond) and be able to negotiate the multiplicity of voices and perspectives present within the range of print, digital and hybrid text forms present in their daily as well as their work lives. Again, in a globalized society, an education for democracy is not merely one of assimilation to a common "truth" but an ability to negotiate new ideas at the intersection of multiple perspectives. The authors in this volume are invested in teaching Critical Literacy as part of a broader understanding of New Literacies. They join this movement advocating for a critical literacy for the reasons outlined by Allan Luke (2013) as "… [use of]the technologies of print and other media of communication to analyze, critique, and transform the norms, rule systems, and practices governing the social fields of institutions and everyday life" (p. 21) to achieve what Henry Giroux (2013) calls a "radical democracy" or "a political, social, and ethical referent for rethinking how citizens can be educated to deal with a world made up of different, multiple, and fractured public cultures" (p. 53).

The volume specifically chooses to tap the field of popular culture for examples of forms and content that lend themselves to such productive critique. The inclusion of popular genres in the classroom provide content, as well as language forms and formats where youth can explore and "critically challenge the diverse cultural discourses, practices and popular media they experience in their everyday existence" (Giroux, 2013, p. 44) – what they face as they grow into adulthood in their own communities of peers and adults, as well as what they witness in the world at large. The chapters explore popular culture texts that are both complex and meaningful to youth and their lives. The authors illustrate ways in which a critical teaching of these texts encourages students to experience literacy as an empowering social practice important for full social participation and transformation in today's world. Teachers and teacher educators face a set of choices within a highly visible site of struggle among English Language Arts educators and policy makers. This volume supports teachers who ask:

INTRODUCTION

- What are and should be the intellectual challenges of the English Language Arts classroom?
- What are the various text forms that appear in academic and social lives of today's citizens?
- What are the goals of an intellectually complex literacy curriculum? What texts lend themselves to such a curriculum? What habits of text analysis and navigation enable students to achieve these goals?

These authors, teachers and teacher educators themselves, share a range of conceptual and empirical evidence to demonstrate the power of creating a critical literacy pedagogy using texts found in the popular culture of today's youth. Theoretical models helpful to teaching a critical literacy are explored. Included are typologies such as Morrell's (2004) description of four types of capital (utilitarian, culture, critical, and recontextualized), Jank's (2000) four themes important to critical literacy (access, domination, diversity and design), Barthes (1975) conception of texts of pleasure vs. texts of bliss, Rosenblatt's (1978) transactional theories of text consumption and production, and Luke and Freebody's (1990) Four Resources model, to name a few. Text variations include postmodern picture books, YA (Young Adult) fiction, adult fiction, graphic novels, science fiction, Steampunk fiction, dystopian and fantasy genres, video games, and even students' lived experiences as texts. The critical literacy pedagogies that accompany study of these texts are both complex and hybrid, providing learners with relevant experiences in using literacy as a vehicle for questioning and transforming the world for social good. Students are positioned to use literacy as part of a social community, both real and imagined, in ways that prepare them not only to be 21st century workers but more importantly to be 21st century citizens, innovating and creating new relationships that keep social justice and equity at the forefront. Each chapter supplies not only theoretical and evidence-based support for this work but suggest syllabi, materials, and activities for readers who may be seeking to introduce or extend their own teaching with similar goals in mind.

In this age of collaboration and competition, an intellectually rigorous English Language Arts education must offer students economic benefits, but not without ensuring that society benefits. To his credit, later in the same speech Obama reminded students that they were also expected to participate in the political process:

> I tell you all this not just because you stand to benefit from changes in laws, but because you're going to have to be a part of helping to shape the law. You're going to have to shape public opinion. You're going to have [to] remember everybody who invested in you. You're going to have to remember the experience of being part of this incredible community. And then, when you go out into the world, whether you are a businessperson, or you are in the military, or you are an academic, or a doctor, or whatever it is that you're doing, you're also going to be a citizen. You're also going to be somebody who has a voice in how this country operates. And you've got to push so that others get the same chance you did.

While the majority of those interested in English Language Arts education argue for the humanities as a site for teaching a deep analysis of issues pertinent to a civic or democratic participation, there is a debate between those who advocate for standardization in education and those who advocate for education to be culturally, linguistically and socially responsive. Advocates for the former regard literature study as leading to assimilation into a common, dominant belief system found in the Western Canon (Stotksy, 2012). Following this line of reasoning, close and intellectually rigorous analysis of texts remains focused on the author's message "within" leading to a directly "knowable" and mutually accepted reality (Cervetti, Pardales, & Damico, 2001). In contrast, a critical literacy represents the opportunity to question dominant ideologies and question the power dynamics involved in how those ideologies benefit some but not others, and using literacy to transform inequities that emerge within this process (Cervetti et al., 2001; Janks, 2013). The authors of this volume would interpret Obama's message above as advocating a critical citizenry where students experience literacy practices that support their political involvement in a "radical democracy." The use of popular culture benefits this latter set of educational goals. As chapter author William Reynolds argues, it is popular culture that creates "cracks" in the common sense, providing opportunities for readers to grapple with the complex and critical issues that arise in contemporary times. A critical reading of Obama's message above would support a pedagogy of activism as the means to "shape the law" and the exemplars provided in this volume provide many examples of the effectiveness of a complex critical literacy in achieving habits of mind to accomplish productive social change as part of a rigorous, complex curriculum.

REFERENCES

Barthes, R. (1975). *The pleasure of the text*. Translated by Richard Miller. New York, NY: Hill.
Carr, P., & Porfilio, B. (2011). The Obama education files: Is there hope to stop the neo-liberal agenda in education? *Journal of Inquiry & Action in Education, 4*(1), 1-30.
Cervetti, G., Pardales, M. J., & Damico, J. S. (2001, April). A tale of differences: Comparing the traditions, perspectives, and educational goals of critical reading and critical literacy. *Reading Online, 4*(9). Available from: http://www.readingonline.org/articles/art_index.asp?HREF=/articles/cervetti/index.html
Giroux, H. (2013). Is there a place for cultural studies in colleges of education? In H. Giroux, C. Lankshear, & M. Peters (Eds.), *Counternarratives: Cultural studies and critical pedagogies in postmodern spaces* (pp. 47-58). Florence, KY: Routledge.
Janks, H. (2000). Domination, access, diversity and design: A synthesis for critical literacy education. *Educational Review, 52*(2), 175-186.
Janks, H. (2013). The importance of critical literacy. In J. Pandya (Ed.), *Moving critical literacies forward: A new look at praxis across contexts* (pp. 31-44). Florence, KY: Routledge.
Luke, A. (2013). Defining critical literacy. In J. Pandya (Ed.), *Moving critical literacies forward: A new look at praxis across contexts* (pp. 19-31). Florence, KY: Routledge.
Luke A., & Freebody, P. (1990). Literacies programs: Debates and demands in cultural context. *Prospect: Australian Journal of TESOL, 5*(7), 7-16.
Morrell, E. (2004). *Linking literacy and popular culture*. Norwood, MA: Christopher-Gordon Publishers.

Obama, B. (2014). Remarks by the president at Worcester Technical High School Commencement Ceremony. Retreived online: http://www.whitehouse.gov/photos-and-video/video/2014/06/11/president-obama-speaks-worcester-technical-high-school#transcript

Ravitch, D. (2012). David Coleman clarifies role of fiction in Common Core Standards. http://dianeravitch.net/2012/12/11/david-coleman-clarifies-role-of-fiction-in-common-core-standards/

Ravitch, D. (2012). Sandra Stotsky the leading critic of Common Core. http://dianeravitch.net/2012/12/11/sandra-stotsky-the-leading-critic-of-common-core/

Rosenblatt, L. (1978). *The reader, the text, and the poem: The transactional theory of the literary work.* Carbondale, IL: Carbondale Press.

Stotksy, S. (2012). *The death and resurrection of a coherent literature curriculum: What secondary English teachers can do.* Lanham, MD: Rowman & Littlefield.

P.L. THOMAS

1. ADVENTURES IN ADAPTATION

Confronting Texts in a Time of Standardization

ABSTRACT

Traditional and accountability-era expectations for students at both K-12 and university levels have included prescribed and template approaches to writing as well as narrow text analysis governed by New Criticism and more recent calls for "close reading." This chapter explores incorporating text adaptations as a guiding set of units for honoring student choice in their writing, reading, and text analysis, what Johns (2008) calls "genre awareness." After exploring the need to shift paradigms away from prescriptive literacy to critical literacy and the paradox of choice, the chapter offers a sample adaptation unit grounded in zombie narratives, anchored by Max Brooks's *World War Z*.

Across the US, children are apt to read, or be required to read, a reasonably common curriculum of writing from a loose cannon of literature, among that experience is likely to include Shirley Jackson's "The Lottery" as a chilling example of the power of fictional short stories. However, when Jackson's story first appeared in *The New Yorker* on June 26, 1948, letters swamped the magazine's office:

> [Jackson] said that of all the letters that came in that summer – they eventually numbered more than three hundred, by her count – only thirteen were kind, "and they were mostly from friends." The rest, she wrote with mordant humor, were dominated by three main themes: "bewilderment, speculation, and plain old-fashioned abuse." Readers wanted to know where such lotteries were held, and whether they could go and watch; they threatened to cancel their *New Yorker* subscriptions; they declared the story a piece of trash. (Franklin, 2013, n.p.)

A number of readers, it seems, believed the story to be non-fiction: "The fact that so many readers accepted 'The Lottery' as truthful is less astonishing than it now seems, since at the time *The New Yorker* did not designate its stories as fact or fiction" (Franklin, n.p.).

Fast-forward to Oprah Winfrey selecting James Frey's *A Million Little Pieces*, her book club prompting the work to be a best-seller and Frey, a well-known writer. However, this fame and celebrity would be short-lived since a controversy erupted once Frey was accused of embellishing his life to make the memoir more appealing to readers:

> The discrepancies and Mr. Frey's reported admissions of falsifying details of his life raise questions about the publishing industry's increasing reliance on nonfiction memoirs as a fast track to the best-seller list. It is not at all uncommon to see new books marketed as nonfiction containing notes to readers saying the author has altered the time sequence of events, created composite characters, changed names or otherwise made up details of a memoir. (Wyatt, 2006, n.p.)

Adding to the controversy was information that Frey originally marketed the book as a novel, but was unable to secure a publisher until he designated the work as a memoir.

What do these events around "The Lottery" and *A Million Little Pieces* reveal? Both a popular interest in and misunderstanding about genre, particularly at the intersection of fiction and non-fiction. For the classroom, particularly educators addressing literacy and critical literacy, that interest and enduring confusion are ideal entry points for addressing genre as a mechanism for fostering critical readers and writers. "This is a story of an ongoing search for a genre-based, social constructivist pedagogy for novice academic classrooms," explains Ann M. Johns (2008), her quest paralleling mine (p. 237). Like Johns, I have come to reject the pursuit of "genre acquisition" (traditionally entrenched and perpetuated by a standards-mania now three decades long) and instead to embrace "genre awareness, which is realized in a course designed to assist students in developing the rhetorical flexibility necessary for adapting their socio-cognitive genre knowledge to ever-evolving contexts" (p. 238).

This chapter will explore and confront what counts as "text" by presenting adaptation as a central mechanism for courses dedicated to literacy and the pursuit of democracy and student liberation (Delpit, 2006, 2012; Freire, 1998; Kincheloe, 2004) – and as a rejection of education as a mechanism for control (Deleuze, 1992; Foucault, 1984). The basis for the discussion below draws from a first year seminar course where students pursue guiding questions about text, genre, adaptation, and reading/writing conventions as an avenue to their own growth as writers broadly and academic writers more narrowly.

ADVENTURES IN ADAPTATION

Soon after I joined my university in 2002, preceded by eighteen years of teaching high school English in rural upstate South Carolina, the faculty adopted a new calendar and curriculum; that curricular change included requiring students take two first year seminars, one of which is writing intensive. This new curriculum also included embracing that faculty from across the disciplines – not just the English department – would teach writing-intensive seminars. Since writing instruction is a primary area of my teaching and scholarship, I have taught a writing-intensive seminar each academic year since the fall of 2008.

Those experiences have allowed me to investigate carefully writing instruction, particularly as that intersects with requiring and allowing choice about texts in classroom settings. My writing-intensive first year seminar has evolved to focusing on *adaptation*; we begin by examining Kurt Vonnegut's "Harrison Bergeron" and the film adaptation *2081* (2009). As I have examined before (Thomas, 2012), the film adaptation of Vonnegut's story reveals a serious misreading of Vonnegut, but examining the two works as separate and dialogic works allows students to consider the sanctity of individual works (Vonnegut's intent in the original story) and the problem of adaptation (the film maker's vision built on Vonnegut's story).

As well, this opening activity addresses text-only traditional stories against the conventions of film. Many students have never read a film critically, but also have only confronted text-only short stories in prescribed and narrow contexts (such as applying New Criticism to the text as is common in Advanced Placement courses). Examining Vonnegut's challenging story against the more conventional messages of *2081* also introduces students to issues about how texts position readers; how genre, medium, and mode impact text content; and how creators of text must negotiate either within or against conventions of genre, medium, and mode when drafting purposefully.

Since the first year seminar I teach is writing intensive, I seek opportunities for students to grow as critical readers and writers – which includes increasing their awareness of genre conventions in varying contexts. First, I introduce students to the unique and often artificial conventions guiding expectations for students as readers and writers. This helps students recognize the power dynamics involved in their education during the K-12 education and how those conventions can help and hinder (Scheele, 2004) their success at the university level. We explore how the conventions guiding K-12 expectations for students tend toward compliance, and not critical or independent thinking. Ultimately, we deconstruct New Criticism, literary analysis, and template paradigms for student essays.

This confrontation of normalizing student behavior through mechanistic approaches to text (New Criticism and the literary technique hunt) and prescriptive dynamics surrounding student writing (prompted essays conforming to five-paragraph models) is then placed against, initially, authentic essays. For example, I often share with students essays by Barbara Kingsolver (see *High Tide in Tucson* and *Small Wonder*), focusing on how her essays contrast the expectations for essays students have experienced in high school. A foundational activity asks students to examine several opening paragraphs from ten or so essays by Kingsolver (see Thomas, 2005, pp. 58-59). Instead of structured introductions and overt thesis sentences, students discover that essays open in a variety of ways, primarily seeking to engage and focus the reader. In the Kingsolver samples, for example, we note that she incorporates a wide range of craft in her openings – allusion, wit, literary quotes, hypothetical "you," questions, narrative, misdirection, figurative language, genre manipulation, one-sentence paragraphing, song lyrics, and dialogue.

These opening activities, again, are guided by building student awareness (Johns, 2008) of conventions forming texts so that students can embrace and develop their own critical literacy (Freire, 1998). As students build their awareness of how school essays and school literary analysis promote artificial conventions (when compared to authentic texts, such as Kingsolver's), they begin to reconsider essay forms, genre (as readers and writer), what constitutes *text*, what counts as *reading* (we consider reading film and graphic novels, for example), and how all of their reconsiderations are confronting who has power, why, and how.

From the opening consideration of Vonnegut's story as film and challenging students' perceptions of the essay through Kingsolver's essays, we move to considering how college and scholarly conventions for reading and writing compare to their K-12 experiences and, again, authentic models. One approach to increasing student awareness of college and scholarly conventions is to confront traditional citation style sheets. Students tend to leave high school thoroughly familiar with MLA citations (often having failed to conform to MLA conventions in a number of assignments, but not really understanding MLA style narrowly or citation conventions broadly). For my course, since I teach in the education department, I ask students to use APA as an entry point to reconsidering citation, plagiarism, research, and scholarship. I also ask students to consider the conventional expectations for citation found in journalism (much different than in academia) and to explore the hyperlink-based citation found in the growing online world of writing (which spans and has even created genres).

Related to this last point, I share with students my own work as a public intellectual, my blogging that merges public and scholarly work. Many of my public blog posts incorporate traditional citations, hyperlinks, embedded video, and images. The hybrid forms of genre, mode, medium, and even tone allow students to explore, confront, and challenge narrow expectations for text, scholarship, and citation.

The foundational and introductory activities, all confrontations of conventions and expectations grounded in specific contexts (K-12 schooling, university, authentic settings), are designed to prepare students for the central mechanism driving our adventure with genre – choice. Many students, especially so-called "good" students (Scheele, 2004), struggle when allowed and required to make choices about their learning as well as the artifacts they produce, artifacts they associate almost exclusively with being evaluated, graded. Next, then, I examine the paradox of choice in a writing intensive course seeking genre awareness and autonomy in the students.

THE PARADOX OF CHOICE

Building a course on essential and enduring questions – what makes poetry, poetry? or what makes a comic book, a comic book? – allows teachers and students the opportunity to gain critical awareness of literacy conventions as an avenue to reading and re-reading the world, writing and re-writing the world (Freire, 1998). But the challenging paradox of offering and fostering autonomy through choice in the classroom is that many students have few experiences with choice and balk at choice when offered because they have been conditioned to avoid risk (as a defense mechanism built up within the punitive grading culture of traditional schooling).

However, Zemelman, Daniels, and Hyde (2012) explain: "The idea of gradual release is quite simple: in the most effective lessons, there is a stepwise transfer of responsibility from the teacher to the student" (p. 39). In other words, a purposeful and systematic release of decisions from the teacher and to the student is not only essential for democratic education that honors human agency, but also best practice. Offering and requiring choice with students, nonetheless, remains challenging, in part because students resist choice.

In my writing intensive first year seminar, choice is central to the two largest elements of the course. The first is that students are asked to draft and submit four original essays throughout the semester, all by choice (students determine the content and form/genre the essays take in conferences with me, although they are confined to non-fiction). The second is that students select a major adaptation unit to experience and then share with the class at the end of the course. Both assignments often cause students a great deal of concern about making the *right* choices and how they will be evaluated.

Writing instruction and assignments have historically been trapped within narrow paradigms of inculcating grammatical and stylistic correctness, conforming to artificial five-paragraph-essay templates, and more recently, fulfilling the prescriptions of a scoring rubric (Kohn, 2006; Wilson, 2006, 2007). As a result, in-school writing and students' expectations for writing are powerfully linked to traditional pedagogy and assessment practices (writing being primarily evaluated against grammatical correctness and how well the writing conforms to the five-paragraph template and prescriptive writing prompts). Student writers and real-world writers, then, have very little in common; thus, when my students are asked to transition away from behaving as student writers and toward acting as real writers do, they are resistant and ill equipped to fulfill that opportunity. Thus, the paradox of choice.

To support students as writers with choice, first, drafting and feedback for original writing must be de-graded (Bower & Thomas, 2013). In other words, the drafting process must be *feedback rich* without assigning grades to each draft. Helping students transition to a de-graded writing environment is complicated, however, by those students also having to shift away from prescriptive and prompt-based writing and toward making their own decisions as writers. This problem is compounded by students' weak grasp of genre, form, and writer's purpose. The paradox of choice, then, is that direct instruction is needed in order to help students acquire the awareness necessary for them to be autonomous.

The texts examined in this writing intensive course all serve to support students as developing writers. We ask, What genres and forms do writers choose, especially in scholarly situations? Simultaneously, students are offered multiple and rich opportunities to mine authentic writing samples for the qualities found in effective and excellent writing while comparing and contrasting what conventions guide both popular and academic writing. As noted earlier, we discuss what techniques, craft, and conventions work in Kingsolver and how her essays compare and contrast with expectations for student essays in academia, highlighting the nuances of conventions among the disciplines. Students then choose genres, forms, and content for their own essays, providing a foundation for my guiding their drafts. For example, I offer a mentoring role of asking if and how their drafts fulfill the purposes and forms they are seeking to produce.

One of the key aspects of exposing students to authentic texts and exploring the expectations of scholarly writing as those are bound to different fields is guiding students as they come to recognize the importance of evidence in many genres and writing forms. The use of evidence, then, leads to the necessity for citation style sheets. In this course and within the requirement that students write four original essays, one of which must be research-based and cited, students often have authentic recognitions of the need for evidence and citations; this contrasts with the mechanical and often artificial ways in which research and citations are addressed in high school.

Conferences during the drafting process also include discussions of possible abandonment of essays. Along with genre awareness and coming to embrace choice, students need the authentic option of abandoning an essay, despite that decision creating some tension in a classroom setting since the students remain obligated to produce an essay. Throughout this process, the focus must remain on student choice and purposefulness with the teacher playing the role of authoritative mentor. The choice paradox is also apparent in the adaptation unit assignment in the course that provides opportunities for students to confront rich ideas that may (or may not) serve as inspiration for their essays.

While I will detail below an adaptation unit focusing on zombies at the end of this discussion, students in this course are asked to choose not only their essay topics and forms but also a major adaptation unit that includes a work adapted in one or more genres and/or media. For example, students can choose a work such as *Watchmen*, the graphic novel (itself compiled from a comic book series), that has been adapted into a film. Often I encourage students to seek out works that have multiple adaptations. Several rich texts have multiple adaptations such as the following:

- The HBO series *True Blood* is based on The Sookie Stackhouse novels and has also been adapted into graphic novels.
- Philip K. Dick's *Do Androids Dream of Electric Sheep?* inspired the 1982 film *Blade Runner* and more recently has been adapted into graphic novels that include every word of the original novel. An interesting aspect of these adaptations is that *Blade Runner* also has several film versions, the theatrical run version and a Director's cut that also was surrounded by a good deal of controversy.
- A fascinating adaptation of the film *The American* is based on the novel *A Very Private Gentleman*, which was itself renamed *The American* once the film was released. Both works are strong texts, but the American in each is significantly different and the works share some basic elements but also differ in important ways.

- George R. R. Martin's A Song of Ice and Fire series (popularly known for *A Game of Thrones*) has spurred an HBO series (*Game of Thrones*) and graphic novels. Along with *True Blood*, these works and adaptations also offer opportunities to examine the enduring power of serialized works – often discouraged by teachers because of traditional prejudices against so-called genre fiction although dedication to serialized genre fiction is a common characteristic of avid and advanced readers.
- Suzanne Collin's *The Hunger Games* trilogy is being adapted into film, representing an important renaissance of young adult literature as a mainstream genre (not just for teenagers).
- Several of Franz Kafka's works have been adapted into graphic novels – *Give It Up! and Other Stories*, *The Trial*, and *The Metamorphosis*. Graphic adaptations of literary fiction have often been marginalized as simplistic versions targeting beginning or struggling (such as narrowly labeled "not on grade level") readers – such as Classics Illustrated, which published graphic adaptations from 1941-1971. Confronting that mischaracterization of graphic texts through Kafka allows students to consider genre, medium, and adaptation as windows into normative biases.
- Non-fiction works in multiple media include works by Howard Zinn, whose popular *A People's History of the United States* is adapted as a graphic novel, *A People's History of American Empire*.
- A rich companion to exploring non-fiction adaptations by Zinn is non-fiction works surrounding Malcolm X: *The Autobiography of Malcolm X* (a controversial autobiography co-authored by Alex Haley), *Malcolm X* (Spike Lee's bio-film), *Malcolm X: A Graphic Biography* (Helfer and Burke), and *Malcolm X: A Life of Reinvention* (Manning Marable). Malcolm X represents a powerful avenue to understanding the complex relationship among genre, medium, and truth/Truth. As Marable shows, Malcolm X himself manipulated the image he wanted portrayed, one also made complex by Malcolm X's relationship within the Nation of Islam.
- As a capstone or introductory adaptation unit, the graphic adaptation of Ray Bradbury's *Fahrenheit 451* serves students well since it captures the tensions remaining regarding graphic texts and canonized literary fiction; graphic texts and science fiction pose hurdles for Bradbury's works (see Boxer, 2009), despite Bradbury himself endorsing the graphic adaptation. A provocative entry point for this unit is that comic books are the only texts still allowed in the book-burning dystopia of Bradbury's classic work.

Another alternative related to considering adaptation, genre, medium, and audience is to introduce and encourage students to consider author studies. Several authors have rich bodies of work, including their own discussions of issues related to genre, medium, and purpose. A few authors to consider include the following:
- Margaret Atwood (Thomas, 2007) represents a career of working within and against genre. Her novels often incorporate complex genre conventions, simultaneously embracing and challenging those conventions. Atwood has written often about science fiction, speculative fiction, and dystopian fiction,

including her public disagreement with Le Guin (Thomas, 2013) that serves well as an entry point into Atwood's works often labeled (despite her complaints) as science fiction – *The Handmaid's Tale*, *Oryx and Crake*, *The Year of the Flood*, and *Madd Addam*. As well, Atwood's canon includes novels, short stories, poetry, non-fiction collections (themselves compiling a wide range of essay forms and purposes), and children's books.
- Michael Chabon is a gifted writer of fiction and essays, and his *The Amazing Adventures of Kavalier and Clay* focuses on the history of the comic book industry in the US. Chabon often mentions and writes about his own growth as a reader and writer as that intersects with the comic book universe; as well, his fictional comic book superhero in *Kavalier and Clay* has been adapted into actual graphic novels.
- Possibly one of the most diverse authors to include in an author study is Neil Gaiman, whose work was originally found in comic books and graphic novels but includes children's books, novels, TV script writing, short stories, and a nearly constant genre and medium bending approach to text. For example, reviews of Gaiman's *The Ocean at the End of the Lane* repeatedly confronted Gaiman's intended audience, struggling with the overlapping world of children with adult themes and plots found in most of Gaiman's works.

A course dedicated to supporting student choice remains a paradox since, as the discussion above about students as autonomous readers and writers details, making choices with literacy both requires and creates awareness. Many students have had their writing and reading lives in school mandated and prescribed for them, leaving them ill equipped and often hesitant to make authentic choices. To create successful adventures in genre, teachers must assume the roles of teacher-student and mentor, guiding students as they build their toolboxes as writers and readers in the context of the many tensions that define and reshape genre, text, reading, writing, and medium.

Finally, below, I detail a genre unit built on zombies with the caveat that this unit is best used as a model for students building their own adaptation units by choice or as an introductory unit preceding students choosing their own additional adaptation units. The discussion that follows should serve as a model for the larger concepts instead of the specific texts identified.

ZOMBIES, GENRE, AND ADAPTATION: A UNIT

Broadly, this is a critical literacy unit, seeking ways in which classroom experiences and assignments can foster rich and authentic opportunities for students to grow in their genre (and medium) awareness (Johns, 2008) as purposeful writers and readers. Some guiding question for the unit include the following:
- What are the conventional expectations for zombie narratives? How are zombie narratives impacted by genre (horror, science fiction, dystopian fiction) conventions and medium contexts?

- How do non-fiction genre and medium conventions impact *World War Z* as a novel?
- What are the defining characteristics of the career and writing of Studs Terkel? How does Terkel's work inform an understanding of journalism, history, oral history, and other genres and forms of discourse?
- How do the genre and medium elements in the zombie unit contribute to coming to know the choices and practices necessary for purposeful and authentic composition? How do those lessons inform a student's expectations for writing in academic settings? In settings beyond academia?

Some instructional and class experiences included in this unit are reading a wide variety of texts with attention to writer's craft (texts detailed below and others relevant to the topics, addressing genre awareness, and modeling essay forms and types students may choose for their writing requirements); class discussions led by the teacher and students; and workshop time for students to read, discuss with peers, conference with the teacher, and write. Several set lessons are planned before the unit begins, but individual lessons should also be created during the unit as student artifacts reveal what aspects of learning need to be addressed along with what interests students express for further learning.

The anchor text for this unit is Max Brooks's *World War Z*, which has companion texts that include *The Zombie Survival Guide* and *Recorded Attacks* (graphic novel). A theatrical release of a film adaptation of *World War Z* also appeared during the summer of 2013. A number of related texts can contribute to this unit and include the following:

- An examination of Max Brooks's web site, focusing on how marketing impacts the texts themselves. Students may be encouraged to research the role of marketing and popularity in genre fiction and, specifically, comic books/graphic novels (Thomas, 2010), science fiction (Thomas, 2013), and young adult literature (Garcia, 2013). (See http://www.maxbrookszombieworld.com/).
- Researching film reviews about the film adaptation to consider the conventions for zombie narratives and examine discussions of adaptation: what constitutes "good" adaptations, for example?
- Researching and gathering artifacts of zombie narratives in fiction, film, and comic books/graphic novels – including a consideration of tone and cross-genre elements (such as *Shaun of the Dead*, a zombie parody that requires the audience have awareness of zombie conventions to respond to the satire).
- Researching Studs Terkel in the context of Brooks's comments about the foundational role of Terkel's non-fiction work (such as *The Good War*) for *World War Z*:

MB: Everything comes from something. If there weren't a Studs Terkel and *The Good War*, there wouldn't be a *World War Z*. That inspired me to write *World War Z* much more than any zombie fiction – an oral history of World War II. It was a book I read when I was a teenager and it never left me. I always thought, "Man, I want to write a book like that." For me, a lot of inspiration comes from real life as opposed to other people's fiction.

> I wrote *The Zombie Survival Guide* as a real guidebook. Take out the zombies and it's *How To Survive A Disaster*. The inspiration for *The Zombie Survival Guide* was growing up in Southern California in the 80s with threats of earthquake and nuclear war. Then in the 90s, we had riots, we had fires, we had floods. In LA we're always living on the edge of disaster and the government never seems to show up. (Townsend, 2010, n.p.)

Student outcomes and artifacts along with assessing student learning for this unit should focus, again, on student choice and collaboration. While in the context of my course as part of a first year writing-intensive seminar I have an obligation to require students produce multiple original essays, often within a somewhat narrow expectation for academic writing (and scholarly citations), requirements for the sorts of texts students produce can vary as widely as students can imagine. A few guiding principles, however, can help shape student compositions, artifacts, and assessing genre awareness as well as critical literacy.

First, the major outcomes for which students are responsible should be guided by student choice influenced by teacher feedback. Once the purpose, genre, form, and media students choose are established, the teacher then helps monitor that work against the chosen parameters. This touches on the second key principle – drafting. Students should be required and afforded time to offer multiple drafts of all artifacts, including essays, that receive peer and teacher feedback. Finally, some expectations of public display of artifacts should be included; for example, at the end of the term, I ask students to choose a showcase piece to include on a course blog. One additional note: Consider asking students to produce at least one text in a virtual format, such as a blog, that incorporates text, video, images, and hyperlinks.

STUDENT VOICES AS NEW VOICES IN THE PURSUIT OF GENRE AWARENESS

Literacy practices historically and during the most recent thirty years of accountability have reduced writing and reading to mechanisms for creating compliant students who can produce prescribed texts and who can interpret texts correctly. That traditional and mechanistic paradigm in no way fulfills democratic or liberatory goals for universal public education. One of the strategies within literacy as compliance is to honor some texts and interpretations while marginalizing and silencing other texts and interpretations.

For example, genres such as science fiction and young adult fiction as well as media such as comic books/graphic novels and film have been indirectly and directly discounted by an authoritarian embracing of print-only texts, literary fiction, and with the rise of Common Core standards, certain types of non-fiction. Seeking genre awareness, instead of student compliance, then, is a commitment to student voices as the new voices of the classroom and then society.

The texts and strategies discussed above are one way to re-navigate texts, genre, reading, writing, citations, and response that acknowledges conventions and norms as a basis for each student determining for her/himself what conventions to embrace, what conventions to resist, and when such purposes are effective. In the adventures in genre discussed here, the *interaction* between student and text is honored, instead of honoring a canonized text and a predetermined response *for* the student. *Adventures in genre* is an education done *with* students, whose voices ultimately matter the most.

ADVENTURES IN GENRE: A LISTING OF TEXTS

Short Fiction

"The Lottery," Shirley Jackson
"Harrison Bergeron," Kurt Vonnegut

Memoir, Autobiography, Biography

The Autobiography of Malcolm X, Malcolm X, Alex Haley
Malcolm X: A Life of Reinvention, Manning Marable
A Million Little Pieces, James Frey

Non-fiction

High Tide in Tucson, Small Wonder, Barbara Kingsolver
The Good War, Studs Terkel
A People's History of the United States, Howard Zinn

Film

2081
The American
Blade Runner
The Hunger Games
Malcolm X
Watchmen
World War Z

Graphic Novel

Do Androids Dream of Electric Sheep?
Fahrenheit 451
Game of Thrones
Give It Up! and Other Stories, The Trial, and *The Metamorphosis* (based on Franz Kafka)
Malcolm X: A Graphic Biography
A People's History of American Empire, Howard Zinn
Recorded Attacks
True Blood

Watchmen

TV Mini-series

Game of Thrones
True Blood

Novel

The Handmaid's Tale, Oryx and Crake, The Year of the Flood, Madd Addam, Margaret Atwood
A Very Private Gentleman, Martin Booth
Fahrenheit 451, Ray Bradbury
The Zombie Survival Guide, World War Z, Max Brooks
The Amazing Adventures of Kavalier and Clay, Michael Chabon
The Hunger Games trilogy, Suzanne Collins
Do Androids Dream of Electric Sheep?, Philip K. Dick
The Ocean at the End of the Lane, Neil Gaiman
Sookie Stackhouse Novels/ The Southern Vampire Mysteries, Charlaine Harris
A Song of Fire and Ice series, George R. R. Martin

REFERENCES

Bower, J., & Thomas, P. L. (Eds.). (2013). *De-testing and de-grading schools: Authentic alternatives to accountability and standardization.* New York, NY: Peter Lang.
Boxer, S. (2009, August 17). Is it time to burn this book? *Slate.* Retrieved from http://www.slate.com/articles/arts/books/2009/08/is_it_time_to_burn_this_book.html
Deleuze, G. (1992, Winter). Postscript on the societies of control. October, 59, pp. 3-7. Retrieved May 1, 2013, from https://files.nyu.edu/dnm232/public/deleuze_postcript.pdf
Delpit, L. (2012). *"Multiplication is for white people": Raising expectations for other people's children.* New York, NY: The New Press.
Delpit, L. (2006). *Other people's children: Cultural conflict in the classroom.* New York, NY: The New Press.
Foucault, M. (1984). *The Foucault reader.* Ed. P. Rabinow. New York, NY: Pantheon Books.
Franklin, R. (2013, June 26). "The lottery" letters. *The New Yorker.* Retrieved from http://www.newyorker.com/online/blogs/books/2013/06/the-lottery-letters.html
Freire, P. (1998). *Pedagogy of freedom: Ethics, democracy, and civic courage.* Trans. P. Clarke. New York, NY: Rowman and Littlefield Publishers, Inc.
Garcia, A. (2013). *Young adult literature: Challenging genres.* Boston, MA: Sense Publishers.
Johns, A M. (2008). Genre awareness for the novice academic student: An ongoing quest. *Language Teaching, 41*(2), 237-252.
Kincheloe, J. (2004). *Critical pedagogy primer.* New York, NY: Peter Lang.
Kohn, A. (2006). The trouble with rubrics. *English Journal, 95*(4), 12-15.
Scheele, A. (2004, May 6) The good student trap. *The Washington Post.* Retrieved from http://www.washingtonpost.com/wp-dyn/articles/A50758-2003May13.html
Thomas, P. L. (Ed.). (2013). *Science fiction and speculative fiction: Challenging genres.* Boston, MA: Sense Publishers.

Thomas, P.L. (2012, Fall). Lost in adaptation: Kurt Vonnegut's radical humor in film and print. *Studies in American Humor, 3*(26), 85-101.

Thomas, P. L. (2010). *Comics and graphic novels: Challenging genres.* Boston, MA: Sense Publishers.

Thomas, P. L. (2007). *Reading, learning, teaching Margaret Atwood.* New York, NY: Peter Lang.

Thomas, P. L. (2005). *Reading, learning, teaching Barbara Kingsolver.* New York, NY: Peter Lang.

Townsend, A. (2010, July 20). "It's sense & sensibility & sleestacks now" the Max Brooks interview, Part two. *Time.* Retrieved from http://techland.time.com/2010/07/20/were-doing-sense-sensibility-sleestacks-now-the-max-brooks-interview-part-two/

Wilson, M. (2007). Why I won't be using rubrics to respond to students' writing. *English Journal, 96*(4), 62-66.

Wilson, M. (2006). *Rethinking rubrics in writing assessment.* Portsmouth, NH: Heinemann.

Wyatt, E. (2006, January 10). Best-selling memoir draw scrutiny. *The New York Times.* Retrieved from http://www.nytimes.com/2006/01/10/books/10frey.html

Zemelman, S., Daniels, H., & Hyde, A. (2012). *Best practice: Bringing standards to life in America's classrooms* (4th ed.). Portsmouth, NH: Heinemann.

WILLIAM M. REYNOLDS

2. NEO-POST-URBAN-NOIR GRAPHIC NOVELS AND CRITICAL LITERACY

The Hard Connection

ABSTRACT

This chapter explores issues in critical media literacy centering on a discussion of comic books and graphic novels, particularly *Sin City: The Hard Goodbye* (Miller, 2005). The discussion includes the entanglement of graphic novels within the context of consumer culture and commodification, the questions surrounding the "legitimacy" of such texts, the impact that these artifacts of popular culture have on the identity formation of youth, the reactions of students to the use of graphic novels in the classroom and the exploration of the issues of race, class and gender that are raised as result of the study of graphic novels in the classroom. It does mean that the so-called 'literary canon', the unquestioned 'great tradition' of the 'national literature' has to be recognized as a construct, fashioned by particular people for particular reasons at a certain time (Eagleton, 1983, p. 11).

The theoretical perspective of this study is a combination of critical theory and literary criticism. The serious study of the history, development and reception of graphic novels is enriched by the application of such theoretical perspectives, places them within a 21st century context and makes connections between popular culture, youth and critical pedagogy. Put another way, for radical literacy to come about, the pedagogical should be made more political and the political more pedagogical. In other words, there is a dire need to develop pedagogical practices which bring teachers, parents, and students together around new and more emancipatory visions of community (Giroux in Freire and Macedo, 1987, p. 6).

INTRODUCTION

Night after night I wait for somebody to come and finish me off. After a while I realize it's not going to be as easy as that. I am a monkey wrench stuck in a great big machine and I've caused some damage and it'll take a good long time for the gears to grind me to powder. (Miller, 2005, p. 194)

Reading does not consist merely of decoding the written word of language; rather, it is preceded by and intertwined with knowledge of the world. Language and reality are dynamically interconnected. The understanding attained by critical reading of a text implies perceiving the relationship between text and context. (Freire & Macedo, 1987, p. 29)

When I was twelve, my friend David and I would save up money and take the city bus from our suburban homes into downtown Rochester, New York. This was a monthly trip. We would both save up our allowance money with much anticipation and eagerly head to the magazine counter at Woolworths on Main Street or the magazine shop a few blocks away. Sometimes they wouldn't let us in to the magazine shop because they sold *Playboy* and cigars in that store. We were there to buy the latest issues of *X-men, The Amazing Spiderman, The Incredible Hulk, The Mighty Thor, Captain America, Iron Man* and *Daredevil*. Sometimes we would even buy a DC comic if none of the Marvel issues came out. Apparently we thought we had developed a discriminating taste. Each graphic treasure cost 12 cents. So buying ten comic books didn't cost too much money. I still have over 200 of those very same comic books today (Silver Age comics is the way in which they are identified presently). David and I would get home and see who could read all the issues first. I remember reading about 1960s teenage superhero angst, the greatness of America, superhuman strength, the underhandedness of evil, and the triumph of goodness. They were twentieth century morality tales with characters in spandex.

Comic books were certainly considered low brow culture. Of course, I like popular action movies as well (see Reynolds, 2007). And, at school all my English teachers would frown when I related stories of Captain America fighting the Red Skull. After all comic books were not literature. They were somehow not worthy. I often wonder if those highbrow/ low brow distinctions and attitudes were the spark that lit the flame of my developing critical consciousness. It probably started with my question—Why not? Imagine my surprise when reading, years after undergraduate and graduate school as an English major, *English in America* (1976 updated 1996) by Richard Ohmann and from *Literary Theory: An Introduction* (1983) by Terry Eagleton that literature and the literary canon were constructs.

> But it does mean that the so-called 'literary canon', the unquestioned 'great tradition' of the 'national literature' has to be recognized as a *construct*, fashioned by particular people for particular reasons at a certain time. (Eagleton, 1983, p. 11)

Reading Eagleton in the 1980s changed my perspective on what counts. I have not taken this brief autobiographical detour to justify or rationalize the credibility of graphic novels. I suppose, however, there are still some that would like to participate in that argument. I do want to discuss the issue, however, of the uses of graphic novels for teacher education classrooms and the demonstration of the critical potential of this artifact of popular culture for the critique of the larger socio-economic political context and the ways in which it is a subject worthy of attention. The labeling and dismissing of comic books and graphic novels as low brow is a political maneuver that obfuscates and dismisses their critical potential and effectively keeps them out of the educational process, but not out of the popular imagination. We can observe the interest in graphic novels in bookstores and libraries. Graphic novels have moved into the forefront of popular culture (Weiner, 2004, p. 58).

> Since 2000, the train carrying graphic novels to readers outside the world of comic book specialty shops has moved even more rapidly. The attention and bookshelf space given to a select group of graphic novels by chain bookstores has raised the medium's profile, while reviews, sound bites, and endorsements for literary graphic novels appearing in respected American Publications such as the *New York Times Book Review* continue to raise the cartooning field's status. In France today, one of every five books sold in bookstores is a graphic novel. (Weiner, 2003, p. 59)

To dismiss graphic novels as simply popular pabulum and as inappropriate texts for critical study is a type of political action that extinguishes their potential for emancipatory knowledge.

Despite that many graphic novels are misogynist, violent and contain brutal content, it may be because of those very qualities they should be analyzed to focus on, as Freire discusses, the text and the context. Of course, not only do graphic novels have potentially critical dispositions, and troubling content, they also are enmeshed within the corporate culture of marketing and production. Graphic novels are not to be taken as either the epitome of critical work or the pawn of corporate marketing. They manifest both potentials. Horkheimer and Adorno (1944) confirm this in *Dialectic of the Enlightenment*. Their notion was that even popular cultural productions (low brow) have the potential to create cracks in the everyday "common-sense," taken-for-granted perceptions of everyday life or can demystify some forms of ideological blindness. They also commented, however, on a paradox because graphic novels or any cultural production (since neither Horkheimer nor Adorno comment on specifically on graphic novels) not only have the potential to critique the socio-economic milieu, but also because of their commercial nature can be and usually are co-opted to maintain the very same milieu. Capitalism is recuperative and any artifact or cultural phenomenon that manifests any resistant or critical potential is eventually co-opted/reified for the market's benefit. Graphic novels become objects to be consumed, collected, and traded. Witness the comic book specialty stores (the specialty stores began to emerge in the 1970s (see Weiner, 2004), racks of graphic novels in chain mega-bookstores, thousands of "collectible" comics for sale on eBay, and of course, the Comic Con fest.

Horkheimer and Adorno discuss the recuperative power of the capitalist market.

> Marked differentiations such as those of A and B films, or of stories in magazines in different price ranges, depend not so much on subject matter as on classifying, organizing, and labeling consumers. Something is provided for all so that none may escape; the distinctions are emphasized and extended. The public is catered for with a hierarchical range of mass-produced products of varying quality thus advancing their rule of complete

quantification....Consumers appear as statistics on research organization charts, and divided by income groups into red, green, and blue areas; the technique that is used for any type of propaganda. (Horkheimer & Adorno, 2010)

This notion of the power of the market and consumer culture to counter act the critical potential of any cultural artifact was also discussed by Gilles Deleuze (1995).

Even art has moved away from closed sites and into open circuits of banking. Markets are won by taking control rather than establishing a discipline, by fixing rates rather than by reducing costs by transforming products rather than by specializing production. Corruption takes on a new power. The sales department becomes the business center or 'soul.' (Deleuze, 1995, p. 181)

Graphic novels exist within this duality of potential and product. In an interview with Slavoj Zizek entitled "Capitalism, Marxism and Kung-Fu Panda," (Zizek, 2010) notes that the point is to wake people up, which in this context can mean awareness of the potential of critically reading graphic novels like *Sin City: The Hard Goodbye*. When graphic novels are considered not worthy of serious study based solely upon the excessive violence and graphic sexuality or on some moral high ground, then that very movement away from critical study may be evidence of a type of what Zizek calls a "cheap moralization" (European Graduate School, 2010) that directs us away from the critical, ideological analysis of these cultural artifacts and their potential for producing awareness of our current historical context. Moralizing is a way of dealing with troubling systemic contexts. Zizek uses this notion of moralizing to demonstrate how it has diverted attention in the context of the economic crisis facing global capitalism. Rather than analyzing the deep recession as a systemic problem within late global capitalism, there is a tendency to reduce that analysis to the discussion of a moral collapse with personalities such Bernie Madoff. If only we could reform these types of individuals, our troubles would fade away. This redirects our attention and our critical focus. In the case of graphic novels, the immediate rejections of this form of art based on simplistic "just say no" judgments negate the critical potential of such work. Graphic novels can be dismissed as not worthy of serious study or as not appropriate for certain or all readers. There are legitimate questions about misogyny, violence and so on, but a simple outright cheap dismissal is not productive.

So, the status and function of graphic novels can be placed into this critical postmodern context of potential and problematic. Perhaps, graphic novels occupy or can negotiate a space between potential and problematic. Graphic novels can be characterized as manifesting varying degrees of "accommodation contestation and resistance" (Freire & Macedo, 1987, p. 17). Having briefly explained this multidimensionality of graphic novels, this essay will discuss the historical development of the graphic novel focusing on the work of Frank Miller and in particular his graphic novel *Sin City: The Hard Goodbye*. It will also place graphic novels within the context of critical pedagogy and critical literacy. Graphic novels cover a wide range of types and manifest numerous characteristics. One such type is neo/post-noir graphic novel. *Sin City* manifests the tendency for these types of stories to be morality tales. In this case the anti-hero, who commits multiple murders and horrific acts in the end, is punished. The fact that good triumphs and evil is punished is appealing. In the end all is right with the world again. Barthes discussed the appeal of morality tales in his book, *Mythologies* (1989). He was discussing the phenomenon of wrestling, but his notion of good and evil and wrestling is applicable to *Sin City*.

> In the Ring, and even in the depths of their voluntary ignominy wrestlers remain gods because they are, for a few moments, the key which opens nature, the pure gesture which separates good from evil, and unveils the form of Justice which is at last intelligible. (Barthes, 1989, p. 25)

NEO-NOIR/POST-NOIR

The neo-noir or post-noir graphic novel can be historically situated. Urban-noir is a term that is also used to identify this genre. Neo/Post- Noir is a genre in most cases associated with films – Neo meaning new and noir meaning dark or black. In the case of film it is the dark tendencies of "traditional" film noir with new technology, extreme violence, more explicit sexuality along with contemporary urban issues. Some of the major characteristics of film noir are also present in neo-noir graphic novels as well.

> The primary moods of classic *film noir* were melancholy, alienation, bleakness, disillusionment, disenchantment, pessimism, ambiguity, moral corruption, evil, guilt, desperation and paranoia. (Dirks, 2010, p. 1)

In films, examples of neo/post-noir would be *Pulp Fiction, Fight Club, Se7en,* and the film adaption of *Sin* City. These primary characteristics or moods and the portrayal of the darker side of life are in graphic novels as well. In the case of graphic novels there are the additional characteristics of extreme violence, dangerous cities, femme fatales, and explicit sexuality. When you experience the art of the graphic novels, particularly *Sin City,* the ambiance of the neo-noir film is evident. Even the staccato style speech of film noir is in the graphic novel.

> The night is hot as Hell. Everything sticks. It's a lousy room in a lousy part of a lousy town. (Miller, 2005, p. 10)

> No good trying to sleep. And it's not the street noise or the stench of this nine dollar flop, either, I'm just too excited. I can't ever sleep when I am excited. (Miller, 2005, p. 69)

There is no doubt that this was, in part, inspiration for the development of the film adaption of *Sin City.* Neo/Post-Noir graphic novels are not comic books.

There is one factor that begins to distinguish graphic novels from comic books – this neo-noir affect. The *Sin City* series are not the only books within this genre.

Other writers and artists contribute to this phenomenon. Neo/post-noir graphic novels are not only produced exclusively in black and white, but in color also. *Criminal* by Brubaker and Philips (2009), (color), *Torso/Fortune and Glory* by Bendis (2001), (black and white), *Fell* by Ellis and Templesmith (2007), (color), *The Dark Knight Returns* by Miller (1997), (color), *Desolation Jones* by Ellis and William (2006), (color), *Sleeper* by Brubaker and Philips (2009), (color), *Powers* (2006), (color) by Bendis and Oeming, and *Daredevil* (2007), (color) by Brubaker and Lark are all examples of neo-noir graphic novels (Culbertson, 2008).

The effort to achieve credibility and therefore a broader market for graphic novels involved attempts at distinguishing these novels from comic books. The distinction is emphasized by reference to the episodic nature of comic books. Comic books seldom, if ever, contain a complete story within one issue. Graphic novels, however, contain a complete story. Even though they might be part of a series (e.g., the *Sin City* books), each text can be read separately.

> Graphic novels as I define them are book-length comic books that are meant to be read as one story. This broad term includes collections of stories in genres such as mystery, superhero, or supernatural, that are meant to be read apart from their corresponding on-going comic book storyline; heart-rending works such as Art Spiegelman's *Maus*; and nonfiction pieces such as Joe Sacco's journalistic work, *Palestine*. (Weiner, 2003, p. xi)

The first graphic novel was "*A Contract with God and Other Tenement Stories*" by Will Eisner (1978), "who coined the term while trying to persuade the editors at Bantam Books to publish the book-length comic book. Bantam declined, but the term stuck" (Weiner, 2003, p. 17). Eisner's graphic novel was a series of four short stories concerning working-class Jewish life in New York during the great depression (Weiner, 2003). It was published in 1978 by Baronet books.

Neo/post-noir graphic novels, a genre within the larger genre of graphic novels, initially appeared in the 1990s and continues into the 21st century. They emerged within the historical progression of the comic book. Histories of the comic book industry (Weiner, 2005, Mann, 2002, Bradford, 2001) give detailed portraits of the variations and struggles of the art form. Elaborating a brief history is relevant (see Mann, 2002). Comic books developed from the Sunday comic pages of the major newspapers. Comic books that began to appear in the late 1930s (*Superman # 1*, 1938) were eventually read by kids and adults, along with soldiers in World War II. These comic books focused on war and tales of the weird. They were not censored. So, they portrayed extreme violence, gore, and heroic soldiers and heroes battling evil. As the decade of the 1940s progressed, comic books became more extreme in their depiction of horror and gore. This trend would be halted. A tide of censorship swelled in the 1950s. Apparently communism and comic books made a deadly pair. The 1950s witnessed censorship efforts with experts who raged against the evil influence of comic books on the youth of America. Dr. Fredrick Wertham, a psychiatrist and author of *Seduction of the Innocent* (1954) vehemently attacked the evil effects of comic books.

The real question is this; are comic books good or are they not good? If you want to raise a generation that is half storm troopers and half cannon fodder with a dose of illiteracy then comic books are good in fact they are perfect. (Wertham as cited in Mann, 2002)

Wertham's vociferous attacks in speeches and in his book eventually led to Congressional hearings. The Senate Subcommittee on Juvenile Delinquency met to hear witnesses on the entire comic book question. The hearing lead to the establishment on October 26, 1954 of the Comic Book Code officially designated as the Code of the Comics Magazine Association of America, Inc. Once the code was issued, comic books had to undergo the code's and the censor's scrutiny. Approval was indicated by a seal on the cover of the comic book that read "Approved by the Comics Code Authority." The current discussions of graphic novels and their acceptability were foreshadowed by the code, which forbade words such as horror, terror and weird amongst others from the covers and pages of comic books (Mann, 2002). There were frequent touch-ups on the original artwork/panels of comic books (e.g. whiting out censored material); Cover art was completely changed so it would be less disturbing.

The decade of the 1960s brought the superhero back into the genre. Stan Lee established Marvel Comics, a brand that remains. Marvel is presently not only in the comic book business but produces films that are adaptations of those same heroes from *Blade* to *Ultraviolet* to *Spiderman I, II and III*, to the *Fantastic Four* and so on. Underground comics also emerged in the 1960s with such characters as *Mr. Natural* (Keep on Truckin) to *Fritz the Cat*. These titles moved away from the superhero characters to contemporary issues and critical social commentary. Since they were "underground"—they could escape the perils of censorship.

The writers/artists were and are not all men. Women writer/artists were producing interesting versions of the comic book genre. Sherry Flenniken produced the series *Trots and Bonnie*. Her comic books appeared to be innocent with child-like art. This enabled her, in the pages of her books, to tackle issues of sexuality and politics (e.g. capital punishment) using images of children. Sue Cole produced a searing graphic/comic book on people imprisoned in South Africa during apartheid, *How to Commit Suicide in South Africa*. Her work was/is openly political.

Frank Miller is a comic book artist who was known in the 1970s for his development of the superhero, *Daredevil* (film adaptation in 2003). He also was involved in the female hero *Elektra*. (Miller is credited as a writer on the film adaptation in 2005). His first graphic novel was *Batman: The Dark Knight Returns* (1986). The Batman graphic novel is frequently cited as the impetus for the current Batman franchise (see *Who 2* biography, 2010). 1991 marked the year that Miller began the *Sin City* story-line. It was within the genre neo-post-urban- noir. "Miller wrote and drew the stories of *Sin City* in black and white to emphasize their film-noir origins" (Who 2 biography, 2010). Miller, it seems, was commenting on contemporary urban life, particularly the dark side of it through the setting, characters, and themes traditional to the noir genre.

Can these neo-post-urban noir graphic novels/comic books be used as legitimate texts for the study of critical literacy? That is the issue we turn to next.

GRAPHIC NOVELS, CRITICAL PEDAGOGY AND CRITICAL LITERACY

Education will unfit anyone to be a slave. That is because education is bold, adventurous, creative, and vivid, illuminating-in other words, education is for self-activating explorers of life, for those who challenge fate, for doers and activists, for citizens. Training is for slaves, for loyal subjects, for tractable employees, for willing consumers, for obedient soldiers. Education tears down walls; training is all barbed wire. (Ayers, 2003, p. 36)

In the summer of 2010 at McGill University in Montreal, I was teaching a course entitled, Literacy and Language Across the Curriculum. I decided that I would try to expand and trouble the students' conventional notions of literacy. I wanted to discuss notions of critical literacy, environmental literacy, and popular culture/ visual media literacy. My attempt was to teach about critical pedagogy and critical literacy while practicing it in the classroom. The students were immediately receptive to the notions of Paulo Freire and Donald Macedo concerning critical literacy, and David Orr and environmental literacy. But when they saw *Sin City: The Hard Goodbye* (Volume 1 of the *Sin City* Series)[i] by Frank Miller on the reading list they were skeptical about the appropriateness of a graphic novel in an advanced literacy class. Questions concerning its appropriateness centered on the subject matter and the sophistication of the text. There was also outright rejection of the text as sexist, violent and vapid. There was a distinct gendered difference in the reaction to the inclusion of *Sin City*. Women students resisted its inclusion. They discussed the misogynistic and violent nature of graphic novels in general and initially dismissed the notion that these types of texts could promote social critique or critical consciousness. The male students, many of whom were already familiar with Frank Miller's work and other graphic novels were less resistant. In fact, many of the male students knew more about graphic novels than I did. The resistance came in the form of understanding the inclusion of apparently low brow, sexist, violent, macho, and graphic popular culture into an advanced class on literacy. Since many of the students knew the *Sin City* series and the film, it was somewhat a paradoxical reaction.

After the reading and discussing of the first book in the *Sin City* series, we watched the film based on the first 3 books. Eventually all twenty-two students wrote papers on their reactions to the graphic novel. Many of the comments by women students reflect the general, initial response to the inclusion of the graphic novel into the class.

> Why did I leave *Sin City* in the car? I guess I knew I'd have to write something immediately, to talk back to the book right away, to calm the angry, almost visceral reactions it elicits from me. The 'irritant effect' of the critical pedagogue is in play. Much as I would like to ignore, throw out, or

perhaps joyfully burn the book, I see your point. I need to unravel why I hate it so much, and why it evokes such antagonism in me. (Joyce, 2010, p. 1)

It never crossed my mind that this graphic novel would be explored with such credibility, in that it had something to say about the world in which we live. Through his dark, violent, masculine and somewhat offensive novel Miller has made it possible for us to discuss the hidden problems of our society. (Do Monte Branco, 2010, p. 1)

Interesting choice for a course book I thought as I picked up *Sin City* at the bookstore. Briefly flipping through the book I'll admit, I was beyond perturbed by the material. How is this going to fit into the topic of literacy and curriculum? There didn't even seem to be many words! And what about those images, way more risqué and violent then I am used to, or usually interested in getting involved with. (Prokosh, 2010, p. 1)

My therapist once told me that we learn most from people or experiences that upset us. Consequently, as I opened *Sin City* and laid my eyes on the images of voluptuous women and excessively bulky men in compromising positions, I knew I would learn from Frank Miller's graphic novel! As soon as I made that realization, I stopped being offended (goodness knows that as a feminist, I had much by which to be offended) and let the images and the text carry me to the land of interpretation – and learn I did. (Di Scala, 2010, p. 1)

The comments by the male students were somewhat different and yet also questioned the inclusion of this graphic novel.

After more than 18 years of schooling, hundreds of books, textbooks, coursepacks and novels, I have finally read my first graphic novel. I was under the impression that a graphic novel was simply a glorified comic book; a notion which I now know was greatly flawed. (Agozzino. 2010, p. 1)

People exist in deep denial and turn a blind eye to the fact that all popular culture contains messages (overt and covert) and is created by people with certain vested political /social consumerist interests and intentions in mind. Yet the easy way is to turn off this awareness, to be "asleep" and see everything as benign, innocent, and believe popular culture is not as influential as other factors in our society that are viewed as being more highbrow, traditional or academic in nature. (Adler, 2010, p. 1)

I never thought I would like graphic novels. Like many people I saw them as glorified comic books, complete with superheroes, villains and fair maidens in despair. After reading *Sin City: The Hard Goodbye* and watching the accompanying Hollywood movie I can still not say that I enjoy graphic novels as a genre but can say that I enjoyed this title and I am now very interested in Frank Miller's view of masculinity, gender, race and religion. (Climan, 2010, p. 1)

So the initial troubled discussion was of the place of popular culture, specifically graphic novels within the context of critical literacy education.

CRITICAL LITERACY, SOCIAL CRITIQUE AND *SIN CITY*

To the domains of reading, writing, and traditional print literacies, one could argue that in an era of technological revolution educators must develop robust forms of media literacy, computer literacy, and multimedia literacies, thus cultivating "multiple literacies" in the restructuring of education.[ii] Computer and multimedia technologies demand novel skills and competencies, and if education is to be relevant to the problems and challenges of contemporary life, engaged teachers must expand the concept of literacy and develop new curricula and pedagogies. (Kellner & Shane, 2007, p. 5)

After the initial discomfort and shock was overcome in the class, we began to discuss the many complex, critical issues that arose when we analyzed *Sin City* for its emancipatory and critical potential. *Sin City* like other graphic novels not only provides a critique of mainstream society in an emancipatory sense but also can reproduce attitudes confirming long standing abuses in society. In this section I will focus on the emancipatory critique. *Sin City: The Hard Goodbye* contains much of this critical potential. I would briefly like to discuss its critical approach to class, religion and sexuality. These notions are the result of reading and the class discussions.

Marv, the anti-hero of this tale, violent, hard-boiled, vigilantly trying to revenge the killing of Goldie the women/hooker he slept with the night before, makes these insightful comments concerning the environment of Sin City. It is Sin City and it reflects the "dark side" of life. Simply portraying that dark side can build awareness, particularly for middle-class readers, and pre-service teachers that this side does, indeed, exist.

> The air cools. The sounds change. The suits and briefcases scurry to their fortresses and bolt their doors and balance their checkbooks and ignore the screams and try not to think about who really owns Sin City. (Miller, 2005, p. 69)

The reader is confronted through the text with images of the dark urban environment. In a majority of the panels in the text that portray the city there is an almost haunting play of light and dark. The reader views flop houses, dark street corners, dimly lit alleyways; even the church is a dark place. The only light is that which comes through small windows partially dimmed by blinds. One of the interesting places that Marv visits in his quest for revenge is Kadies. This is a dark nightclub/strip club in the city.

> In this town just about everything you can name that's worth doing is against the law. It works out better for everybody this way. Cops and politicians make their fortunes by looking the other way while crooks like Kadie get away with charging ten bucks a drink. But here at Kadie's my drinks are

always free. The sweet old transsexual would break my arm if I tried to pay. (Miller, 2005, p. 51)

The artistic representation of the "hidden" part of the city enables the discussion of several critical implications. These critical conversations centered on the fact that certain parts of the urban environment are either hidden or ignored. In the context of Montreal, we discussed the underside of the city. Kadie's strip joint began discussions on not only the phenomenon of plethora of strip clubs, and peep shows in Montreal, but the entire notion of the objectification of women. Usually those discussions do not enter into the study of literacy as decoding. In environments that are not urban, particularly in the rural south, discussions focus on the ignored poverty-stricken areas of a town. This leads inevitably to questions of race and class. Why in these poverty-stricken sections of town is the population predominately Black? Did Frank Miller intend these conversations to occur after reading his graphic novel? There is, of course, no way of reconstructing the author's intention. But, they can and do occur when there is a critical pedagogical disposition in the class or discussion. So, in the portrayal of hidden urban environments discussions can arise that lead to questioning of misogyny, race, class and social justice.

Another issue that emerged in the discussion was religion. Admittedly Miller's book is anti-Catholic so the potential of the text to replicate existing attitudes is present, but there is also the critique of religion present. *Sin City* is run by a corrupt church. The critical discussion of the church in Sin City opened up the critique of place of religion in current political debates in American and Canadian society. In the text, after Marv brutally eviscerates Kevin the serial cannibalistic serial killer of prostitutes, he decides to go to the source of evil in Sin City Cardinal Roark. After dispatching Roark's guards, Marv confronts the religious leader. We witness the corrupt depravity of the cardinal in the ensuing confrontation.

> He was just a boy when he first came to me and I was just a priest. He came to give confession. He was a *tortured* soul. *Tormented* by the guilt. But the eating...it filled him with *white light* ... with *love* for every living thing. Tearful, he swore to me that he felt the touch of *God Almighty.* (Miller, 2005, p. 190)

Roark it turns out is a cannibal as well.

> He didn't just eat their bodies, You Pig! He ate their souls! He loved them in a way that was absolute and clean and perfect.
> And you joined in.
> Yes, oh yes. The women were nothing, *whores*. Nobody missed them. Nobody *cared.* (Miller, 2005, p. 191)

Eventually Marv kills Roark. The critical discussions and comments on course papers demonstrate, once again, the critical potential of this cultural artifact. Topics that emerged centered on the role of religion in politics, pedophilia in the Catholic

Church, the use of religious symbols (i.e., wearing crosses) and the overall power of religion.

> There is something inherently wrong when religious men devalue any human life. As I examine religion in our society this devaluing of human life is very real. Take for example, the many children that have been molested by our so called pious priests. (Do Monte Bronco, 2010, p. 7)

> Second, I think Miller is making a point about the ridiculous power of the clergy that existed in the past. As we all know many of these priests abused children and took advantage of their power to satisfy their needs. There are so many stories that are coming out today about sexual abused committed by clergy. Therefore I see that Miller feels that they too belong to Sin City. (Vicere, 2010, p. 5)

> One is not a Christian simply because s/he wears a cross around his/her neck. One is not religious because s/he has received a title decreeing him/her as such. It is in interesting in the novel the two clerical figures portrayed hide behind religion in order to mask their own criminal intent. (da Silveira, p. 8)

So the discussion of religiosity and sexuality were evident. The critical pedagogical/literacy process provided a space for them to emerge.

The critique of sexuality in Frank Miller's novel provided the most wide ranging discussions. Pornography, misogyny, objectification, homophobia, transgender, and transsexuality were topics that received attention. One example that opened up a long discussion on homophobia was the character of Lucille. She is Marv's parole officer and provides Marv with drugs that help him with his attitudes. When we first view Lucille she is clad only in a thong. But she perplexes Marv.

> Lucielle's my parole officer. She is a dyke but God knows why. With that body of hers she could have any man she wants. The pills come from her girlfriend who's a shrink. She tried to analyze me once but got too scared. (Miller, 2005, p. 37)

Lucille is eventually kidnapped by the cannibal Kevin and forced to watch him consume her hand. Marv's analysis of Lucille's lesbianism provoked a very heated and interesting discussion in class concerning homophobia.

> Lucille represents an interesting dilemma. She, like Goldie, is both sex object and caregiver in Marv's eyes, yet she is a lesbian. She provides him with his medicine and tries to protect him from himself. She is his advocate. However, she is also extremely attractive. Marv cannot reconcile why such an attractive women would be a lesbian. Perhaps all men justify lesbianism by telling themselves that only un desirable women sleep with other women. The male ego cannot reconcile the fact that a woman may simply choose to not get into physical relationships with men. (Pappas, 2010 p. 4)

The end of the course papers focused primarily on the topics of sexuality and objectification.

It is interesting again here to note that the woman is seen as the instigator of sexual activity at the beginning of the novel. She is the one moving towards the man, enticing him into the sexual act. The woman is portrayed as Biblical Eve, seducing the man and the end bringing him to his final demise. In these first three pages no text is provided. The lack of text avoids giving women a narrative, she has no voice and he story is untold. (da Salivia, 2010, p. 4)

We are exposed to a scantily clad female on the first Page of the book. She is shown from lips to thighs. Her eyes are not depicted, her identity has been removed. All that is left are body parts whose primary function is sexuality. Lips, breasts and crotch are all this woman is reduced to graphically. Right from the start she is being set up as a sexual object on display. (Najarian, 2010, p. 2)

It is interesting that in the critical analysis of sexuality in the graphic novel not only the issues swirling around the text were discussed, but the text itself was also seen as an object of criticism.

The hard connection between critical literacy and graphic novels returns us to the original premise that graphic novels exist within this paradox of critique and reproduction. The discourse of despair is that graphic novels are considered by most educators as not pedagogically appropriate so the reading of these texts may very well remain within the context of replicating existing values and attitudes. It is only when pedagogy becomes critical and literacy intertwines that these texts become a language of possibility for critique.

Put another way, for radical literacy to come about, the pedagogical should be made more political and the political more pedagogical. In other words, there is a dire need to develop pedagogical practices, in the first instance,that brings teachers, parents, and students together around new and more emancipatory visions of community (Giroux in Freire & Macedo, 1987, p. 6).

This is the hope, of course that critical pedagogy/literacy can lead us all to think more deeply and critique more effectively.

NOTES

[i] The Sin City Series includes: Book 1: The Hard Goodbye; Book 2: A Dame to Kill For; Book 3: The Big Fat Kill; Book 4: The Yellow Bastard; Book 5: Family Values; Book 6: Booze Broads and Bullets; and Book 7: Hell and Back.

[ii] Kellner, D. (1998). Multiple literacies and critical pedagogy in a multicultural society. Educational Theory. 48(1), 103-122. Kellner, D. (2004). Technological transformation, multiple literacies, and the re-visioning of education. E-Learning, 1 (1), 9-37.

REFERENCES

Adler, R. (2010). *Representation and identity: How popular culture strongly influences who we are and how we view our world.* Unpublished class paper, McGill University, Montreal, Quebec, Canada.

Agozzino, M. (2010). *Bullets, breasts, and blood: The removal of imagination in the art of reading.* Unpublished class paper, McGill University, Montreal, Quebec, Canada.

Atlasphere. (2007, March 10). *NPR interview with 300's Frank Miller*. Retrieved from http://www.theatlasphere.com/metablog/612.php.

Ayers, W. (2003). The mystery of teaching. In *The Jossey-Bass reader on teaching* (pp. 26-37). San Francisco, CA: Jossey-Bass.

Barthes, R. (1989). *Mythologies* (22nd ed.). (Trans. A. Lavers). New York, NY: Noonday Press.

Bucher, K. T., & Manning, M. L. (2004). Bringing Graphic Novels into the classroom. *The Clearing House, 78*(2), 67-72.

Climan, D. (2010). *A personal response to: Sin City: The Hard Goodbye by Frank Miller*. Unpublished class paper, McGill University, Montreal, Quebec, Canada.

Culbertson, G. (2008). *Top ten noir inspired comics*. Retrieved from http://www.moviezeal.com/top-10-noir-inspired-comics/

da Silveira, L. (2010). *Review of Sin City*. Unpublished class paper, McGill University, Montreal, Quebec, Canada.

Di Scala, M. (2010). *Sin City: Reading the world through a graphic novel*. Unpublished class paper, McGill University, Montreal, Quebec, Canada.

Dirks, T. (2010). *AMC film site*. Retrieved from: http://www.filmsite.org/filmnoir.html.

Do Monte Branco, V. (2010). *Covering up society's sins: Sex, drugs and religion*. Unpublished class paper, McGill University, Montreal, Quebec, Canada.

Eagleton, T. (1983). *Literary theory: An introduction*. Minneapolis, MN: University of MinnesotaPress.

European Graduate School (Producer). (2010). *Slavoj Zizek: Capitalism, Marxism and Kung-Fu Panda*. [Video]. Available from: http://www.egs.edu/faculty/slavoj-zizek/videos/capitalism-marxism and-kung-fu-panda/.

Freire, P., & Macedo, D. (1987). *Literacy: Reading the word and the world*. New York, NY: Routledge.

Giroux, H. (1987). Introduction: Literacy and the pedagogy of political empowerment. In P. Freire & D. Macedo, *Literacy: Reading the word and the world* (pp. 1-28), New York, NY: Routledge.

Horkheimer, M., & Adorno, T. (2010). *The culture industry: Enlightment as mass deception*. Retreved from: www.marxists.or/reference/archive/adorno/1944/culture industry.

Joyce, L. (2010). *Tumbling thoughts: Gut level reactions to Frank Miller's Sin City*. Unpublished class paper, McGill University, Montreal, Quebec, Canada.

Kellner, D., & Shane, J. (2007). Critical media literacy, democracy, and the reconstruction of education. In D. Macedo & S. Steinberg (Eds.), *Media literacy: A reader* (pp. 9-23). New York, NY: Peter Lang.

Mann, R. (Producer/Writer/Director). (2002). Comic book confidential [DVD]. United States: Home Vision Entertainment.

Miller, F. (2005). *Sin city: The hard goodbye*. Milwaukie, OR: Dark Horse Books.

Najarian, N. (2010). The consumption of women in Sin City. Unpublished class paper, McGill University, Montreal, Quebec, Canada.

Ohmann, R. (1996). *English in America: A radical view of the profession*. Hanover, NH: University Press of New England.

Orr, D. (2004). *Earth in mind: Environment and the human prospect*. Washington, DC: Island Press.

Pappas, C. (2010). *Women in Sin City: The hard goodbye*. Unpublished class paper, McGill University, Montreal, Quebec, Canada.

Prokosh, K. (2010). *A critical response to Sin City and popular culture*. Unpublished class paper, McGill University, Montreal, Quebec, Canada.

Reynolds, W. M. (2007). Under siege and out of reach: Stephen Seagal and the paradox and politics of new age masculinity. In D. Macedo & S. Steinberg (Eds.), *Media literacy: A reader* (pp. 340-352). New York, NY: Peter Lang.

Viciere, S. (2010). *Reflection on popular culture and Sin City*. Unpublished class paper, McGill University, Montreal, Quebec, Canada.

Weiner, S. (2004). *Faster than a speeding bullet: The rise of the graphic novel*. New York, NY: Nantier Beall Minoustchine Publishing.

Who 2 biography. (2010). *Frank Miller, artist/writer.* Retrieved from: http://www.answers.com/topic/frank-miller

Wright, B. (2001). *Comic book nation: The transformation of youth culture in America.* Baltimore, MD: The John Hopkins University Press.

Zizek, S. (2010a). *Capitalism, Marxism and Kung-Fu Panda.* Retrieved from: http://www.egs.edu/faculty/slavoj-zizek/videos/capitalism-marxism-and-kung-fu-panda/

Zizek, S. (2010b). *Living in the end times.* New York, NY: Verso Press.

LINDY L. JOHNSON, TOBIE BASS & MATT HICKS

3. CREATING CRITICAL SPACES FOR YOUTH ACTIVISTS

ABSTRACT

This chapter describes how an experienced high school English teacher created critical spaces to support a group of Latin@ students as they used new media to create awareness of and opposition to the harsh anti-immigration policies in the southeastern United States. Drawing on a popular culture framework (Hagood, Alvermann, & Heron-Hruby, 2010; Morrell, 2004), the authors discuss the recontextualized model of pop culture that focuses on providing opportunities for students to construct new knowledge and to transform pop culture texts for new, unforeseen purposes (Marsh, 2008). The authors illustrate how using the Latin@ students' lived realities as popular culture texts in the classroom encouraged the students to become producers and eventually activists in their school and in the community at large. The students used social media as an activist tool, produced an online and print-based newsletter, and created a collaborative digital story with the intent of representing themselves to the world at large. The chapter concludes with a lesson plan and specific activities for helping students interrogate how marginalized groups of people have been represented and how they can be (re)presented through new and digital media.

INTRODUCTION

In a crowded 11th grade classroom in a large public high school in the *Nuevo South*, Mr. Hicks, an experienced English teacher, began the day's lesson by writing three essential questions on the board: "Where are Latinos/Latinas represented in our society? What are the dominant images? How are they represented?" Mr. Hicks' students – many of whom are Latin@, and many of whom are from mixed-immigration status families – walked up to the board and began listing their answers to the questions: wet-back, criminals, job-takers, dumb, poorly-educated, ignorant, useless, gang-bangers, all look alike, not going anywhere in life. There were also some positive responses, such as: big part of the economy, hard workers, artistic, dedicated. The students' responses became the starting point for students to engage in critical conversations about the lack of authentic and non-essentialized representations of Latin@s.

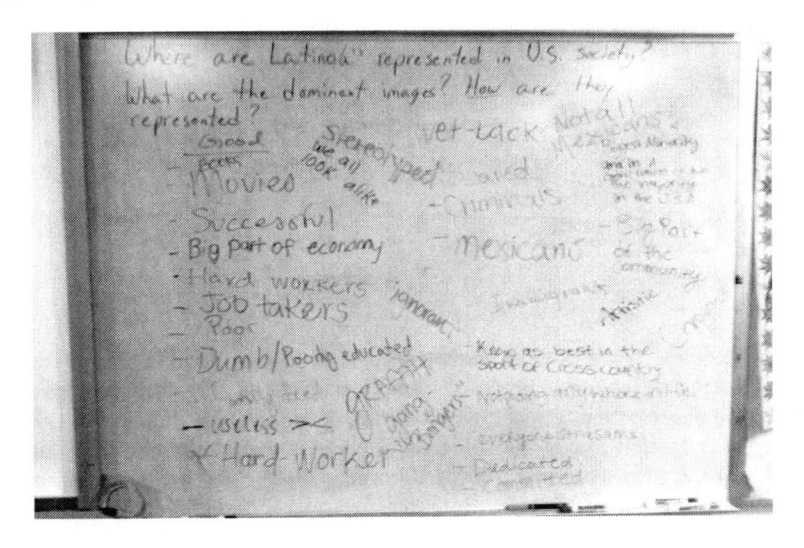

Figure 1. Representations of Latin@s.

In this chapter, we examine how Mr. Hicks, an experienced high school English teacher at a Title I school in Georgia, created critical spaces to meet the needs of his Latin@ students. Using the *recontextualized model* of popular culture (Marsh, 2008), we consider how Hicks positioned his students as producers who used their own lived realities as popular culture texts. Through his role as both English teacher and soccer and cross country coach, Mr. Hicks had learned of the challenges many of his students faced as they were finishing high school and pursuing postsecondary options while also dealing with changing immigration policies, and the resulting ramifications on their friends, family and community. Some of Mr. Hicks' students were undocumented themselves; others came from mixed status families. The changing state and federal policies related to immigrants created a complicated web of questions and answers for all students with varying immigration statuses. In addition, immigrant students were living amidst a culture of fear, largely stemming from increased numbers of local and national deportations and harsh anti-immigrant state legislation that abruptly and effectively separated families. Mr. Hicks fostered critical literacy with his students by engaging them in reading and analyzing complex texts such as legislative and university policies, remediating written scholarship essays into multimodal digital stories, and creating newsletters to educate their community on local, state, and national policies affecting students from immigrant families. In the following chapter, we explore the ways in which the students' lived experiences in Mr. Hick's classroom became popular cultures "texts" worthy of study. We discuss how Mr. Hicks encouraged his students through the use of new media technologies (Facebook, Instagram, and digital storytelling) often associated with popular culture to become activists and advocates for their own lives.

CONCEPTUALIZING POP CULTURE

Many scholars have argued that using popular culture in the classroom can engage and motivate students (Jenkins, 2011), make classroom learning more relevant (Alvermann, 2010), serve as a bridge for in and out of school literacies (Alvermann, 2008; Mahiri, 1998; Morrell, 2002, 2004), lead students to become better producers and consumers of popular culture (Kellner, 1995, Morrell, 2004), and help students think more critically about society (Giroux, 2009). Yet even in schools where innovative teaching is encouraged, and in spite of the benefits outlined by researchers, teachers often struggle to incorporate pop culture into their classroom because to do so would challenge their conception of what it means to be a "real" teacher (Chandler-Olcott & Lewis, 2010). Alvermann (2008) suggests that it may be our unexamined assumptions about the *nature of text* that has caused classroom practice to be slow to respond to the rapid changes we've seen in digital technologies (and thus access to popular culture). If we fail to examine these assumptions – and the implications for teaching that go along with them – "then we may find ourselves schooling young people in literacy practices that disregard the vitality of their literate lives and the needs they will have for their literate and social futures at home, at work, and in their communities" (Lewis & Fabos, as quoted in Alvermann, p. 14). When teachers position popular culture texts as those worth studying, it calls into question what counts as text. This was certainly the case in Mr. Hick's classroom where students navigated federal policies that had life-altering consequences. As we will discuss throughout this chapter, in Mr. Hick's class, the everyday lives of his students (and the new media they are so often immersed in) became central texts that were studied and analyzed not only among undocumented students, but among immigrant and non-immigrant students, as well. In conceptualizing how Mr. Hicks helped his students to draw on their life texts, we have found Morrell's (2004) definition of pop culture, which draws from cultural studies and a postmodern lens, particularly helpful:

> Popular culture is seen as a site of struggle between the forces of resistance of subordinate groups in society, and the forces of incorporation of dominant groups in society. Popular culture in this usage is not an imposed 'mass culture,' or a 'people's culture,' it is more of a terrain of exchange between the two. (p. 46)

Morrell emphasizes the importance of teachers understanding the philosophical debates and theoretical frameworks that have influenced the multiple ways that scholars and researchers define popular culture. While there is not room in this chapter for a thorough discussion of the historical context of this movement, we want to point out that we find Morrell's rationale for teachers developing an understanding of these debates particularly compelling. Morrell argues that knowledge of this framework "allows teachers to help students understand how their everyday practices are also considered as popular culture, and often inform the cultural products promoted and marketed by the culture industries" (p.51). In this chapter, we want to foreground students' everyday lives (and the new media they are so often immersed in) as central texts – popular culture texts – worthy of study and inclusion in the curriculum.

Marsh (2008) outlined four models typically used when teachers incorporate popular culture into the classroom: the *utilitarian model*, the *cultural capital model*, the *critical model*, and the *recontextualized model*. Understanding these four models can help educators go beyond using pop culture for "fun" or to "hook" students into traditional and canonical literature, and may help teachers reexamine their assumptions about how to bring in students' lives, questions, experiences, and everyday culture as part of the curriculum. Marsh explains that the model most frequently used in schools is the *utilitarian mode*. This approach seeks to connect school content that is often seen as irrelevant to students' lives and focuses on how pop culture texts connect to traditional literacy practices. The *cultural capital model* seeks to build on the authentic experiences of students who have been marginalized by the educational process. In this model, teachers encourage students to bring in texts that are normally ignored in schools such as trading cards, music lyrics, and comic books (Hagood, Alvermann, & Heron-Hruby, 2010). Encouraging students to bring in texts from their own lives that are meaningful can help students to see themselves and their lives as deserving of study. In the *critical model*, pop culture is conceptualized as everyday culture that should naturally be a part of the school curriculum. This model emphasizes popular media as a serious site for social knowledge to be discussed, interrogated, and critiqued. Instruction seeks to develop students' understanding of how texts are produced and consumed.

The recontextualized model incorporates aspects of the other models, but with a specific focus on providing opportunities for students to construct new knowledge and to transform pop culture texts for new, unforeseen purposes. The youth in Mr. Hicks class began to use Instagram, for example, for new, unforeseen purposes. While mainstream media focuses primarily as Instagram as a promotion of celebrity culture, narcissism, and "selfies," the young people in Mr. Hicks' class used it to promote and spread information about the undocumented student movement. We argue that it was because Mr. Hicks foregrounded his students' lived experiences as important texts to study that students then took up new media technologies to become producers rather than just consumers. Not only were pop culture texts used in unique and powerful learning experiences; Mr. Hicks' students recontextualized and reproduced their own everyday culture, their life stories as the curriculum. We believe that there is as of yet still much unrealized potential in ELA classrooms for helping students develop tools to become producers of popular culture rather than just critical consumers (Morrell, 2004). But it is important to note in order for students to become powerful producers they must engage with texts that they truly care about and that are embedded in their everyday social practices.

ANTI-IMMIGRANT DISCOURSE IN THE SOUTH

We argue that becoming producers is especially important for immigrant students in the *Nuevo South*. These young people are negotiating their identities – already complicated by adolescence – while also being positioned by the larger community's anti-immigrant discourses. The state of Georgia continues to uphold some of the harshest policies regarding immigrants- both through aggressive, anti-immigrant state laws and through restrictive higher education policy. For example, House Bill 87, the "Show me your papers" law has created a culture of fear that surrounds many young people in our state's classrooms. In the last two decades, the foreign-born population has increased in Georgia by almost 300% (Migration Policy Institute, 2011). Consequently, students from immigrant families now make up a large percentage of Georgia high school classrooms. Georgia joins a small number of other conservative states such as South Carolina and Alabama, by enacting oppressive, formidable policies that limit undocumented students who want to attend college or university. On top of onerous state legislation and increased deportations nationwide, the University System of Georgia Board of Regents enacted a ban in 2011 that prohibits undocumented students from applying to the state's top five competitive universities.

In 2012 and 2013, state legislators in Georgia proposed bills that, if passed, would have prohibited undocumented students from attending any state institution of higher education. Such restrictive, anti-immigrant measures highly diminish students' motivations for continuing their education, even for finishing high school, and contribute to further shaping negative public discourse regarding immigrants. For the many K-12 teachers working with undocumented students around the state these policies became deeply troubling and complex issues. The following headline and ensuing public commentary in local newspaper the *Athens Online Banner-Herald* illustrates the dominant ideology surrounding immigrant students in Georgia, and the public discourse positioning them:

> Teacher and coach Matt Hicks has become an expert in how students can apply to college without Social Security numbers since the state Board of Regents placed restrictions on which Georgia public colleges undocumented students can attend.

The first two comments below the article provide a picture of how many local Georgians view the issue of education for undocumented students:

> As teachers don't you think it might be a good idea on teaching them how to become LEGAL? I understand that you want everyone to have an education, but how about educating them on being in this country legal. People everyday become citizens and do the LEGAL way.

> And with this mindset, he therefore is part of the problem. Teaching students how to circumvent rules and laws should be grounds for his termination. (Shearer, 2012)

The two reactive comments above represent a common conservative mindset that positions undocumented students in the state of Georgia and other places around the U.S. in deficit and limiting ways. As described in the opening anecdote, many students are well aware of the negative ways that they are positioned in the mainstream and dominant discourses in the South. In Mr. Hicks' class, examining how students were being positioned and how students wanted to position themselves became central to the curriculum. As Wortham, Murillo, and Hamann (2002) note, it is critical for research to examine how students adopt identities and have identities imposed on them. Mr. Hicks and his students began to identify, deconstruct, and problematize the public identities of Latin@ youth, taking critical first steps in preparation for agentive re-conceptualization of those identities. In emphasizing the difficult context within which most teachers, such as Hicks, work, Morrell (2004) asserts:

> These challenging classrooms, however, are also the perfect site for struggle for those literacy educators who are dedicated to the cause of social justice and want to be major players in helping those students who have traditionally not had access to the literacy skills needed for advancement and empowerment in our society. (p. 10)

For Hicks, teaching within such a challenging dominant discourse also presented a unique opportunity to meet the needs of his students. In the next section, we describe how Mr. Hicks created space within the conservative culture of Georgia and the structured schedule of high school for students to develop their own voices.

CREATING SPACE

At Mr. Hicks' high school, students attend an enrichment period called "Jagtime" (named after the school mascot – Jaguars) for 40 minutes three days a week. In Fall of 2011, one of Mr. Hicks' most talented and successful students, Karla, came to him in tears about her limited options following graduation due to her immigration status. It was then that Hicks decided to propose to the school's administration that he facilitate a Jagtime dedicated to supporting the almost 150 undocumented students at the school in their transition to college. In this way, Hicks was building upon the idea of a *cultural capital model* of popular culture; he was advocating for students to bring their lives into the school. Further, he was advocating that students' lives and their concerns become the text of the curriculum. Hicks proposed that students would investigate post-graduation options, apply for college, and write scholarship essays. In order to protect the students' from being publicly labeled by immigration status, Hicks named his Jagtime "Post-Secondary Options with Hicks," and word spread quickly among students that this was a "safe space" where students could find support in working toward their post-graduation plans (college or otherwise) regardless of their immigration status.

By FERPA (Family Educational Rights and Privacy Act, 1974) regulation, a teacher is prohibited from asking about a student's documentation status. Although Mr. Hicks did not ask, some students opened up to him on their own, signifying a trusting relationship and a call for help. Law mandates that public school teachers do not share immigration status information they may know with authorities in order to protect all students. The rotating groups of Jagtime students did not consist soley of undocumented students; students from mixed-status families, including siblings who did not share the same documentation status also attended Jagtime. Many young people do not become aware of their documentation status until they are in high school- seeking a driver's license or applying to college, for example. Until very recently and still for many young people, immigration status is not a conversation topic even among close friends and family. Because of the real-world implications, Hicks knew that the students he cared about needed answers about what their post-secondary options were, and so in fall of 2011, "Post-Secondary Options with Hicks" Jagtime began.

As critical educators, we know that teaching is always political. And we know that the political climate surrounding us and our students affects learning and achievement. Hicks began his Jagtime with little understanding or support from colleagues. He knew that students' (and their families') immigration status was a sensitive topic and remained cautious about the information he shared about his students. He was well aware that his project could easily be shut down at any point and that he could be reprimanded for engaging in such a politically divisive topic with his students. But over time Hicks' Jagtime session became known as an "institution" among the students and his colleagues.

A central organizing feature of this "enrichment" period was that Mr. Hicks conceptualized the time as having emerged out of an authentic need and real questions with which students were grappling. As Hull and Katz (2006) write, one's identity and sense of self has "much to do with how and why we learn; the desire to acquire new skills and knowledge is inextricably linked to who we want to be as people" (p. 43). Because this was an enrichment period, Hicks had freedom to choose class texts. In addition, he was not bound by preparing students for an end-of-course test. Instead, the assessment came from the real world answers students sought and found as they applied for scholarships and college admissions. The "text" for Jagtime was the lived experiences of the students – their everyday culture and something that many students take for granted: the ability to attend post-secondary institutions of learning. Undocumented students are not permitted to receive any state or federal loans, grants, or scholarships, and for students from mixed-status families, the application process can be muddled with fear and lack of clarity. Hicks and his Jagtime students began by collecting information on available scholarships and trying to make sense of the constantly changing policies that limited post-secondary educational opportunities for immigrant students.

STUDENT-PRODUCED CURRICULUM

In Fall 2011, Karla, Hicks' student intern, researched and produced a 35-page booklet called "The Ultimate Guide for College Bound Undocumented Georgia Students" that explained current policies, compared college costs, and highlighted scholarships open to undocumented students.

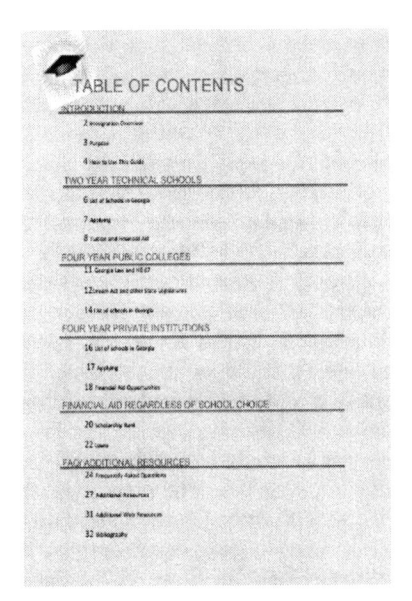

Figure 2. Karla's guide.

This hard copy booklet was printed and passed out by students around the school and e-mailed by students to friends and family members around the state. Eventually, the booklet was published online by Cobb County School districts and circulated widely through a variety of blogs and websites dedicated to helping undocumented students. Karla's published booklet sparked other students' interest in researching more current information, networking, and finding ways to communicate and share information. Mr. Hicks began using Karla's booklet as the class curriculum. In using Karla's booklet, Hicks began to rely on students' voices and knowledge to help shape classroom learning. This set a precedent for collaborative learning and student-led recontextualization of their life-to-school learning experiences.

Throughout 2011 and 2012, new and returning groups of students from Jagtime began working on their scholarship essays and initial steps toward college applications by sharing their stories. They addressed common scholarship and admissions prompts such as: "How has your family background affected the way you see the world?" and "Why do you want to get a college education?" For college admissions officers and scholarship competitions, the answers to these questions offer a window into the student's world that cannot be described by grades or SAT scores. For any high school student, answering these questions honestly is an important and personal part of both the academic and psychological process of preparing for college and the future. For students whose immigration status or the immigration status of their parents is an extenuating factor, these questions often lead to long conversations with parents, the sharing of difficult stories, and an emerging maturity in the voice of the student. Jagtime provided a space for students to help design the curriculum, learn from each other, and draw strength from peers' similar experiences. A collective identity began to emerge – one that resisted the negative, anti-immigrant public discourse and offered students the agency to move forward in productive ways as they began to develop a shared sense of purpose.

BLURRING THE BOUNDARIES: LEVERAGING SOCIAL MEDIA TO BRIDGE THE IN AND OUT OF SCHOOL DIVIDE

When students found that the 40 minute Jagtime sessions didn't provide enough time for them to complete their scholarship information, they turned to Facebook. Karla created a private Facebook group then invited Hicks and the other students in Jagtime to be members. Since students were already using social media regularly, they quickly became active members of the private Facebook group. Moving some of the "overflow" of the Jagtime conversations into an online social networking space was initiated by students, and symbolized an important moment in the identity development of these students. Instead of Hicks fielding repeated questions and being positioned as the sole distributor of knowledge, he and his students could both ask and answer questions, and share their information with other students who had similar questions.

While initially Karla had been the primary producer of content, using the tool of Facebook helped students connect with each other and collaborate on information. The group became a powerful network for investigating answers to questions that many adults, including school counselors, had no idea how to answer. For example, students would ask, "How do I fill out a college application if I don't have a social security number?" or "How much will it cost me to go to the local community college?" While these questions might seem simple to answer, the answers were difficult to find in Georgia because laws were constantly changing and policies were in flux.

Social media sites such as Facebook are often criticized by teachers as being a waste of time, and a major distraction to students. Yet students in Hicks' Jagtime used Facebook in innovative and productive ways. Facebook's non-hierarchical and interactive platform seemed to serve as a scaffold for students' development from passive consumers to producers. Participating in this network helped to reposition students as producers rather than only consumers of information. It also helped students understand that the information they researched and the answers they discovered had important, even life-altering, consequences for themselves and their peers. In this way, Jagtime students continued to form a collective identity, as they shared stories, experiences, and knowledge with each other. Some students "came out" as undocumented either in the physical space of Hicks' classroom, or online in the private Jagtime Facebook page. The development of a collective identity in online spaces is found in the larger DREAMers activist movement nationwide, where the sharing of stories "through various social media and digital platforms has allowed youth to challenge, and at times, supplant mass media representations through more locally constructed and participatory forms of messaging" (Zimmerman, 2012, p. 39). Throughout the 2011 Fall Jagtime face-to-face meetings and online interactions, students sought answers, applied for scholarships, shared stories, and gained knowledge about college possibilities. Neither teacher nor students could imagine how this group's emerging collective identity would become even more necessary and instrumental in the following semester.

RE(PRESENTING): MOVING FROM PRODUCERS TO ACTIVISTS

During the Spring 2012 legislative session, Georgia legislators proposed two different bills that attempted to ban undocumented students from *all* higher education institutions. In Jagtime, students continued to write essays for scholarship applications, but questioned to what end as they followed closely the legislative proposals and associated local news reactions.

Students became increasingly frustrated and a loss of hope threatened student motivation in Hicks' Jagtime and in school overall. In an attempt to offer a platform for Jagtime students to express their voices, Tobie Bass, a friend and colleague of Hicks, proposed the idea of collaborating on a digital story (see lesson plan for detailed instructions). While the students were interested in the project, they had not created digital stories before. And, while Mr. Hicks was intrigued by the idea, he was uncertain about how it would all come together. The only technology available in his classroom was his school-issued laptop, he had never created a digital story, and his dedication to his students and the sensitive issues of immigration status made it hard for Hicks to allow other adults into his classroom. Technology issues did present ongoing challenges such as restricted internet access. However, after much discussion and planning among Hicks, Bass, and Johnson, coupled with feelings of frustration about impending legislation, Hicks decided to embark on the creation of a collaborative digital story.

As noted in the introduction, Hicks introduced the idea of the digital story to his Jagtime students with a "chalk talk" activity; he asked students to "relay" to the board to write quick answers to the questions, "Where are Latin@s represented in our society? What are the dominant images? How are they represented?" As students came to the board, the list became more disturbing. Some of the students' responses included: wet-back, criminals, job-takers, dumb, poorly-educated, ignorant, useless, gang-bangers, all look alike, not going anywhere in life. There were also some positive responses, such as: big part of the economy, hard workers, artistic, dedicated. The students' responses became the starting point for engaging in critical conversations about the lack of authentic and non-essentialized representations of Latin@s.

Another important component of engaging in critical dialogue came through connecting students' own personal experiences with other historically marginalized groups of people. During subsequent Jagtimes, Hicks engaged students in critically analyzing stereotypical images of Native Americans and African Americans prevalent in old textbooks and comic books. Hicks and students also googled images of various groups of people to see what came up as popular hits. Students were able to connect their own experiences of being misrepresented with other marginalized groups of people. They then began to move from critical consumption to thinking about the importance of producing images of themselves, or self-representing. Students voiced their feelings and shared ideas about what they wanted the world to know about them, in a sense re-shaping the stereotypes and the negative, anti-immigrant rhetoric surrounding them. Then, students were encouraged to begin documenting themselves through photographing objects, places, and people that were important to them. They took pictures with their phones, searched the web for images, and asked their parents for old photographs. Hicks and Bass asked students to bring in other texts – song lyrics, quotes, and phrases that they felt would help represent how they saw themselves. Students searched their iPods for music, emailed favorite quotes from their English class, recorded their voices on a phone or Hicks' laptop, and wrote with pen and paper about who they were, who they wanted to be, how they wanted to be represented, and what was most important to them. The original plan was for students to engage in all aspects of producing the digital story, but restricted internet access at the school removed the possibility of using any sort of online platform (which would have allowed students to work as collaborating editors and designers), so Bass eventually took on the job of curating editor.

Telling a collective story takes time; the multiple voices must feel fairly valued, presenting both individual and group. Through design discussion, trial and error, feedback in Jagtime, remixing at night, more feedback in Jagtime, and so on, the digital story came to life. Hicks and Bass then began assembling students' words and images with an open and uncertain understanding of where it might lead. Digital stories need a cohesive storyline running throughout, to which end the Jagtime group decided on the title "(re)presenting." There was a long discussion about who the audience might be for this story and why. Students emphasized that they wanted to send it first to their families, friends, and other teachers. But they also wanted the school Superintendent, the state Governor, the Georgia State Legislature, and even President Obama to see it. Before releasing the digital story, parents viewed the video, signed media release forms, and were encouraged to ask questions. Hicks spoke on the phone with one parent, and led the students in Jagtime through long discussion about creating digital footprints.

As critical educators, we argue that too often our students' own stories and histories are neglected in classroom settings. Yet, Giroux writes that one of the most essential pedagogical practices that teachers undertake is foregrounding students' experiences. He urges teachers to help students "draw on their own voices and histories as a basis for engaging and interrogating the multiple and often contradictory experiences that provide them with a sense of identity, worth, and presence" (2009a, p. 453). Watching students unpack the ways that Latin@ are represented in our society helped all of us realize the wealth of knowledge and the "multiple and contradictory experiences" they were living in that needed to be analyzed, scrutinized, critiqued, and then "re"presented. Thus, we don't want to undermine the importance of critical consumption and deconstructing images and texts. However, we do want to emphasize that the most transformative experiences seemed to occur when students reimagined and represented their own versions of who they were and who they wanted to be.

In producing this digital story, we argue that students and teachers developed "new and literate identities" (Hull & Katz, 2006) in which they not only imagined their social futures, but also sought to transform how others saw them. The process of putting together (re)presenting helped us all to reimagine our roles- as students and as teachers. Observing, responding to, and participating in the creation of the video with students strengthened our relationships with students. Importantly, it also transformed our thinking about the ways in which students are capable of using digital tools to collaborate on work, learning, and activism.

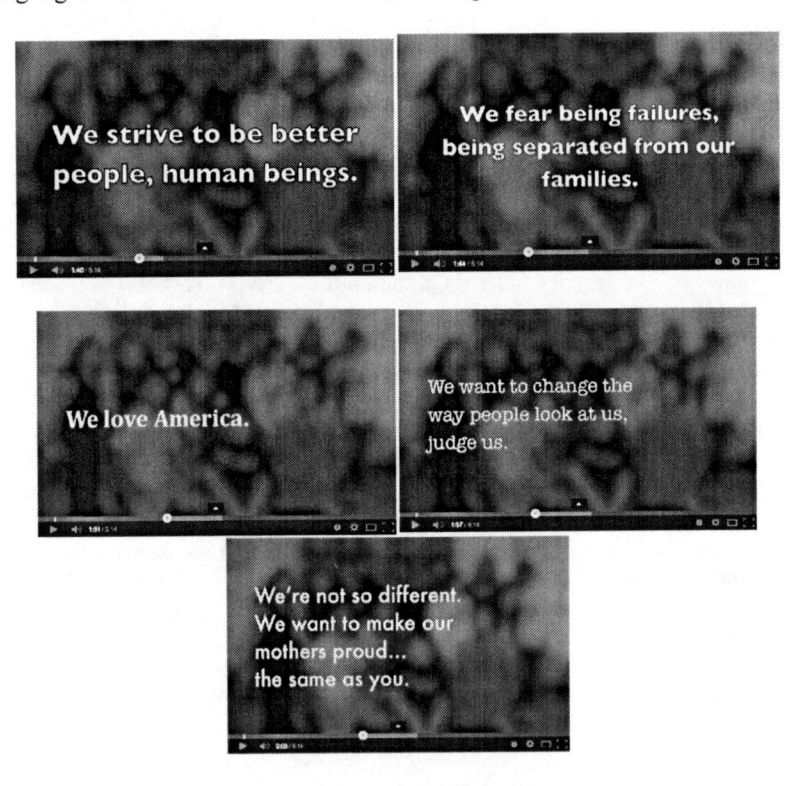

Figure 3. Images from (re)presenting.

Many researchers have demonstrated that creating digital stories provides rich opportunities for students to improvise, experiment and play, all of which can lead to the development of new literate identities (Hull & Katz, 2006; Nelson, Hull, & Roche-Smith, 2008; Vasudevan, Schultz, & Bateman, 2010). At the same time, it is important to recognize that not all multimedia compositions students create are emancipatory or serve to challenge old stereotypes. In fact, Norton reminds us of the "complex relationship between social structure on the one hand, and human agency on the other, without resorting to deterministic or reductionist analyses" (Norton, date, cited in Hornberger & McKay, 2010, p. 352). Rogers, Winters, LaMonde, and Perry (2010), for example, emphasize the importance of youth being supported as they create digital stories in which they "negotiate their subject positions and challenge dominant cultural representations and ideologies" (p. 310).

This was certainly the case in the creation of the digital story. Just pointing out the essentialized and negative ways that Latin@s are currently presented isn't enough, and on its own can serve to reify the deficit discourse. While we recognize the constraints, the continued difficulties immigrant families face, and the complexity of power operating in society around Jagtime students, our focus builds on the agentive uses of students' lived experiences as popular culture texts in the classroom. Indeed, the last frame of the Jagtime digital story "(re)presenting" reads, "A document doesn't define who we are, we do."

UNDOCUFILES: INTERPRETING AND ANALYZING FEDERAL POLICY

In June of 2012, President Obama announced an executive order called DACA (Deferred Action for Childhood Arrivals), which provided for young undocumented immigrants to apply for a 2-year amnesty. During Jagtime that fall, DACA was a major focus for students, as deferred action would potentially allow undocumented students to get a driver's license. While a drivers' license makes it somewhat easier to apply and get into college and work, students still faced the challenge of how to pay for college; Georgia's policies required that higher education institutions in the state charge undocumented students four times the tuition that a student paying in-state tuition would be charged. In addition, undocumented students cannot receive any federal loans or state funding which makes college costs much more difficult to manage in comparison with students who have documented status.

Hicks and his students began to compile the information they were learning about DACA into a one-page document they titled "Undocufiles." Wading through the President's executive order and figuring out how local agencies and colleges in Georgia were interpreting the order, and what that meant for post-secondary options for the students was a complex task. Students quickly began to take responsibility for finding information themselves; they texted ideas, and relevant article links to articles to Hicks to share with the whole class. Hicks brought in a few laptops so that small group of students could work together to research information and discuss why they might want to include it in Undocufiles. Over the course of the semester, four issues of Undocufiles were created and printed.

Students passed the Undocufiles around the school and even the most reserved students asked their favorite teachers to hang Undocufiles on their doors. Undocufiles became pseudo "safe space" stickers in classroom windows demonstrating to students that this teacher was an ally. Many students around the school were becoming aware of and supporting their peers by reading Undocufiles, asking questions, and asking what they could do to help.

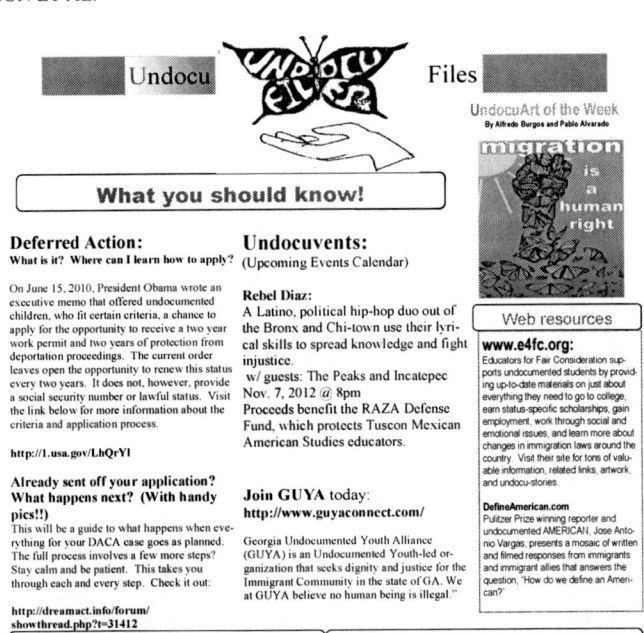

Figure 4. Undocufiles Edition 1 on paper.

Undocufiles via Instagram: Learning from Our Students

By March of 2013, students had shared their Undocufiles and the digital story, *"Re"presenting* at local community forums and conferences. Hicks continued to learn much about his students' inclinations toward activism. In an effort to gain a wider audience, Hicks thought that uploading Undocufiles to Twitter might be a good solution since so many of his students already were on Twitter. Uploading Undocufiles to Twitter, however, required clicking on links to access charts or images, which students wanted to see but were less likely to do on their phones. In addition, several Jagtime student-activists who followed the undocumented artist movement closely were unsatisfied with the limitations of Twitter as a social media platform.

Figure 5. Instagram art and activism posted from Jagtime.

David, a senior who was doing an internship in Hicks' class, suggested Instagram as a platform that would work particularly well for sharing artwork and other images. When Hicks and David brought this idea to Jagtime, they learned that several students were already frequent users of Instagram. The students were excited about this new development in Undocufiles and quickly taught each other how to navigate and post to their feed. Almost instantly, Jagtime students were connecting not only to each other, but to a vast network of other undocumented student-activists across the country through their new Instagram feed. Zimmerman (2012) argues that "Given the effects of legal status on youth's social marginalization, isolation, and self-esteem, new media technologies have become an important mechanism of communication and connection" (p. 39). For the Jagtime students, communicating newly discovered information to a larger audience was an important stage in the development of their collective identity. Through the use of remixed text and art on their Undocufiles Instagram feed, the students in Jagtime carried their activism even further by connecting to the larger movement of DREAMers.

The DREAM movement has garnered national attention as the voices of undocumented youth are spotlighted, advocating for fair and humane immigration reform and ultimately, a path toward a productive life studying and working in the U.S. Following the footsteps of the DREAMers movement across the nation, some of Hicks' students began to "come out" as undocumented during the class by writing and sharing their stories, winning scholarships to private universities, and speaking at local forums. Of course, this was never a requirement of Jagtime, and many students did not share their immigration status with the group. It is important to note that the work produced in Jagtime reached far beyond the nearly 150 undocumented students at the school to a much broader group of youth around the school – Latin@s and non-Latin@s, immigrants and non-immigrants. In fact, Jagtime student producers have contributed in many ways to community activism and awareness of the complex issues surrounding higher education that immigrant students continue to face. Several Jagtime students have also joined groups such as GUYA (Georgia Undocumented Youth Alliance) and FU (Freedom University), becoming activists outside of their school community. GUYA (Georgia Undocumented Youth Alliance) leads protests and keeps people up to date via social media. Both GUYA and FU are volunteer-led groups that actively advocate for education and human rights for immigrant youth in Georgia.

Conclusion

For the past three years, Jagtime has been a short but powerful time for students to take part in active learning that directly affects their educational futures. It is uncertain if Jagtime will continue in the future. It is certain, however, that due to Hicks' commitment to his students, many young people's lives and educational futures have been and continue to be impacted. Jagtime students experienced a unique collaboration of building life texts into school learning, forming collective identity around advocacy, and producing knowledgeable voices as individuals and as a group. Their unique use of personal stories, their construction of new knowledge, and their production of texts illustrate outstanding examples of recontextualizing life experiences as pop culture texts. Through face-to face classroom learning and new media, Hicks and his students have blurred boundaries, making more fluid the borders of institutional, intellectual, and emotional literacies.

CREATING CRITICAL SPACES FOR YOUTH ACTIVISTS

SAMPLE LESSON PLANS

PART ONE

Opener:

http://www.learner.org/resources/series203.html

Scroll down to "Workshop 8" and click the small tan VoD icon. Skip over to 27:35 min. for "Final Shots," which provides a 3-minute intro on how to author and name your world and the importance of that activity. The activity at 30:41, "Two Rounds," shows different representations of Native Americans and the student's responses/reactions to the image representations. This short video segment provides a foundation for the project, illustrating the power of representation through images.

Activity:

Chalk Talk Succinct questions are written on board and students quickly relay to write their answers.
1. Where are Latin@s represented in U.S. society?
2. What are the dominant images?
3. How are they represented?

Homework:

Questions to reflect on after Chalk Talk:
1. What is missing from the list we made today of how Latin@s are represented in this society?
2. Specifically, what is important in your life right now, that's not on that list?(It doesn't have to be specifically about being Latin@!)

PART TWO

Opener:

Follow-up discussion based on the chalk talk and the questions posed for homework reflection.

Activity:

Show students a digital story that uses images, text, music, and voice. Ask students to dissect the digital story in small groups by answering the questions:

1. What story does the video tell?
2. How do the different components (image, text, music, voice) work together to tell the story?

Homework:

Find two images that you would like to represent you. What is important in your life? Bring the images (on your phone, email, text, or photograph) and be prepared to explain why you chose them.

PART THREE

Opener:

http://www.pbs.org/wnet/jimcrow/resources.html

Quick review of how the teacher from "Two Rounds" (Part One) structured her discussion.
– How did she get her students describing/talking about the images?
– Where did the discussions go from there?(i.e. What do we remember?)

How can we use that protocol to unpack the following images of African American caricatures: Sambo, Mammy, Pickaninny, and Uncle Tom?
– Adjectives
– Implications
– Etc.
In this case, students' prior knowledge of African American history and oppression gave them a framework with which to talk about stereotypical/derogatory images.

Activity:

Provide the students with laptops – one per group.

Ask them to search and save images of stereotypical "Mexicans/Mexican Americans or Latin@s"

They should choose three and follow the protocol within their groups.
– 3 adjectives
– Write a few sentences about outsiders' perceptions
– Come up with a few dangers/implications of these images/perceptions

Whip Around: Go around the room and each group presents one image and their findings

Homework:

Hand each student a small notecard. Ask them to quietly reflect on the day's lesson. In a sentence or two, students answer the following questions:
1. What patterns seemed to emerge?
2. How are you/your family and culture not represented in these images?
3. What would you like to see brought in?

PART FOUR

Opener:

Students share images they have collected to represent themselves in small groups and then in whole group.

Activity:

Explain your images to each other and turn in your answers to the following questions:
1. Why did you choose that image?
2. What does that image say about you?
3. How do you want people to react when they see this image?

Homework:

Answer the questions:
1. What story do we want to tell?
2. What do we care about/love?
3. What do we fear? What are our worries?
4. What do we hate?
5. What do we want to change?
6. How are we different?
7. How are we the same?

PART FIVE

Opener:

Show a compilation video of what the students have submitted thus far.

Note: With working tools and more time, students can create their own digital stories or participate more in the video creation and editing process. In this case, due to limited group time together and technical restrictions at the school, Bass used iMovie and YouTube to edit the video with guidance and feedback from students.

Activity:

Frame by frame, students watch and pause video to discuss homework questions below, crafting a collaborative outline of how to fit together their images, text, and music.

Homework:

Watch the video alone and answer the questions below.
1. Who is your audience? In other words, who would you like to represent yourself to?
2. How do you think your audience sees you? (Use adjectives to describe how you think they see you. For example, intelligent, lazy, etc.)
3. How would you like to self-represent to your audience? In other words, how would you like to change the way they see you? (Use adjectives to describe how you want them to see you. For example, ambitious, unique, etc.)
4. What ONE image do you think would help you accomplish your self-representation? (The image can be a person, place, or thing, a photograph, artwork, etc.)
5. What is ONE sentence, phrase, or word that identifies something important to your self-representation?(Do you have a favorite quote, motto, or something you like to say?)
6. What is ONE song, song lyric, or poem that you feel would help you self-represent who you are?
7. What is ONE place that you feel is important to your self-representation?
8. Why is it important to self-represent?

PART SIX

Opener:

Whole-group viewing of video.

Activity:

Discussion and voting on final edits.

Homework:

Share with your parents for their feedback.

REFERENCES

Alvermann, D. E. (2008). Why bother theorizing adolescents' online literacies for classroom practice and research? *Journal of Adolescent & Adult Literacy, 52,* 8-19.

Alvermann, D. E. (2010).Introduction. In D. E. Alvermann (Ed.), *Adolescents' online literacies* (pp. 1-4). New York, NY: Peter Lang.

Alvermann, D. E., Moon, J. S., & Hagood, M. C. (1999). *Popular culture in the classroom: Teaching and researching critical media literacy.* Newark, DE: International Reading Association/National Reading Conference.

Freire, P., & Macedo, D. (1987). *Literacy: Reading the word and the world.* Westport, CT: Bergin & Garvey Publishers.

Giroux, H.A. (2009a). Critical theory and educational practice. In A. Darder, M. Baltodano, & R. D. Torres (Eds.), *The critical pedagogy reader* (pp. 27-51). New York, NY: Routledge.

Giroux, H.A. (2009b). Teacher education and democratic schooling. In A. Darder, M. Baltodano, R. D. Torres (Eds.), *The critical pedagogy reader* (pp. 438-457). New York, NY: Routledge.

Hagood, M. C., Alvermann, D. E., & Heron-Hruby, A. (2010). *Bring it to class: Unpacking pop culture in literacy learning.* New York, NY: Teachers College Press.

Hill, M. L. (2009). *Beats, rhymes + classroom life: Hip-hop pedagogy + the politics of identity.* New York, NY: Teachers College Press.

Jenkins, H. (2011). From new media literacies to new media expertise: "Confronting the challenges of a participatory culture," Revisited. *A manifesto for media education.* Retrieved from http://www.manifestoformediaeducation.co.uk/2011/01/henryjenkins/

Kirkland, D. (2009). Standpoints: Research and teaching English in the digital dimension. *Research in the Teaching of English, 44*(1), 8-22.

Kist, W. (2005). *New literacies in action.* New York, NY: Teachers College Press.

Lewis, C., & Fabos, B. (2005). Instant messaging, literacies, and social identities. *Reading Research Quarterly, 40*(4), 470-501.

Luke, C. (2000). New literacies in teacher education. *Journal of Adolescent & Adult Literacy, 43,* 424-435.

Mahiri, J. (2001). Pop culture pedagogy and the end(s) of school. *Journal of Adolescent & Adult Literacy, 44,* 382-385.

Marsh, J. (2008). Popular culture in the language arts classroom. In J. Flood, S.B. Heath, & D. Lapp (Eds.), *Handbook of research on teaching literacy through the communicative and visual arts* (Vol. II, pp. 529-536). New Jersey: Simon and Schuster.

Migration Policy Institute. (2011). *MPT data hub: Migration facts, stats, and maps.* Retrieved from http://www.migrationinformation.org/datahub/state.cfm?ID=GA

Millard, E. (2003). Toward a literacy of fusion: New times, new teachings and learning? *Reading, Literacy and Learning, 37*(1), 3-9.

Morrell, E. (2004). *Linking literacy and popular culture.* Norwood, MA: Christopher-Gordon Publishers.

Norton, B. (2010). Language and identity. In N. Hornberger & S. L. McKay (Eds.), *Sociolinguistics and language education* (pp. 349-369). UK: Multilingual Matters.

Shearer, Lee. (2012, April 7). Rules for undocumented students hit teachers, too. *The Athens Banner Herald.* Retrieved from http://onlineathens.com

Shore, I. (2009). What is critical literacy? In A. Darder, M. Baltodano, & R. D. Torres (Eds.), *The critical pedagogy reader* (pp. 282-301). New York, NY: Routledge.

Umana, K. (2011). *The ultimate college guide for college bound undocumented Georgia students.* Retrieved from http://www.cobbk12.org/pebblebrook/Guidance/Georgia%20College%20Guide%20for%20Undocumented%20Students.pdf

Wortham, S. E. F., Murillo, E. G., & Hamann, E. T. (2002). *Education in the new Latino diaspora: Policy and the politics of identity*. Westport, CT: Ablex Pub.

Zimmerman, A. (2012, June). *Documenting DREAMs: New media, undocumented youth, and the immigrant rights movement*. Retrieved from http://ypp.dmlcentral.net/publications/108

TONYA PERRY

4. TEACHING STUDENTS TO THINK CRITICALLY

Using Young Adult Literature in the 21st Century Classroom – The Watsons Go to Birmingham – 1963

ABSTRACT

Adolescents in the 21st century have an expanded view of literacy. The inclusion of varied quality young adult literature in the classroom expands the voices that have access and engagement in reading. Using such rich literature in the classroom can lead to a *hybridity* of texts that can open dialogue across cultures and generations. Young adult literature, works written for youth to invite them into the world of reading and capture their imaginations and perceptions of a world, is worthy of study and rich in its ability to teach students about text itself and the global society. Young adult literature in the classroom can be a bridge to show students, including marginalized groups, their voices in literature and capture students' interest and build academic stamina. A text, such as *The Watson's Go to Birmingham – 1963*, can be used to demonstrate how a young adult literature text deepens students' thinking through a "prism" approach.

> You feel like you need to [change your hair] so that we can all look alike. But that's not right. – *Middle School Student, 2000*

> It reminded me of the discussion about [different types and availability] of shampoo also-just because I as a white person do not have to think about my hair. – *Pre-Service Teacher, 2013*

> The eighth graders and I had just finished reading *The Watsons Go to Birmingham – 1963* chapter seven when Joseph, a student in the front row, asked a question that the other students were obviously thinking. With twenty-five students in the class, and only one student of color (not Joseph), he was perplexed.
>
> "What's a conk?" he asked. "I know it's some kind of hairdo. I get that. But I don't get why it made Byron's mom so mad!"
>
> The other students were listening, ready to hear a response from me. "Let's talk about hair – natural hair and processed hair. Natural hair is the biological version of your own hair, its own texture and color that you were born with

> that has not been altered by anything. I don't mean a haircut. I mean the texture, the structure, or color somehow is changed."
>
> "What do you mean by texture?" Joseph asked.
>
> "Well, I'm an African American, and right now, my hair is processed or changed by chemicals found in a perm. It's pretty strong stuff. It makes my hair turn from curly to straight. If I leave it in too long, it will burn my scalp. Momma from the story might call this a conk if she were here."
>
> Joseph looked perplexed. He did not know that this was not my natural hair. "Why would you want to put that in your hair?"
>
> Joseph then begins to research "perms" while in class.

The decline of the reading level of America's teens has been partially tied to students reading "less challenging" texts, compared to canonical pieces of literature (Stotsky, 2010; Allen, 2011). However, young adult literature, works written for youth to invite them into the world of reading and capture their imaginations and perceptions of a world, is worthy of study and rich in its ability to teach students about text itself and the global society. In fact, the opposite must be true. In today's classrooms, a majority of the secondary class novels are overwhelmingly canonical by definition (Gibbons & Stallworth, 2012; Wolk, 2010). Even though there are a plethora of texts available to teachers, it is the canon that is still assigned in many of the classrooms in the United States. Then, if students are assigned, and presumably are reading the canon but the reading scores are still low, then why is it that reading the assigned canonical literature has not strengthened the reading comprehension scores for students?

The answer is complex. Students today are still reading, but they are reading quite differently than the generations preceding them (Burns & Botzakis, 2012; Kaiser Foundation, 2004; Wilhelm, 2008). Students find pleasure in nonfiction, media, fantasy, and young adult literature and other texts that are not traditionally valued in an academic setting. So, even though the books in the canon are being assigned and teachers are working with students in class and out of class to understand the texts, I propose that students are not learning the skills that they need in order to do the "heavy lifting" to comprehend. Students need to understand and practice "how" to read texts, all texts. The answer is not to rid ourselves of the traditional canon, but the answer lies in expanding the canon and using other works in tandem with more challenging, sometimes less engaging pieces.

I've had the privilege of teaching *The Watsons Go to Birmingham* to suburban and urban middle school students and pre-service teachers enrolled in the Young Adult Literature course at the university. The reading of a text like *The Watsons* has an impact on both the middle school students and pre-service teachers. One, the deep thinking that a discussion about "hair" and other topics can spur allows a window into the lives of others that may be unconsidered and unquestioned. Two, the tie to time periods, people, and human experiences strengthen the discussion and the lens through which to conduct close examination and reading of the text.

Using a text like the *Watsons* can lead to inquiry into complicated issues that require additional reading, which I believe is the goal of becoming a life-long reader as well as a functional one.

Adolescents in the 21st century have an expanded view of literacy. Unlike the generations before, this group can access more information at a faster rate than any other. In addition, students now have access to countless texts – video clips, music lyrics, graphic novels, online magazines, Internet articles, young adult literature and so much more – that represent many cultural perspectives about many different subjects in multiple forms. This access, this expanded definition of literacy – *multiple literacies*, if you will, impacts how postmodern educators define literacy development and the inclusion of different types of texts, including young adult literature, in the present-day classroom (Alvermann, Hinchman, Moore, Phelps, & Waff, 1998; Perry, 2006).

The inclusion of varied quality young adult literature in the classroom expands the voices in the classroom literature (Engles & Kory, 2013; Metzger, Box, & Blasingame, 2013; Pytash, Morgan, & Batchelor, 2013; Stallworth, B.J., Gibbons, L., & Fauber, L. , 2008), increases the richness in conversations (Groenke, Maples, & Henderson, 2010), and promotes engagement in reading (Ostenson & Wadham, 2012; Perry & Stallworth, 2013; Rybakova, Piotrowski & Harper, 2013;). Using such rich literature in the secondary and pre-service teacher classroom can lead to a *hybridity* (Kincheloe & Steinberg, 2012) of texts that can open dialogue across cultures and generations. Despite the dialogue students have about young adult literature and the impact it has on student engagement in the classroom, it is still under attack. Hayne, Kaplan, Nolen (2011) stated, "YAL struggles for legitimacy and prestige." They call for more empirical research, and rightly so, in the field of young adult literature.

Young adult literature in the classroom can be a bridge to becoming a life-long reader (Lesesne, 2010), show students, including marginalized groups, their voices in literature (Perry & Stallworth, 2013), and capture students' interest and build academic stamina (Wilhem, 2008).

"Why would you want to put that in your hair?" Joseph asked with an expression of concern.

I had a decision to make. I could open up and be honest or I could give the safe answer. I chose the former.

"My hair is naturally curly, the kind of hairdo that looks more like an afro. That's my natural hair."

Some students snickered. I continued.

"To some of you, I imagine an afro looks very different from your own hair. When you think of an afro, it may make you feel like giggling. But it doesn't make me giggle. It is who I am and what my natural hair can do in its natural state."

Another student chimed in, "So your hair can stand up like that?"

> "Yes, if I did not have the perm, it sure could," I added.
>
> Nobody laughed.
>
> "Why don't you wear it that way?" Joseph questioned.
>
> I thought, "My students really want to discuss this."

Novels rich in ideas, characterization, complexity of thought, and development of the journey bring about rich learning, discussion, and inquiry that can only be sparked in students when they are thinking critically and engaged in the deep meaning of texts. Young adult literature provides entre into this world of others who experience life similarly and sometimes differently from the reader that allows adolescents to discuss experiences, themes, and challenges with a purposeful critical eye (Wolk, 2009). *The Watson's Go to Birmingham – 1963*, filled with many opportunities to discuss the past, present, and future, as it is the 50th anniversary of the Birmingham Civil Rights Movement, can be used to demonstrate how a young adult literature text can be used as a "prism" for thinking in the classroom. Looking at the young adult text from multiple perspectives can deepen students' understanding of their own world. In addition, this type of thinking teaches students to analyze, synthesize, and evaluate text, integral skills for reading proficiency for the Common Core and beyond.

COMMON CORE STATE STANDARDS

More than 40 states have adopted the Common Core State Standards (CCSS) as the new standards for the 21st century student. The standards include a focus on teaching students to think critically and to become independent readers of both fiction and non-fiction texts (National Govenors Association, 2010). Listed in the appendix of the CCSS are a group of suggested exemplar texts for each grade level, many of which have been staples in ELA classrooms across the country for decades (Connors 2013; Stallworth & Gibbons, 2012). The list contains, however, no contemporary YAL since 1980s. Although not intended by the CCSS, this limited exemplar list sends the message to some educators that the only literature, or at least the best, to teach is the canonical literature. This, however, is not the case; YAL can also be used to meet the requirement of text complexity of the CCSS (Burns & Botzakis, 2012; Connors, 2013; Ostenson & Wadham, 2012; Rybakova, Piotrowski, & Harper, 2013).

Text complexity, as defined by the CCSS (2010), has three equally important parts: quantitative, qualitative, and readers' consideration. Quantitative measures of complexity are based numbers related to Lexile and grade-level equivalency. The computation, according to the CCSS, is based on "Quantitative measures of text complexity, such as word frequency and sentence length" that is computed using several different measures. *The Watson's Go to Birmingham,* for example, has a Lexile of 1000 and grade equivalency of 5.5, according to the Lexile Framework for Reading. Qualitative measures of complexity are based on words, measurements that a computer could not measure, such as meaning and nuances.

The CCSS defines this as "Qualitative dimensions of text complexity, such as levels of meaning, structure, language conventionality and clarity, and knowledge demands." In *The Watsons*, for instance, attention to double-consciousness, having the ability to navigate two worlds, and understanding the different meanings of actions based on culture, is an advanced qualitative concept immeasurable by numbers and formulas. The third part of text complexity is readers' consideration. A teacher and student must take into consideration other factors that impact a reader. CCSS defines this as "Reader and task considerations, such as students' knowledge, motivation and interests." Before assigning, *Watsons*, for example, a teacher may want to think about students' knowledge of the Civil Rights Movement. This does not mean that the reader should avoid subjects that are unfamiliar; however, this does suggest that the teacher will have to construct meaningful ways for students to learn more through research and inquiry before and during the reading of the text.

When students are able to read a text from multiple lenses, then they are better prepared to participate in meaningful, thought-provoking conversations about author intent, use of language, impact of sociocultural influences, narrator voice, perspective of protagonists, historical lens of the antagonist, and so much more. Teaching students to think critically using young adult literature will give the students a rich experience and valuable practice with a text. This certainly meets the standards of the Common Core and beyond.

OVERVIEW OF THE WATSONS

The Watsons is a YAL novel that tells the story of a family, the Watsons, who live in cold Flint, Michigan. It begins with an overview of the family – father, a humorous character who creates laughter for the family; mother, a woman who was born in Alabama; Byron, the oldest child, a teenager who finds multiple ways to get into trouble; Kenny, the middle child and narrator of the story, who struggles with his place in the family, at school, and with friends; and Joetta, the youngest and only girl sibling, who enjoys being a part of the family. Byron gets into trouble and this family decides that a trip to Birmingham, Alabama is what is needed for the teen. The family plans a trip in 1963, a difficult time in history, especially for African Americans. Once they arrive to Birmingham, Kenny experiences the bombing of a church, which greatly impacts him as a character in the story. The story combines the everyday human experience of a family with the reality of a time period that impacts their decisions.

> "That stuff will hurt your hair. But you still use it?" Joseph relentlessly continued.
>
> "Yes, for now." I added. "I really don't like it, class. But I still use it."
>
> Another student chimed in, quietly, pensively,
>
> "You feel like you need to so that we can all look alike. But that's not right."

This chapter will incorporate different literary perspectives as one way to demonstrate the depth of the thinking that can be applied to young adult literature. The accompanying lesson will illustrate how to use the technique with middle school and high school students in the classroom to maximize student learning. At this time, I plan to focus on the "prism" using cultural studies, black aesthetics, feminism, deconstruction, and archetypes as the lenses to view the text in meaningful forms. The lesson will include suggestions for varied products for students to demonstrate their understanding of the text using music, art, digital media, and theatre.

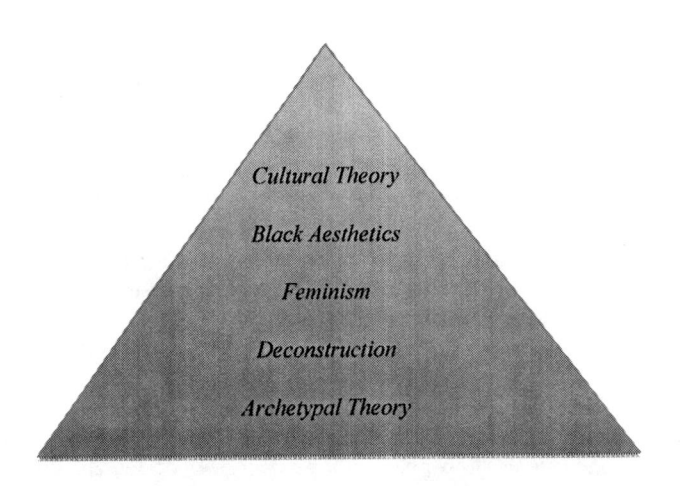

Cultural Theory

Black Aesthetics

Feminism

Deconstruction

Archetypal Theory

EXAMINING WATSONS USING A CULTURAL LENS

A cultural studies approach to literature allows students to examine the text using a cultural lens to understand the work. Smith and Murfin (n.d.) posit in their essay, quoting Giroux and Bakhtin, that cultural studies, "should show works in reference to other works, economic contexts, or broad social discourses (about childbirth, women's education, rural decay, etc.) within whose contexts the work makes sense"(n.d.) The idea that culture is continuously connected, forming and becoming is important. "Culture, rather, is really a set of interactive *cultures*, alive and growing and changing, and cultural critics should be present- and even future-oriented" (n.d). It is almost impossible to examine a small aspect of any culture without interacting with other influences of that culture that impact its being (Moore, 1997).

In order for students to understand an aspect of a text from a cultural standpoint, particularly one different from their own, a part of their own perspective will need to become secondary to the characters' primary way of seeing the world. In *The Watsons*, Anne felt as if she was lured into seeing the characters from a cultural standpoint. Because she saw them as a family first, she adored and laughed with them before she became wholly aware of their different cultural backgrounds and stances. When the church bombing occurred, she was already a part of the family.

> I was struck by the [church] bombing scene, which of course, was quite shocking and emotional. But I was particularly struck by the scene because, up until that moment, race had played such a small role in the novel. I almost could not believe it happened, even though as a student of history, I should have expected it. As a white girl in the 2010s, I have shared the horror and shock of this black family in the 1960s – that is very powerful.

Reading from a cultural stance also allows the course instructor to bring in other resources, such as articles, to support or oppose the text. In class, I used Peggy McIntosh's "Invisible Knapsack" to discuss issues of white privilege that the characters only alluded to through their experiences during the 1960s. Combining the nonfiction article with the book assisted the students in their understanding of privileges experienced by majority groups that are not a part of everyday consciousness. One of the topics we discussed was hair products. I shared with students that, until the last two decades, hair products for all peoples were not readily available in local stores. And to be honest, the products still may not be available for everyone, depending on where the store is located. This point resonated with Jake who made a connection.

> The thing that I thought was interesting [from the reading] was when Byron, I think, got the chemical hair treatment. I do not remember what it was called but it was meant to straighten his hair. It reminded me of our discussion of "white privilege" (Peggy McIntosh), and I assume that he wanted to do this in order to have hair more like a white person would have. It reminded me of the discussion about [different types and availability of] shampoo also – just because I as a white person do not have to think about my hair. I just buy shampoo and do not have to worry [about finding the right kind of shampoo for my texture].

Another aspect of culture is the socioeconomic impact on one's thinking and decision-making. The level of income impacts, perhaps, how the characters see themselves and how others, perhaps, perceive them. Two students in class believed that the family's status based on finances impacted the behavior of the characters, particularly the male siblings.

> Byron and Kenny place a large emphasis on socioeconomics, particularly poverty and class standings of themselves among others....The boys are so concerned about what others will think. In one chapter, Byron assumes they are on welfare because they are buying grocery on credit. Byron is shamed by this. This shows the class struggle that the Watsons, particularly the sons, feel a pressure to conform to.
>
> Class was prevalent throughout the book. It demonstrated how, even as a kid, class is a concern of children and that they are aware of these distinctions.

> This can be a source of pride and /or shame. For instance, when Kenny notices the bully's shoes, Kenny feels pity for him and ashamed of himself for having more. His leather gloves were a source of pride until he saw the exceptionally worn shoes of his nemesis.

In addition to the racial and socioeconomic cultures, one student identified another cultural group that the Kenny is a part of – the students with a physical condition. Because of Kenny's lazy eye, he is picked on by his schoolmates, including his own brother. The cultural dynamics of this ostracized group demonstrate the psychological pain students endure under hostile circumstances, but also the role of Kenny when there is a reversal of power when he is put in an unfamiliar position as an oppressor.

> Kenny experiences ostracization in his school culture because of his physical appearance, his lazy eye. This has no bearing on his intelligence. He wonders how his brother and Larry Dunn can be so mean to him and "bully" him. However, when Rufus and his brother move to town, Kenny takes pleasure for a short period of time in having someone else receive the brunt of the mean behavior instead of him.

READING THE WATSONS USING THE LENS OF BLACK AESTHETICS

Langley (2007) discusses the importance of looking at literature about African Americans and other peoples of the Diaspora with the lens of Black Aesthetics. This examination of literature constructs a way to identify, critically think, and analyze African American (and other diasporic groups) culture (Langley, 2007). Having an opportunity to study and celebrate "blackness" gives students yet another perspective to examine literature.

In *The Watsons*, looking at the literature from the Black Aesthetics lens allows the students to examine the text from one particular group, viewing from the lens based on history, customs, and ideology specific to a group. In the class, students were able to find examples of signifying, black sociopolitics, identity and ideology.

Students found examples of humor and banter playful and brilliant among the family members. Using signifying language, the family members manipulated talk among each other and with friends to express themselves that may have been misunderstood outside of the group. The language used was loaded with meaning, sometimes multiple meanings, that built on the richness of the text.

> There is an informal language that is representative of a community .... Bryon and Kenny used signifying as a way to communicate. Byron and his friend [Bumphead] had their own sort of language. Momma [and Daddy Watson] also signified.

Using this lens, students had to think as if they were a part of the 1960 time period to understand fully the depth of planning and worry Mrs. Watson experienced as an

TEACHING STUDENTS TO THINK CRITICALLY

African American heading South. This lens allowed students to delve into the journey from the perspective of the characters from a historical lens.

> Mrs. Watson's trip planning was memorable because she had to consider what locations would be safe to stop at for a black family traveling South in 1963. I take a lot of road trips across the Southeast and safety is something I take for granted (in regard to my skin color). I like reading a book from another perspective because, if I'm honest, most of the books I read have mostly white characters. I learned about other people's experiences by reading this.

Another student linked the definition of blackness and identity to whiteness and change. Her premise was that to change "blackness" was to deny one's heritage. This change then would then attach itself to some "other" way of being.

> In African America literature, the "conk" or any manipulation of an African American's "natural hair" can represent a refutation of their own "blackness" and conformity to the white definitions of beauty.

Laura discussed the idea of double-consciousness, always being aware of the two ways in which an idea or action can be communicated or received. Students had not considered that in Black Aesthetics, the minority culture always was conscious of the majority culture's beliefs, values, and interpretations, but the reverse was not necessarily true. When Joetta received a doll from her neighbor, it saddened Laura. This led to lively class discussion: Should black children only have black dolls?

> I think the idea of double-consciousness is very evident in the *Watsons Go to Birmingham*. The part with the angel was sad to me. The sister [Joetta] was given a white angel statue and was told that it looked like her, but she knew that it didn't. The woman who gave it to her simply meant that the girl was sweet and angelic, not white, but the little girl interpreted that gesture as strange and upsetting. She knew she did not look like the angel.

LOOKING AT THE WATSONS USING A FEMINIST LENS

Feminist literary criticism analyzes language and literature by revealing how gender impacts a text, both masculine and feminine (Moore, 1997). By examining the characters from a feminist lens, the students are able to think critically about what the text is saying about the role of women in the work and how gender impacts the text.

In *The Watsons,* one student saw the youngest child as the protector, a juxtaposition of her role as a female and youth. Finding the balance in the novel between innocence and authority as a female character was crafted carefully.

> I think it was interesting that Joey was the one trying to protect Byron. She is the youngest and the girl, meaning she would typically be the one needing

> protection .... It can be seen in Joey ... she is a girl who does girlish things and acts like a protector who challenges authority for a loved one. Joey has two roles she is balancing throughout the book as a female character.

The three female characters in the text, the students decided, were secondary to the men in the story. However, without them, the story would not have been possible because of the role of "wholeness" they played in the novel. Terry believed that each female character was central to create the completeness needed for the novel.

> The three main characters (Joey, mom, and grandmother) take on the strong roles to keep the family together. The females form a three-tier system: mind, body, and spirit. Grandmother Sands takes on the role of the mind, the wise ancestor and foundation....Joey acts as the spirit or conscience of the family. She makes everyone rethink his/her actions. Mother Wilona is the body. She is the physical connection to the characters and is the center to the family web. The three combined form a system of strong female roles representing completion of mind, body, and spirit.

LOOKING AT THE WATSONS USING AN ARCHETYPAL LENS

Archetypal lens allows students to analyze a work to look for the timeless similarities or patterns that may exist from one work to another. According to Sproul (1979),

> Prototypes are relevant only for the direct inheritors of the world that they effected. Archetypes, on the other hand, have universal application. And, whether or not they took place in time, it is not their historicity but their timelessness that people value. Archetypes reveal and define form, showing how a truth of the moment has the same structure and meaning as an absolute and eternal one. Prototypes were true once and may still be so; archetypes are true always. (p. 27)

Using Joseph Campbell's work, students studied the journey of a hero to determine if there was a hero in the text, and if so, who was the hero. The students could not agree – half decided that no hero existed while others believed Bryon was the hero by the end of the novel. The journey of the hero has different stages. The students in the YAL course used evidence from the text to support their stance.

> Byron demonstrates one stage of the hero based on Joseph Campbell's model, the Freedom to Live, an acceptance of the reality and difficulty of life in 1963 for African Americans. Byron tells Kenny in Chapter 15, "things ain't never going to be fair ... but you just gotta understand that that's the way it is and keep on steppin'." This is the point that demonstrates Byron is the hero of the story and truly gives up himself for others.

Another student recognized Byron's development from boyhood to manhood during the visit to Birmingham. Before the trip, Byron was unruly and troublesome, but in Birmingham, Byron is a mannerly rule-follower who enjoys spending time with the other men in the family.

> Atonement with the Father is another stage in the journey of a hero. Byron is confronted early on by his father who is trying to exert his authority when he is defied by Bryon. Byron, later in the novel, is attracted to rather than repelled by his father when in Alabama at the lake walking with his father. This demonstrates his willingness to show his father that he has changed and accepts his role as the son.

Bryon is the one responsible for helping Kenny recover from his emotionally traumatic experience at the church. Kenny retreats into himself after the incident and hides to sooth his wounded spirit. Byron sees that he is needed as a brother and not a torturer and provides comfort to Kenny when no one else can help him through this difficult time. Byron then shows his return to Brother, a responsible sibling.

> The crossing of the return thresh is another stage of the hero. Byron reached out to Kenny while he hid under the sofa and spoke wisdom and life into his brother .... This demonstrates Byron's return to "brother" and fulfilling his role to Kenny by protecting and offering advice, an action that did not happen often during Byron's journey as a delinquent teenager.

LOOKING AT THE WATSONS USING DECONSTRUCTION

The Deconstruction lens allowed students to look closely at words and ideas for multiple meanings/impacts in this context. Balkin (1995-1996) states that

> the deconstructor looks for unexpected relationships between different parts of a text, or loose threads that at first glance appear peripheral yet often turn out to undermine or confuse the argument. A deconstructor may consider the multiple meanings of key words in a text, etymological relationships between words, and even puns to show how the text speaks with different (and often conflicting) voices. (n.d.)

Using this approach, students examined the language politics in the text and concepts such as the Wool Pooh, resurrection, the word "weird," and the character's role and name, Grandma Sands.

Characters in the text use language for many purposes. Each verbal and non-verbal communicative gesture expresses something different about the character in relationship to the larger story.

> A close reading of the text reveals a language politics which situates power in terms of comprehension, participation, and exclusion. Both verbal and non-verbal communication play roles in this meta-communicative work. One is

> the repetition of understanding in Kenny's talks with his father. Another is the emphasis on the language of music and its importance in their lives. Third is the absence of language as a power tool, the silent treatment used by Byron to punish his family. Fourth, Kenny's use of language is to tease but also to apologize.

Several students attempted to deconstruct the role of the Wool Pooh in the text. The idea that he only shows up around the natural elements and disasters demonstrates that he is quite the opposite of the childhood Winnie-the-Pooh character in Kenny's imagination.

> The ending few chapters really brought in the character "Wool Pooh," who at first seemed harmless, but in the scenes [in the water and] in the church, he took an entirely new meaning. Kenny sees Wool Pooh when he goes into the church and he thinks it has taken Joetta's life .... Whether this is a spiritual experience or some illusion is up for debate, but the Wool Pooh's influence on the last few chapters is apparent.

The idea of a resurrection to depict the change Kenny undergoes after leaving the church was an interesting notion. The student deconstructed words such as "rebirth," "resurrection," and "change."

> Chapter 14 was about change in Kenny – he goes into the bombed church and innocent, relatively self-centered kid, and emerges from the church a different person – a rebirth of sorts. Kenny's rebirth sparks a change in Byron's attitude and his family's view about each other.

At the end of Chapter 1, Kenny refers to his family as the "Weird Watsons." One student deconstructed the term "weird" from the first chapter to the last to make a comparison of the two meanings.

> Weird Watsons is a term Kenny used to describe his family. "Weird" can be defined as strikingly odd or unusual. This describes the family when they are all outside crying after Byron has been pulled from the frozen car side window. The other definition suggests something supernatural. This could refer to the spirit that led Joetta from the church. In both cases, weird depicts a type of behavior, comical and serious, that impacted the family in important ways.

Terry deconstructed the name and role of the grandmother, actually agreeing with the author on the appropriateness of the two.

> The same "sands" is unique. Naming is an important part of culture and identity. Grandma Sands's name shows she is an ancestor connected to the earth. She is what "grounds" the family as they look to her for direction.

LESSON: EXAMINING WATSONS THROUGH A PRISM

Students learn the different types of lenses to examine literature. This practice in small groups allows opportunities for discussion. To facilitate this in manageable ways, I use note cards for students to jot down their thoughts. This keeps the responses succinct so that I can quickly review their thinking about the text and a particular lens.

When students enter the class, I ask for their individual read on Chapter One using the lens that they were assigned. The students then turn in their notecards. Students then assemble in their small groups with classmates who have the same lens to examine the chapter. The groups discuss their findings from the chapter and compose a group list of their ideas. Students then turn in a second notecard responding to this question: "What do you see now in the reading that you did not see before the group discussion?"

After the groups turn in their analysis of Chapter One from one particular lens, I then jigsaw the groups so that each group has at least four different perspectives about the chapter. Each person becomes the expert using his lens and shares his/her understanding with the new group. The students in this newly formed group must design a thesis statement that unifies their ideas about the chapter.

Students then agree and write down the group thesis statement and write a multi-paragraph response. As the students learn more about the different ways to examine the chapters, this process then extends to multiple chapters to examine with a different lens.

By end of the text, students will be able to construct an analysis essay using one of the ideas created during the reading. In addition, students then can create an authentic representation using music, theatre, digital media, or art to depict the change they see in their understanding of the text. This is not a characterization piece; rather, it is a meta-cognitive analysis of student thinking throughout the learning process.

One example of this artistically may be a mask from a feminist lens. I might ask students to create a three-part mask with Joetta, Wilona, and Grandma Sands to depict who they are and what they represent from a feminist standpoint using evidence from the text.

Using music, students can compose a song using a simple tool, such as the digital tool GarageBand, putting lyrics into melodies. The words, rather than a retelling, could be an analysis of the three female characters in the text and their roles to the larger story. An example might be as follows:

> Grandma Sands
>
> Ever present, earthly, whole, realistic, passing time, passing wisdom, bending to hold another generation through a tough situation
>
> Shares hope and vision for the future with the ones who gain strength from her presence

> The life she lived has not been easy – Jim Crow, boycotts, separate expectations, second class citizenship
>
> But she persevered like the sands of time, flowing from top to bottom, waiting her turn to rise to the top again.
>
> Grandma Sands

A theatrical representation from a feminist standpoint might be a reader's theatre. A student would write the script using the exact words from the female characters from the text and rearrange them in a manner to support a reading of the work. Only short interpretative lines may be included to help the audience understand the overall message. A short version may read like this for Grandma Sands:

> "The Family Heart"
>
> "Give your granny a hug"
>
> It's been a long time since I've seen you, my loves
>
> "You call this child bad"
>
> He is still in my heart.
>
> "My fambly, my beautiful fambly"
>
> Nothing can separate us – distance, Jim Crow, time
>
> "Things are different from what they were when you left"
>
> Life changes but my heart is still the same for you.
>
> "I am your Grandma"
>
> I am the foundation of this family, the center
>
> "Give your granny a hug"
>
> I've missed you. I love you. I pass to you my heart.

Example of Initial Guiding Questions for the Prism Activity

Feminist Lens	Cultural Lens
1. Who are the women in the chapter? 2. What are the roles of the women? 3. How does society see them? How do you see them as the reader? 4. How would the novel change without the women? How would the novel become stronger with more of a presence?	1. What are the cultural groups that the characters are members of? From which groups are they excluded? 2. How did they gain membership? 3. How does culture impact the actions of the character(s)? 4. What role does the culture play in the chapter (s)?

Deconstruction Lens	*Black Aesthetics Lens*
1. What are words that are key to the text? 2. How do these words impact the larger meaning of the text? 3. What are the multiple meanings of the words and what is the textual evidence to support your different definitions of the words? 4. How does language impact meaning in this chapter?	1. What is present in this chapter that is overwhelmingly tied to African American culture and what is your evidence? 2. How does this idea or action impact the chapter? 3. How does it impact different types of readers? 4. How can this idea or action be perceived in different contexts? Is it ineffective or effective here?

Archetypal Lens

1. Who is the hero(ine) in the story?
2. What stages of the journey does the hero seem to experience? What is the evidence for this?
3. How is the hero's journey in the novel different from the model we've discussed?
4. How might this hero's journey look if you were to create a model just for this character?

Getting students to think critically takes planning and forethought. It takes careful construction of learning opportunities that will push students to think differently, deeply, and critically about the work. Young adult literature in the classroom can do just that for students, and this type of thinking and learning can be applied to other texts. The important point here is to expose students to the types of literature that can expand their thinking and conversations and apply those skills to other types of texts as well. Young adult literature is an excellent springboard to a world of literature in different genres. Use of *The Watsons* in both the middle and pre-service teacher college classroom created discussions that led to the reading of other extended texts and literatures. To deny students access to the richness of young adult literature will deny them of windows into the culture of others and an opening into the world of expansive reading opportunities.

REFERENCES

Abrams, M. H. (1999). Archetypal criticism. In *A glossary of literary terms* (7th ed.), Fort Worth, TX: Harcourt Brace College.

Allen, R. (2011, August). Looking for the literary canon. *Association for Supervision and Curriculum Education Update, 53*(8), 1-8.

Alvermann, D. E., Hinchman, K. A., Moore, D. W., Phelps, S. F., & Waff, D. R. (Eds.). (1998). *Reconceptualizing the literacies in adolescents' Lives*. Matwah, NJ: Erlbaum.

Balkin, J.M. (1996). Deconstruction. Retrieved from http://www.yale.edu/lawweb/jbalkin/articles/deconessay.pdf

Burns, L. D., & Botzakis, S. G. (2012). Using *The Joy Luck Club* to teach core standards and 21st century literacies. *English Journal, 101*(5), 23-29.
Connors, S. P. (2013). Challenging perspectives on young adult literature. *English Journal, 102*(5), 69-73.
Engles, T., & Kory, F. (2013). Incarceration, identity, formation, and race in young adult literature: The case of *Monster* versus *Hole in My Life*. *English Journal, 102*(4), 53-58.
Groenke, S. L., Maples, J., & Henderson, J. (2010). Raising "hot topics" through young adult literature. *Voices from the Middle, 17*(4), 29-36.
Hayn, J. A., Kaplan, J. S., & Nolen, A. (2011). Young adult literature research in the 21sst century. *Theory into Practice, 50*, 176-181.
Kaiser Family Foundation. (2004). *Teens, tweens, and magazines*. Retrieved November 9, 2005, from http://www.kff.org/entmedia/upload/Tweens-Teensand-Magazines-Fact-Sheet.pdf
Kincheloe, J. L., & Steinberg, S. R. (2012). Indigenous knowledges in education: Complexities, dangers, and profound benefits. In S. R. Steinberg & G. S. Cannella (Eds.), *Critical qualitative research reader* (pp. 341-361). New York, NY: Peter Lang.
Langley, A. C. E. (2008). *The Black aesthetic unbound: Theorizing the dilemma of eighteenth-century African American literature*. Columbus, OH: Ohio State Press.
Lesesne, T. S. (2010). *Reading ladders: Leading students from where they are to where we'd like them to be*. Portsmouth, NH: Heinemann.
McIntosh, P. Unpacking the invisible knapsack. Retrieved from http://www.nymbp.org/reference/WhitePrivilege.pdf
Metzger, K., Box, A., & Blasingame, J. (2013). Embracing intercultural diversification: Teaching young adult literature with Native American themes. *English Journal, 102*(5), 57-62.
Moore, J. N. (1997). *Interpreting young adult literature: Literary theory in the secondary classroom*. Portsmouth, NH: Heinemann.
National Governors Association Center for Best Practices, & Council of Chief State School Officers. (2010). *Common core state standards: English language arts & literacy in history/social studies, science, and technical subjects*. Retrieved from http://www.corestandards.org/the-standards.pdf
Ostenson, J., & Wadham, R. (2012). Young adult literature and the common core: A surprisingly good fit. *America Secondary Education, 41*(1), 4-13.
Perry, T. B. (2006). Multiple literacies and middle school students. *Theory into Practice, 45*(4), 328-336.
Perry, T. B., & Stallworth, B. J. (2013). 21st-century students demand a balanced, more inclusive canon. *Voices from the Middle, 21*(1), 15-18.
Pytash, K. E., Morgan, D. N., & Batchelor, K. E. (2013). Recognize the signs: Reading young adult literature to address bullying. *Voices from the Middle, 20*(3), 15-20.
Rybakova, K., Piotrowski, A., & Harper, E. (2013). Teaching controversial young adult literature with the common core. *Wisconsin English Journal, 55*(1), 37-56.
Smith, J. M., & Murfin, R. C. (n.d.). What is cultural criticism? Retrieved from http://www.usask.ca/english/frank/cultint.htm
Sproul, B. C. (1979). *Primal myths: Creation myths around the world*. San Francisco: Harper Collins.
Stallworth, B. J., & Gibbons, L. (2012). What's on the list ... now? A follow-up study of the book-length works taught in secondary schools. *English Leadership Quarterly, 34*(3), 2-3.
Stallworth, B. J., Gibbons, L., & Fauber, L. (2008). It's not on the list: An exploration of teachers' perspectives on using multicultural literature. *Journal of Adolescent and Adult Literacy, 49*, 478-489.
Stallworth, B. J. (2006). The relevance of young adult literature. *Educational Leadership, 63*(7), 59-63.
Stotsky, S. (2010). *Literary study in grades 9, 10, and 11: A national survey. Forum: A publication of the Association of Literary Scholars, Critics, and Writers*. Association of Literary Scholars, Critics and Writers. Retrieved from http://coehp.uark.edu/literary_study.pdf
Tatum, A. W. (2005). *Teaching reading to Black adolescent males: Closing the achievement gap*. Portland, ME: Stenhouse.

Wilhelm, J. D. (2008). *You gotta be the book: Teaching engaged and reflective reading with adolescents* (2nd ed.). New York, NY: Teachers College Press and Urbana, IL: National Council of Teachers of English.

Wolk, S. (2010). What should students read? *Phi Delta Kappan, 91*(7), 8-16.

Wolk, S. (2009). Reading for better world: Teaching for social responsibility with young adult literature. *Journal of Adolescent & Adult Literacy, 52*(8), 664-673.

AMBER M. SIMMONS

5. CLASS ON FIRE

Using the Hunger Games Trilogy to Encourage Social Action

ABSTRACT

This chapter explores ways to utilize students' interest in fantasy literature to support critical literacy. Focusing on Suzanne Collins's The Hunger Games series (2008, 2009, 2010), the author addresses how elements of the trilogy relate to violent acts in our world, helping student understand that violence and brutality toward children is not fiction, but very real, and that they can play a role in its abolishment, just like Katniss, through social action projects. Issues such as hunger, forced labor, child soldiers, and the sex trade that appear in both the fictional series and our world are discussed, encouraging students to assess their world and advocate for change. Examples of social action projects that utilize multiple literacies are suggested as a way to inspire students take action in the community and to stand up to injustice and brutality in hopes of creating a better world and a better human race.

Using popular literature to pique student interest, this chapter explores how to incorporate the books in the Hunger Games series into the ELA classroom to support literacy and critical goals.

INTRODUCTION

The Hunger Games trilogy by Suzanne Collins, comprising *The Hunger Games* (2008), *Catching Fire* (2009), and *Mockingjay* (2010), is a pop culture sensation. With more than 26 million books sold and box office receipts grossing $68.3 million on the opening day of the film adaptation of the first novel, this postapocalyptic, dystopian series clearly appeals to a wide audience that is not limited to a specific age, group or gender.

The Hunger Games, the first book in the series, introduces readers to Panem, a country in North America that is controlled by a wealthy area referred to as the Capitol, which is dependent on 12 poorer districts to supply its inhabitants with the necessary resources to maintain their political dominance and luxurious lifestyle. As punishment for a past rebellion, every district must provide via a lottery system a male and a female tribute between the ages of 12 and 18 to fight to the death in a high-tech arena. Only one tribute walks away the victor.

P. Paugh et al. (eds.), *Teaching towards Democracy with Postmodern and Popular Culture Texts*, 77–95.
© 2014 Sense Publishers. All rights reserved.

Katniss Everdeen, a 16-year-old girl from District 12, volunteers to be a tribute when the name of Primrose, her younger sister, is drawn. Peeta Mellark, the baker's son who is in love with Katniss and provided her with bread when she was starving, is selected as the male tribute. The book then follows the pair to the Capitol, where they are transformed by stylists to win popularity with the viewing public, sent into an arena with 22 other tributes to murder one another, survive together by gaining the public's sympathy as star-crossed lovers, and incite rebellion in the districts through their unconventional victory. The second and third books, *Catching Fire* and *Mockingjay*, recount the events surrounding the rebellion and the eventual overthrow of the Capitol (see Table 1 for a more detailed summary of each book). With a thick love story, action-packed adventure, and shocking twists and turns, the Hunger Games trilogy is a rich meal for the imagination.

There are many reasons to love the series, but one reason I find it so compelling is that Katniss Everdeen is the most accurate depiction of a teenager that I have ever encountered in adolescent literature. Yes, I am a fan of Harry Potter (Rowling, 1997) and Frodo Baggins (Tolkien, 1954) and the Pevensie children (Lewis, 1950) but Katniss Everdeen seems the most *real*. She is oxymoronic with her uncertain impulsivity and her role as a leader and a pawn. She is strong and brave, features I observe daily in my students, but fragile to the point of breaking. Her black and white sense of right and wrong, betrayal and loyalty, is a trait of youth; as she matures, she is introduced to the ambiguity – the gray – of human nature. Considering her similarities to today's teens, does Katniss Everdeen, the "girl on fire" (Collins, 2008, p. 147), a description inspired by her opening-ceremony outfit that blazed with flames, have the power to set our classrooms on fire? To make them burn with desire and urgency and even anger?

By incorporating the Hunger Games trilogy into the classroom, teachers can encourage students to look at current issues of violence and domination in our world, relating them to the injustices faced by the 12 districts of Panem while using students' out-of-school literacy practices, "learning [that students] consider powerful and important" (Moje, 2008, p. 98). Addressing issues of violence through popular literature is important, for as Downey (2005) pointed out, students are desensitized to violence, and one goal of educators is to resensitize them so that they understand the reality of brutality and injustice. In *Entertainment Weekly*, Stephen King (2008) wrote that the Hunger Games series is "violent and jarring" (para. 3). That may be true, but the trilogy is fiction and, therefore, unthreatening to most students. By pairing popular novels with real-world violence, novels that are defined as fantasy or science fiction are kept from being romanticized (Moje, Young, Readence, & Moore, 2000) and in fact help "students deconstruct dominant narratives and contend with oppressive practices in hopes of achieving a more egalitarian and inclusive society" (Morrell, 2002, p. 72).

However, "once students recognize the reality [of violence], they express feelings of helplessness and a sense of inevitability" as well as the "weight of responsibility" (Downey, 2005, p. 37). This is where the fire metaphor that Collins

Table 1. Summary of the trilogy.

Book 1: *The Hunger Games*
The Hunger Games introduces readers to Panem, a country in North America that is controlled by the wealthy Capitol that depends on 12 poorer districts to supply them with the necessary resources to maintain their political dominance and luxurious lifestyle. As punishment for a past rebellion, via a lottery system, every District must provide a male and female tribute between the ages of twelve and eighteen to fight to the death in a high-tech arena. Only one tribute walks out the victor. Katniss Everdeen, a sixteen year old from District 12, volunteers as tribute when Primrose, her younger sister's name, is drawn. Peeta Mellark, the baker's boy who is in love with Katniss and provided her with bread when she was starving, is selected as the male tribute. Haymitch Abernathy, a previous victor from District 12and a drunk, attends the games with the pair as their mentor. Once at the Capitol, they are transformed by stylist, Cinna, in order to gain public popularity that might lead to rich audience members donating gifts that might aid in their survival. During an interview, Peeta declares his love for Katniss, a ploy she believes is a strategy for gaining more public support. When sent in the arena, 11 of the 24 tributes are killed in the first day. A skilled hunter, Katniss's knowledge of the forest and skills with a bow and arrow help her survive and escape many life threatening situations. She allies with Rue, the youngest tribute from District 11, and displeases the Gamemakes and President Snow when she decorates Rue's body with flowers when she is eventually killed by another tribute. The Gamemakers then announce that there can be two winners if the victors are from the same District. At this news, Katniss sets out in search for Peeta. Playing into the "star-crossed lovers" façade, they ban together and receive gifts from sponsors that keep them alive until the grand finale. When Katniss and Peeta are the last two standing, the Gamemakers change the rules again, stating there can only be one winner. Unwilling to kill each other and determined to beat the Gamemakers at their "game," Katniss and Peeta act as if they are going to commit suicide by eating poisonous berries. Knowing that two victors are better than no victor at all, the Gamemakers declare them both winners. After the ordeal, Haymitch reveals to Katniss that she has incited President Snow's fury at so openly defying the rules. Knowing she has put her family in danger, she quickly tries to convince the authorities that "love" made her act so irrationally, declaring it was not an act of open defiance. On the way home, Katniss tells Peeta that her actions of love in the arena were an act to keep them alive, a truth that leaves Peeta heartbroken.
Book 2: *Catching Fire*
As winners of the Hunger Games, Katniss and Peeta are subjected to participate in a "Victory Tour" of the country. Katniss is visited by President Snow who threatens her with the consequences of inciting any further rebellion. While in District 11, Katniss speaks of Rue, her young ally. The audience reacts by saluting Katniss when a man whistles Rue's tune that she used to sing to the Mockingjays, an act that costs him his life. After returning to District 12, Katniss encounters two runaways from District 8 who tell her of other rebellions and their belief that District 13, previously thought to have been demolished in the rebellion, actually still exists. It is then announced that for the next Hunger Games, previous victors will be forced to compete again, an event known as the "Quarter Quell" that happens every 25 years. Katniss and Peeta are forced into the arena again. Katniss promises to herself that she will protect Peeta. While in the arena,

Katniss and Peeta join up with Finnick and Mags from District 4, Beetee and Wiress from District 3 and Johanna from District 7. They soon find out that the arena is set up like a clock, meaning each danger is triggered in a specific parameter during a particular hour. The alliance decides to create a trap to eliminate two contenders using the electricity from the force field that surrounds the arena. Katniss is charged with directing the lightening rod, and the shock of the blast knocks her out, leaving her temporarily paralyzed. When she wakes up, she is on her way to District 13. It is then revealed to her that there was a plan among most of the tributes to break out of the arena. While they succeeded in escaping, Peeta and Johanna were captured by the Capitol. Gale, Katniss's best friend from District 12, tells her that in retaliation, District 12 was bombed and destroyed. However, he managed to get her family out in time.

Book 3: *Mockingjay*

Safe in District 13, Katniss is coerced in becoming a symbol of the rebellion: "the Mockingjay," so named for the pin she wore during the Hunger Games. Before agreeing, Katniss demands that she be allowed to kill President Snow. Peeta and Johanna are rescued from the Capitol, but Peeta has been brainwashed to hate Katniss and tries to kill her during their reunion. After securing many of the districts, the rebels attack the Capitol. During the assault, many of Katniss's allies are killed, and killing President Snow becomes impossible as he has surrounded himself with all of the Capitol children to use as a human shield. During the attack on the Capitol, bombs are dropped on the children and the rebel medical team rushes in to help, including Katniss's sister, Prim. Prim dies as another set of bombs explode, making Katniss catatonic with grief. The Capitol is secured and President Snow is found guilty for crimes against humanity; however, it was president Coin, District 13's President, who ordered the bombing of the children, not President Snow. The bombing tactic was also originally developed by her best friend, Gale. Although he was not directly involved in Prim's death, their friendship is forever altered. President Coin then suggests holding a Hunger Games using the Capitol's children as retribution for all of the Hunger Games that killed District children. Knowing that President Coin is no better than President Snow, Katniss shoots her with an arrow when she was supposed to execute Snow. During the riot that follows, Snow chokes on his own blood and dies. Katniss is taken into custody where she tries to kill herself with a cyanide pill, but Peeta stops her. When on trial, Katniss is acquitted due to temporary insanity and she, her mother, Haymitch and Peeta return to District 12. As Peeta recovers from his brainwashing, Katniss finds herself falling in love with him. Together they make a book that pays respect to past fallen tributes and begin to heal. In the epilogue, Katniss speaks as an adult, revealing that she and Peeta had two children, who represent the future of Panem. While She and Peeta still have nightmares and traumatic, emotional scars, they teach their children about their past so as to ensure it does not happen again. When Katniss feels the evils of the world around her, she, plays a "game" where she remembers every good thing she has seen a person do since the fall of the Capitol. The irony of this game is not lost on her, but she admits that there are worse games to play.

employs so effectively throughout the trilogy can be appropriately transferred to the classroom via social-justice education and social-action projects. By raising awareness and advocating for change, such projects encourage students to assess their world and take action against the social problems they observe (Wade, 1997), allowing them to make a "real and material change in what people do, how they interact with the world and with others, what they mean and what they value, and the discourses in which they understand and interpret the world" (Atweh, Kemmis, & Weeks, 1998, p. 25). According to Morrell (2002), students will then be "motivated and empowered by the prospect of addressing a real problem in the world" (p. 76) and will use multiple literacies in hopes of changing it.

This article addresses how elements of the Hunger Games trilogy relate to social injustices in our world and presents activities for the language arts classroom that can foster literacy and help students understand that violence and brutality toward children are not fiction but fact. The activities can engage students to play a role in the abolishment of harm toward children, just as Katniss does, by using their literacy skills to participate in social-action projects. For example, the hunger and starvation experienced by the districts can relate to issues of hunger in the United States by comparing the Capitol's wastefulness to that of the U.S. population. The forced labor in the districts correlates with various types of involuntary employment around the world. The idea of children set against one another in combat is relevant to the use of child soldiers in many African countries. And Finnick's description of how victors are sold as sex objects is a means for revealing the booming sex trade and sex-slave industry that occur in all major countries, even the United States. Although focusing on these dark issues may seem too heavy for adolescents, it is equally difficult for teachers because "one of the great difficulties in teaching about horrific periods of history, the underbelly of human experience, is addressing how to help students comprehend the incomprehensible" (Downey, 2005, p. 33). The horrors with which students will become familiar may alter their conception of humanity, but the social-action projects in which they can participate will show them that, as long as there are people like Katniss and themselves who are compassionate and brave enough to stand up to such brutality, there is hope for a better world and a better human race.

CRITICAL LITERACY AND SOCIAL JUSTICE

Similar to Katniss's development throughout the trilogy, "through words and other actions, we build ourselves in a world that is building us" (Shor, 2009, p. 282). To understand the world's role in our self-development, critical literacy is a "pedagogical process of teaching and learning, by which students and teachers interrogate the world, unmask ideological and hegemonic discourses, and frame their actions, in the interest of the larger struggle for social justice" (Darder, Baltodano, & Torres, 2009, p. 279). According to Freire and other critical theorists, a critical-oriented mindset can be developed through conscientization and problematization. The term *conscientization (conscientizacao)* implies obtaining a critical consciousness that enables one to demythologize reality (Freire, 1970/1986). Once one obtains a critical consciousness, that person has obtained "awareness of oneself as a knower" (Berhoff, 1987, p. xiii) and is able "to take action against the oppressive elements of reality" (Freire, 1970/1986, p. 19).

According to Greene's (1993b) explanation of the purpose of the language arts classroom, developing a critical consciousness is essential in helping students articulate their experiences, empower others, and imagine the world differently. With this in mind, social-justice education is especially amenable to the language arts classroom because reading and talking about fiction make a difference in how we live together democratically (Davis, 2010). It is therefore natural for social-action projects to stem from the critical reflection of literature, especially those texts drawn from popular media sources (see Alvermann, Moon, & Hagood, 1999) because the projects can engage students in meaningful experiences through – not just with – literature (see Rosenblatt, 1938) and provide "transformative practice [that] engages students as critical thinkers, participatory and active learners, and envisioners of alternative possibilities of social reality" (Nagda, Gurin, & Lopez, 2003, p. 167). Doing so helps "encourage student voice and responsibility" (Mantle-Bromley & Foster, 2005, p. 72), skills that are relevant to the language arts classroom and students' developing sense of citizenry.

SOCIAL ACTION IN THE CLASSROOM

Golden and Christensen (2008) reminded critics that social-action projects are "academically rigorous" and that social justice does not supersede learning the skills needed to "traverse the world" (p. 60); on the contrary, social-action projects require students to take their learning into the community to benefit the greater good through the use of their learned skills. With this in mind, teachers have incorporated such projects into their classrooms in various ways, but all projects have one thing in common: they allow students to express their feelings and desire for change to the wider community. For example, Plemmons (2006) incorporated a social-action project in his classroom when students were outraged about the destruction of historical landmarks in their county. The students took pictures of specific landmarks and wrote poems from each landmark's perspective, giving these inanimate objects a voice. Plemmons then had the photos and poems published and delivered copies of the students' work to doctors' offices, libraries, banks, historical societies, and tourist sites to bring awareness to the community that their cultural heritage was being neglected and needed to be preserved. In addition, Darts (2006), an art teacher, described how her students incorporated performance and multimedia artwork to combat hate and violence instigated by discrimination. Students led small-group discussions on such topics as bullying and displayed artworks around the school to advocate for respect and tolerance. Through artistic and language skills, Darts's students attacked issues they faced in their everyday lives – racism, discrimination, and bullying – and became active participants in change.

Furthermore, after reading several newspaper articles that portrayed "OCHS students as being a bunch of 'druggie, loser, good-for-nothing' kids" (p. 32), Mancina (2005) engaged her students in an action-writing project that aimed to change the community's view of their school and student body. Also using writing as a platform for change, Borsheim and Petrone (2006) encouraged students to critically question the world by providing them with examples of authors whose research questioned the status quo: for example, Eric Schlosser's (2002) *Fast Food*

Nation and Barbara Ehrenreich's (2001) *Nickel and Dimed*. Students then researched issues important to them and distributed information throughout the community in the form of documentaries, letters, and brochures.

Inspired by Bomer and Bomer's (2001) action-writing project that encouraged students to write to city officials about police brutality, Epstein (2010) aimed to incorporate social action into her own classroom. By writing about complex social issues, her students were able to articulate their opinions and passion about political issues while fulfilling reading and writing standards. As Epstein continued to include these writing assignments in her class, she hoped that "students will eventually develop a sense of identity beyond that of 'student' to one of informed, concerned activist" (p. 365).

These action projects not only strengthened the literacy goals of each teacher's classroom by enhancing communication skills and building critical thinking (Sedlak, Doheny, Panthofer, & Anaya, 2005), they also lent "reality, importance, and purpose to reading, making it a part of students' 'here and now'" (Wilhelm, 2002, p. 160) and served as a source of empowerment, showing students that they had the ability to speak out to support change in their community.

Social Justice and the Hunger Games

Teachers of adolescents can engage students in similar projects by using as a catalyst the Hunger Games trilogy, a text that is currently in students' "here and now."

HUNGER

Collins (2008) introduces the effects of hunger as a major theme early in the series when Katniss describes the following:

> Starvation's not an uncommon fate in District 12. Who hasn't seen the victims? Older people who can't work. Children from a family with too many to feed. Straggling through the streets. And one day, you come upon them sitting motionless against a wall or dying in the Meadow, you hear the wails from a house, and the Peacekeepers are called in to retrieve the body. Starvation is never the cause of death officially. It's always the flu, or exposure, or pneumonia. But that fools no one. (p. 28)

This passage tells us that the people of District 12 do not receive enough resources to sustain the population and that those in charge turn a blind eye to the cause of so many deaths (see Table 2 for a brief description of each district). Later, the reader learns that the Capitol is full of gluttonous people who waste food that could haveeasily saved thousands of lives across Panem (Collins, 2008). The overabundance of food and people's wastefulness are especially clear in *Catching Fire* (2009), in which it is revealed that citizens of the Capitol drink a liquid that makes them throw up, effectively emptying their bellies, so that they can continue

Table 2. The districts of Panem.

District	District Attributes
The Capitol	The Capitol is in the Rocky Mountains. The inhabitants of the Capitol are frivolous, shallow, and gluttonous. They are concerned with luxuries and outrageous fashions and are generally ignorant and/or uncaring of the poverty and starvation in the districts.
District 1	District 1 provides the Capitol with items such as diamonds, gems, and fine materials. This district illegally trains children, known as "careers," to participate in the games. It is thought to be near the Rocky Mountains.
District 2	District 2 provides the Capitol with many of their "Peacekeepers," and it is the source of the Capitol's weapons. Because of the Capitol's dependency, this district is favored and often given preferential treatment, which also suggests that it may border the Capitol. "Career" tributes are also trained in this district.
District 3	District 3 tributes are skilled in electronics and other elements of engineering because their industry involves technology. Wiress and Beetee, allies of Katniss in *Catching Fire*, provide a means for the tributes to destroy the arena's force field. It is assumed that District 3 is close to Silicon Valley.
District 4	Tributes from District 4 are strong swimmers and skilled with knots. That is because they are the fishing district. Finnick Odair, another ally from the Quarter Quell, comes from this district, which possibly lies near the Gulf of Mexico.
District 5	District 5's industry is power. It is unclear where this district is located. Foxface, a clever girl who dies accidentally by stealing Peeta's poisonous berries, is from this district.
District 6	District 6 provides transportation, suggesting that it is near Detroit. The two tributes from this district are "morphling" addicts, an indication that it may also produce pharmaceuticals.
District 7	District 7 produces lumber and paper. Johanna, another ally from *Catching Fire*, is dangerous with an axe and reveals that the smell of pine needles reminds her of home. These clues imply that District 7 is near Oregon and Washington.
District 8	Because the two District 8 runaways in *Catching Fire* are traveling on foot, it can be surmised that it is close to District 12. The district's industry is textiles and clothing.
District 9	District 9's industry is grain, which suggests that it is in the Midwest. Little else is known of this district because its tributes die early in the games.

District	District Attributes
District 10	Because the tributes from this district are dressed in cowboy costumes during the games and the tributes for the Quarter Quell wear cowbells, it is assumed that the industry is livestock. This leads one to believe that the district is close to Texas.
District 11	Rue, Katniss's young ally during the games, comes from this poor district. The industry is agriculture, and small children are forced into the highest trees to pick fruit. District 11 is thought to be in the South because growing fruit requires a warm climate. Because of Katniss's tenderness toward Rue, District 11 sends her a loaf of bread during the games.
District 12	Katniss and Peeta are from District 12, the poorest district in Panem. The industry is coal mining. Katniss illegally hunts game in the forest to feed her family, but others die of starvation. Katniss reveals that District 12 was once called Appalachia.
District 13	District 13 is secretly rebuilding and represents a threat to the Capitol because its industry is nuclear energy. The underground community is militant in its efficiency and is governed by President Coin. District 13 is a week away from District 12 by foot, so it is assumed that it is close to New England.

to gorge on delicacies provided at a feast. As Katniss witnesses this spectacle, she thinks, "all I can think of is the emaciated bodies of the children on our kitchen table as my mother prescribes what the parents can't give. More food" (Collins, 2009, p. 80). The irony of starving children lying on the kitchen table, a place associated with bounty and reserved for meals, is not lost on the reader and adds to the horror of the image while magnifying the wastefulness of the Capitol.

Hunger in America

Collins revealed in an interview that "the sociopolitical overtones of *The Hunger Games* were very intentionally created to characterize current and past world events, including the use of hunger as a weapon to control populations" (Blasingame & Collins, 2009, p. 726). Still, hunger as a method of control is not what initially disturbs the adolescent and adult in the United States; it is the blatant waste of food while others starve that makes our stomachs twist. Why does it make us so uncomfortable? Because if we look at patterns of wastefulness in the United States, we are more closely associated with the Capitol, the bad guys, than with the districts. For example, we overconsume food, which contributes to the country's high obesity rate, but waste vast quantities at the same time. According to the U.S. Environmental Protection Agency (2012), in 2010 approximately 34 million tons of food were thrown away. These facts force us to question how our standard of living affects others and the environment.

According to the Food and Agriculture Organization (2000), 792 million people worldwide, and 20% of the population in developing countries, suffer from chronic food deficits. In 2004, Timothy Jones, an anthropologist, concluded a 10-year study that showed that an average individual U.S. household wastes 14% of food purchases (William Reed Business Media, Nov. 25, 2004), supporting our nickname as the "throw-away generation." To address these issues, Atlanta Community Food Bank (2011) devised a curriculum called Hunger 101 (www.acfb.org/projects/hunger_101) to educate and empower students to support change in their communities. The program, which is aligned with state academic standards, has been adopted by multiple food banks and food salvage programs around the country to inspire social responsibility in the school system. The program includes local facts about hunger, suggests that students explore definitions of hunger and food security and factors that contribute to hunger, and understand the nutritional consequences of hunger, all while fostering critical thinking skills. Students are asked to think of practical and effective solutions to hunger and provide short-term and long-term initiatives to empower them to take action in their own communities.

Although 22.3% of children in my state (Georgia) live in poverty (U.S. Census Bureau, 2010), the area in which I teach is relatively middle class and the students have had little experience with poverty. As I have argued before (Simmons, 2011), some middle class students may choose to ignore critical issues of inequality because they have latched on to the idea that everyone is an individual and "equal." Therefore, having read the Hunger Games series, students who have not experienced need can use the text as a reference when discussing hunger, its reality, its causes, and its consequences.

Taking Social Action

Inspired by Hunger 101 and teachers' social-action projects, educators can foster social responsibility in students by allowing them to choose a project that addresses hunger. Working individually or in small groups, students can start a food bank, help advertise for a local hunger walk (the one in my metropolitan area raised $214,000), encourage home gardens or create one for the school, inform students about foods that can be frozen and eaten later instead of thrown away, or organize a letter writing campaign. Some of these activities may seem unrelated to the language arts classroom, but putting such programs into motion and ensuring their success require the use of many ELA skills. For example, the projects incorporate research, technology, expository and persuasive writing skills, public speaking, reflection, and creativity, not to mention the reading of the mentor text, *The Hunger Games*.

While implementing these projects, it is important to note that some students are financially unable to contribute to money or food collections. However, these projects are a valuable opportunity to show all students that multiple ways exist to better one's community and that money donation or food donation – collection activities that are most popular in public schools and churches – are not necessary to make a difference. Instead, students can use their passion, skills, and knowledge, as well as the resources of the classroom, to create change.

For instance, one specific issue that is relevant to students' lives is wasted food from the school cafeteria, which provides a valuable opportunity for a letter writing campaign. Pat Meadows, a director of child nutrition, told Vreeland (August 23, 2010), a reporter, that it is against federal law for school food to leave the premises, making it impossible to donate the excess. In response, their county schools reduced waste by "batch cooking," preparing foods as they were served, ensuring that items were used on an as-needed basis and saving uncooked material for the next day. If your school does not participate in such methods, students can begin a letter writing campaign to county school officials informing them of the benefits of batch cooking and how it can reduce food waste. Considering that *The Hunger Games* references how propaganda was used to persuade citizens of Panem to side with either the Capitol or the rebels, such a project can focus on persuasive writing skills and rhetorical devices, encouraging students to avoid illogical reasoning and fallacies while still appealing to the audience's emotions and sense of ethics and logic. Such projects vary in complexity, time requirements, and resources needed and can be implemented throughout the school year or in a specific unit.

SLAVERY: INVOLUNTARY LABOR, FORCED WARRIORS, AND THE SEX TRADE

Hunger is not the only issue experienced by citizens of Panem; forced labor, violence, and sexual exploitation are also daily truths for those living in the districts. This reality exists not only for adults in the novels; children about the age of our students submit to many forms of modern slavery to survive.

Involuntary Labor

For example, those living in the districts are forced to work to provide food, energy, or other materials so that citizens in the Capitol can continue to live in luxury. Gale is a prime example of this forced labor. To feed his family, at the age of 18 he is lowered into the mines to collect coal, most of which is sent to fuel the Capitol (Collins, 2009). Even though no one is holding a whip to his back, this is still a form of slavery, for Gale must engage in a hazardous occupation, receive an unfair wage, and gain little reward for his hard work while those in the Capitol reap the benefits of his efforts.

In real life, the situation is similar for many victims. The International Labor Organization (as cited by the U.S. Department of State, 2006) reported that at least 12.3 million people around the world are trapped in various forms of forced labor, from sweatshops to farm work to prostitution. Approximately $20 billion in wages is stolen from these workers, leaving them in debt bondage or poverty.

An especially violent example of forced labor in Sierra Leone is the mining of conflict diamonds, also known as blood diamonds, which are sold by rebels to fund armed conflict. To intimidate the locals, rebels often murder, mutilate, and enslave the population and force them to mine the diamonds (United Nations Department of Public Information, 2001). In District 12 (see Table 2 for details on the 13 districts), the Peacekeepers also resort to such tactics to ensure that the Capitol receives enough coal from the mines. For example, after Gale is found hunting in the woods to supplement his poor wages, he is brutally whipped for the crime (Collins, 2009). This brutality keeps the population dependent on the mines for its sole means of survival.

Brutality is further highlighted when Katniss meets Bonnie and Twill, two runaways from District 8. Katniss describes District 8 as a "place stinking of industrial fumes, the people housed in run-down tenements" (Collins, 2009, p. 142). Bonnie and Twill tell Katniss of the uprising in their district, giving an account of how citizens were required to work in factories, make goods for the Capitol, and live in squalor. When the workers rebelled,

> there was a lockdown. No food, no coal, everyone forbidden to leave their homes. The only time the television showed anything but static was when suspected instigators were hanged in the square. Then one night, as the whole district was on the brink of starvation, came the order to return to business as usual. (Collins, 2009, p. 145)

Violence and fear in both Panem and our world keep people in situations in which they are forced to work in dangerous conditions, receiving only the bare essentials to ensure that their bodies survive and are able to perform the same tasks day after day.

Forced Warriors

Forcing children into violent situations that require them to kill or be killed is the major theme of the Hunger Games series. As punishment for the districts' rebellion to the Capitol's rule, the Capitol created the Hunger Games to remind the districts of its power. Katniss describes the games in this way:

> Taking the kids from our districts, forcing them to kill one another while we watch – this is the Capitol's way of reminding us how totally we are at their mercy. How little chance we would stand of surviving another rebellion. Whatever words they use, the real message is clear. "Look how we take your children and sacrifice them and there's nothing you can do. If you lift a finger, we will destroy every last one of you." (Collins, 2008, p. 76)

Forcing children to fight to the death, according to President Coin, the leader of District 13, represents "'vengeance with the least loss of life'" (Collins, 2010, p. 369). In real life, forcing children to fight battles is also a form of vengeance, as children of people who oppose an invading army are forced to become members of that same army, as has been the case in some areas of Sierra Leone, Ethiopia, and

Uganda (Annan, 2000). It is as if to say, "You fight against us; you fight against your children" – a sick but effective tactic.

According to the International Rescue Committee (2011), approximately 300,000 children globally are trained to be "instruments of war" (para. 1) and "as many as 50 countries currently recruit children under age 18 into their armed forces" (Annan, 2000, p. 1). In *A Long Way Gone: Memoirs of a Boy Soldier* (2007), Ishmael Beah, recruited into the army in Sierra Leone when he was 13 years old, tells of the horrifying effects of using children as soldiers. Sharing his experience, Beah revealed to the United Nations Economic and Social Council that he fought because he "had to get some food to survive, and the only way to do that was to be a part of the army. It was not easy being a soldier, but we just had to do it" (2007, p. 199). Annan (2000) confirmed Beah's reasoning when he reported that children offer their services as soldiers to get regular meals and medical attention. Similarly, because of hunger, children in Panem sign up for tesserae, a year's supply of grain and oil for one person that can be bought in exchange for placing their names multiple times in the lottery. Doing so increases their chances of being selected for the games (Collins, 2008), showing how starvation and hunger remain the major incentives for putting oneself in danger.

When philanthropic organizations attempt to reintegrate child soldiers into society, the emotional and social wounds prove to be more devastating than any physical harm the children may have encountered (International Rescue Committee, 2011). When UNICEF removed Ishmael Beah from the front lines, he reported symptoms of Posttraumatic Stress Disorder. His symptoms included violence toward UNICEF staff members, horrible nightmares about the violence he inflicted on others, debilitating migraines, and an inability to come to terms and forgive himself for the atrocities in which he played a role (Beah, 2007). Therefore, it would be appropriate to pair Beah's memoir with the Hunger Games series because it allows students to draw comparisons between the characters' experiences, reactions, guilt, suffering, and eventual healing and those of Beah, showing how what we believe to be fiction is reality for some children.

In *The Hunger Games*, Annie, Finnick's wife and a former tribute, illustrates the lasting emotional, mental, and social effects of witnessing and participating in violence. Because she saw the beheading of District 4's male tribute (Collins, 2009) Annie cannot stand arguing, loud noises, or any talk that references violence or the Hunger Games. Her tragic past experience has debilitated her capacity to function in a "normal" community. Furthermore, at the end of the series, Katniss discloses her and Peeta's moments of panic when she reveals that "there are still moments when he clutches the back of a chair and hangs on until the flashbacks are over. I wake screaming from nightmares of mutts and lost children" (Collins, 2010, p. 388). Although they have become more adept at functioning in society after their ordeal than Annie was, it is still clear that Katniss and Peeta's experience as tributes in the Hunger Games left them afflicted with emotional scars that will be prevalent throughout their adult lives.

The Sex Trade

Being a victor and surviving the violence of the Hunger Games does not mean that one can retire and live out one's days in peace. Finnick's story of what happened to him after his victory is a prime example of the continued exploitation of Panem's children. Collins (2010) writes,

> "President Snow used to ... sell me ... my body, that is," Finnick begins in a flat, removed tone. "I wasn't the only one. If a victor is considered desirable, the president gives them as a reward or allows people to buy them for an exorbitant amount of money. If you refuse, he kills someone you love. So you do it." (p. 170)

Katniss suggests that Finnick was not the only victor to endure such intimidation. Although Haymitch, Katniss's mentor, was not blackmailed into prostitution, he suggests that the Capitol killed his family and girlfriend to warn victors of what would happen if they didn't obey President Snow. He told Katniss, "I am the example. The person to hold up to the young Finnicks and Johannas and Cashmeres" (Collins, 2010, p. 172). Listening to Finnick's story and realizing that attractive, young female victors were also subjected to prostitution made Katniss reflect on what might have happened to her had she been the sole survivor of the 74th Hunger Games.

Unfortunately, child prostitution is not a fictional horror created out of Collins's imagination. According to the Juvenile Justice Fund (2012), more than 2,800 men in my state (Georgia) have been involved with an adolescent prostitute, and 250 girls are victimized every month. Despite these alarming statistics, underage prostitution is considered a "low visibility" crime (U.S. Department of Justice, 2007, p. ii); as a result, the gruesome techniques used to manipulate young girls into preforming such acts are not widely known. For example, according to the U.S. Department of Justice (2007), 50% of girls engaged in prostitution are controlled by pimps who sometimes beat and threaten them by telling them that their families will be harmed if they do not cooperate. Furthermore, "often traffickers tell children that if they escape or cooperate with law enforcement, previous cash advances to their families and other money 'owed' will be collected from their parents, who may also be physically harmed" (p. 5). Finnick shows the effectiveness of such tactics when he submits to President Snow's demands out of fear that someone he loves would be hurt if he refuses. Like the rich people in Collins's series who are willing to pay a high price in exchange for sex with victors, those seeking to sexually exploit underage children are participating in sex tourism, traveling to countries with developed sex industries and spending large sums to engage in sexual acts with "exotic" adolescent girls.

Taking Social Action

As mentioned in the previous section, students can engage in multiple social-justice activities that do not require money donation, although some worthwhile, long-term initiatives do require such tactics to enable change. One example is Loose Change to Loosen Chains (LC2LC), "a student-led campaign for elementary to college students to combat modern-day slavery while learning about the reality of injustices today" (International Justice Mission, 2012). This organization has raised more than $10 billion by collecting loose change that people have lying around the house.

Figure 1. Sample social-action project.

To initiate this program at their school, students can participate in a multimedia project that encourages them to use their creativity, writing, and digital literacy skills to create a logo, slogan, posters, and a challenge video. Using an empty milk jug, students can glue their slogan and logo onto the container and distribute the containers to each classroom (see Figure 1). Students can hang their posters, which include researched statistics on modern slavery, and feature their challenge video during the school announcements. In this way, loose change can be collected schoolwide to end slavery. Although this project does involve money collection, students are not obligated to contribute; moreover, by requiring donations in the form of change and leaving the jug in the classroom all year, participation remains anonymous. Even a penny can contribute to a greater cause.

FINAL THOUGHTS

Although I agree with Banks (2003) that "an education that focuses on social justice educates both the heads and hearts of students and helps them to become thoughtful, committed, and active citizens" (p. 18), a focus on such difficult topics may lead to complaints that the curriculum is "too depressing." Zandy (1994) sympathized, stating that "we all want to divert our eyes, our awareness" (p. 47). But language arts teachers have a responsibility to make our students conscious of such difficult issues, not to turn away from them. We should strive to provide a venue in which students can use their language skills to promote change and contend with social responsibility and justice (Greene, 1993a; hooks, 1994).

Furthermore, Johnson (2005) wrote that "hope is often seen as quaint, religious, and naïve" (p. 48), and in the classroom there is much focus on social problems but little emphasis on how to fix them. Suzanne Collins's trilogy provides a way to illuminate social tragedies affecting adolescents around the world and to assure our students that, when paired with action, hope is not naive. Through social-action projects that address hunger, modern slavery, and other societal problems (e.g., poverty, child labor and labor laws, war crimes, drug use, ineffective public works programs, forms of apartheid or segregation, class inequality, abuse of authority, government corruption), students can realize that to create change, they cannot just read about human misfortune and social calamity, lament its existence, and hope for change. They must act, or their hope is in vain.

In the last novel of Collins's series, *Mockingjay* (2010), Katniss warns President Snow that "fire is catching" (p. 186), meaning that if the people of the districts suffer, the Capitol will, too. This warning is relevant to our world as well. If global citizens continue to suffer from injustice and exploitation, humanity will pay a high price. Fire, like passion, is powerful, and if harnessed it can be used for good or for ill. In our language arts classrooms, we have an abundance of fire in the form of passionate students. And if the fire is kindled, we can encourage students to use their literacy skills to serve others, creating a more compassionate and just society. Like an ember that fuels a fire, reading can stoke our students into becoming socially responsible citizens, causing them to spit and blaze in the face of injustice and spread their fire throughout the community.

STEPS FOR IMMEDIATE IMPLEMENTATION

– Gauge your students' interest in and knowledge of the Hunger Games trilogy. Because of the books' current popularity, students may have already read them, making it unnecessary to read all the novels in class. Depending on the current critical consciousness of your students, either ask them to give examples of social issues being addressed in the novels or guide them toward the social issues by pulling relevant quotes from the texts. Lead a discussion about how these issues are at work in each of the books.

- Provide students with examples of how these issues are apparent in our own world by guiding them to social-advocacy websites, reading supplementary newspaper articles, or watching news programs about the social issues on which your class decided to focus.
- Ask students how such social ills can be changed.
- Introduce ways that outreach groups take social action: letter writing campaigns, public service announcements, bumper stickers, educational posters and pamphlets, fundraisers, etc.
- Engage students in a project that educates the public on a social issue and advocates for change, focusing on language arts skills such as research, persuasive writing, and digital literacy.

Distribute widely! It is important that students know they will be reaching a wide audience that includes their community and peers. Ask the editor of the school newspaper if it will feature students' work or, if your school has a broadcasting system, ask if students can broadcast their public service announcements or videos. Make posters and pamphlets that educate the public on chosen social issues and distribute them to local libraries, doctors' offices, and other businesses. If participating in an activity such as a canned-food drive, involve the local grocery store. Although educating students on these issues is important, having students educate others and create change is what makes it social action.

LITERATURE CITED

Beah, I. (2007). *A long way gone: Memoirs of a boy soldier*. New York, NY: Farrar, Straus and Giroux.
Collins, S. (2008). *The hunger games*. New York, NY: Scholastic.
Collins, S. (2009). *Catching fire*. New York, NY: Scholastic.
Collins, S. (2010). *Mockingjay*. New York, NY: Scholastic.
Lewis, C.S. (2004). *The chronicles of Narnia*. New York, NY: HarperCollins. (Original work published 1950)
Rowling, J.K. (1997). *Harry Potter and the sorcerer's stone*. London: Bloomsbury.
Tolkien, J.R.R. (2004). *The lord of the rings trilogy: The fellowship of the ring*. New York, NY: Houghton Mifflin. (Original work published 1954)

REFERENCES

Alvermann, D. E., Moon, J., & Hagood, M. C. (1999). *Popular culture in the classroom: Teaching and researching critical media literacy*. Newark, DE: International Reading Association.
Annan, K. (2000, July 26). *Speech to the Security Council*. Retrieved November 10, 2011, from www.un.org/cyberschoolbus/briefing/soldiers/soldiers.pdf
Atlanta Community Food Bank. (2011). *Hunger 101*. Retrieved September 15, 2011, from www.acfb.org/projects/hunger_101

Atweh, B., Kemmis, S., & Weeks, P. (Eds.). (1998). *Action research in practice: Partnerships for social justice in education.* New York, NY: Routledge. doi: 10.4324/9780203268629

Banks, J. A. (2003). Teaching literacy for social justice and global citizenship. *Language Arts, 81*(1), 18-19.

Blasingame, J., & Collins, S. (2009). An interview with Suzanne Collins. *Journal of Adolescent & Adult Literacy, 52*(8), 726-727.

Bomer, R., & Bomer, K. (2001). *For a better world: Reading and writing for social action.* Portsmouth, NH: Heinemann.

Borsheim, C., & Petrone, R. (2006). Teaching the research paper for local action. *English Journal, 95*(4), 78-83. doi: 10.2307/30047094

Darder, A., Baltodano, M., & Torres, R. (2009). Introduction. In A. Darder, M. Baltodano, & R. Torres (Eds.), *The critical pedagogy reader* (2nd ed., pp. 1-21). New York, NY: Routledge.

Darts, D. (2006). Art education for a change: Contemporary issues and the visual arts. *Art Education, 50*(5), 6-12.

Davis, T. (2010). Can literature really make a difference? Toward a chastened view of the role of fiction in democratic education. *Journal of Educational Controversy, 5*(1). Retrieved April 28, 2012, from www.wce.wwu.edu/Resources/CEP/eJournal/v005n001/a002.shtml

Downey, A.L. (2005). The transformative power of drama: Bringing literature and social justice to life. *English Journal, 95*(1), 33-38. doi: 10.2307/30047395

Ehrenreich, B. (2001). *Nickel and dimed: On (not) getting by in America.* New York, NY: Metropolitan.

Epstein, S. E. (2010). Activists and writers: Student expression in a social action literacy project. *Language Arts, 87*(5), 363-372.

Food and Agriculture Organization. (2000). *Malnutrition.* World Health Organization. Retrieved October 21, 2011, from www.who.int

Freire, P. (1986). *Pedagogy of the oppressed* (M. B. Ramos, Trans.). New York, NY: Continuum. (Original work published 1970)

Golden, J., & Christensen, L. (2008). A conversation with Linda Christensen on social justice education. *English Journal, 97*(6), 59-63.

Greene, M. (1993a). The passions of pluralism: Multiculturalism and the expanding community. *Educational Researcher, 22*(1), 13-18.

Greene, M. (1993b). What are the language arts for? *NAMTA Journal, 18*(12), 123-132.

hooks, b. (1994). *Teaching to transgress: Education as the practice of freedom.* New York, NY: Routledge.

International Justice Mission. (2012). *Youth.* Retrieved July 9, 2012, from http://www.ijm.org/get-involved/youth

International Rescue Committee. (2011). *Child soldiers.* Retrieved November 15, 2011, from www.rescue.org/child-soldiers

Johnson, B. (2005). Overcoming "doom and gloom": Empowering students in courses on social problems, injustice, and inequality. *Teaching Sociology, 33*(1), 44-58. doi: 10.1177/0092055X0503300104

Juvenile Justice Fund (2012). *A future, not a past: Stop the prostitution of children in Georgia.* Retrieved July 9, 2012, from www.afuturenotapast.org/

King, S. (2008, September 8). The Hunger Games [Review of the book *The Hunger Games*, by S. Collins]. *Entertainment Weekly.* Retrieved October 30, 2011, from www.ew.com

Mancina, H. (2005). Empowering students through a social-action writing project. *English Journal, 94*(6), 31-35. doi: 10.2307/30046500

Mantle-Bromley, C., & Young, A. M. (2005). Educating for democracy: The vital role of the language arts teacher. *English Journal, 94*(5), 70-74.

Moje, E. B. (2008). Foregrounding the disciplines in secondary literacy teaching and learning: A call for change. *Journal of Adolescent & Adult Literacy, 52*(2), 96-107. doi: 10.1598/JAAL.52.2.1

Moje, E. B., Young, J. P., Readence, J. E., & Moore, D. W. (2000). Reinventing adolescent literacy for new times: Perennial and millennial issues. *Journal of Adolescent & Adult Literacy, 43*(5), 400-410.

Morrell, E. (2002). Toward critical pedagogy of popular culture: Literacy development among urban youth. *Journal of Adolescent & Adult Literacy, 46*(1), 72-77.
Nagda, B.R.A., Gurin, P., & Lopez, G.E. (2003). Transformative pedagogy for democracy and social justice. *Race, Ethnicity and Education, 6*(2), 165-191. doi: 10.1080/13613320308199
Plemmons, A. (2006). Capturing a community. *Schools: Studies in Education, 3*(1), 83–113. doi:10.1086/588863
Rosenblatt, L. M. (1938). *Literature as exploration.* New York, NY: D. Appleton-Century.
Schlosser, E. (2002). *Fast food nation: The dark side of the all-American meal.* Boston: Houghton.
Sedlak, C. A., Doheny, M. O., Panthofer, N., & Anya, E. (2003). Critical thinking in students' service-learning experiences. *College Teaching, 51*, 99-103.
Shor, I. (2009). What is critical literacy? In A. Darder, M. Baltodano, & R. Torres (Eds.), *The critical pedagogy reader* (2nd ed., pp. 282-304). New York, NY: Routledge.
Simmons, A. M. (2011). Fusing fantasy film and traditional adolescent texts to support critical literacy. *SIGNAL Journal, 34*(2), 25-30.
United Nations Department of Public Information. (2001). *Conflict diamonds: Sanctions and war.* Retrieved September 14, 2011, from www.un.org/peace/africa/Diamond.html
U.S. Census Bureau. (2010). *American community survey profile: 2008–2009.* Retrieved September 14, 2011, from www.census.gov/newsroom/releases/archives/american_community_survey_acs/cb10-cn78.html
U.S. Department of Justice. (2007). *Commercial sexual exploitation of children: What do we know and what do we do about it? Issues in international crime (National Institute of Justice Special Report).* Washington, DC: U.S. Government Printing Office. Retrieved September 14, 2011, from www.ojp.usdoj.gov/nij
U.S. Department of State. (2006). *Trafficking in persons report.* Washington, DC: U.S. Government Printing Office. Retrieved July 9, 2012, from www.state.gov/documents/organization/66086.pdf
U.S. Environmental Protection Agency. (2012). *Basic information about food waste.* Retrieved March 24, 2012, from www.epa.gov/osw/conserve/materials/organics/food/fd-basic.htm
Vreeland, T. (2010, August 23). What does Tulsa's public schools do with leftover cafeteria food? *WorldNow and KOTV.* Retrieved September 14, 2011, from www.newson6.com/global/story.asp?s=13068129
Wade, R. C. (1997). Community service learning and the social studies curriculum: Challenges of effective practice. *Social Studies, 88*(5), 197-202. doi: 10.1080/00377999709603778
Wilhelm, J. D. (2002). *Action strategies for deepening comprehension.* New York, NY: Scholastic.
William Reed Business Media. (2004, November 25). U.S. wastes half its food. *Food Production Daily.* Retrieved September 14, 2011, from www.foodproductiondaily.com/Supply-Chain/Half-of-US
Zandy, J. (1994). Human labor and literature: A pedagogy from a working-class perspective. In D. B. Downing (Ed.), *Changing classroom practices: Resources for literacy and cultural studies* (pp. 37-52). Urbana, IL: National Council of Teachers of English.

PATRICIA PAUGH

6. THE POSTMODERN PICTURE BOOK

Developing Textual Author "ity" in Elementary Readers

ABSTRACT

Young children in today's society need experiences that position them as agents who understand how texts work and how to manipulate texts for a variety of social purposes – most importantly to practice literacy as social actors who contribute productively to the world in which they live. This chapter explores the postmodern picture book, a genre that provides a venue for classroom teachers to engage even the youngest of students as "designers of meaning." The chapter highlights the constellation of features found in postmodern pictures books through an analysis of several texts readily available to classroom teachers and librarians. It presents a typology of features draw from classroom research on this genre and includes a lesson plan designed to support pre- and in-service teachers in closely analyzing these texts with a critical literacy focus in mind.

INTRODUCTION

> It is through our own narratives that we principally construct a version of ourselves in the world, and it is through its narrative that a culture provides models of identity and agency to its members. (Bruner, 1996, p. xiv)

About ten years ago, as high stakes tests invaded classroom consciousness, a teacher in one of my reading assessment classes laughingly shared a satirical "rewriting" of a state test question by one of her fourth graders. This student created a Romeo & Juliet-like love story based on fictional fourth graders. The writing included a short passage (the love story) accompanied by five comprehension questions modeled directly on the testing format. In this playful writing sample I saw mastery of the genre of test taking but also mastery that did not sacrifice the author's own intentions. She demonstrated control of literacy as a social practice by playfully and intentionally mixing genres; creating a narrative of romance located in her current social context (a topic of priority for female students reaching the "tween" years) parodied as a school-valued assessment. In contrast, during a more recent visit to an urban school in a different city, I noticed a hallway bulletin board featuring a group literacy project. The elementary students, in small groups, had dissected four sample literature responses from the state testing website. Rationalizations for why each response had earned a score of 1, 2, 3, or 4, written by each group were posted nearby. It was apparent that the featured end goal of the activity was memorization of the language expected for a good score on the test. Unlike the fourth grade love story cited above, there was little indication of playful flexibility or innovative thought in the compliant (and eerily similar explanations) written next to each group's model response posted in that hallway. If the intention of schooling in today's world is for students to gain a greater awareness of the world around them, and to be active in recognizing the possibilities for their own roles in that world, then literacy should serve to activate the social imagination. The first response to the high stakes test serves as an excellent example of a student who is learning to read and write the "words" expected in school, but also reserves her right to play with and manipulate those words for her own intentions. The second writing example lacks such demonstration of ownership. To paraphrase Freire and Macedo (2013), how can teachers prepare our youngest students to be, like our fourth grader above, flexible and independent owners of the "words" they need for school success while simultaneously learning to be authors who use their words to interact purposefully and intentionally in the "world?"

The purpose of literature study is to promote a "critical analysis of the status quo that can open students to new perspectives, prepare [them] for current and coming challenges to traditional ways of being, and perhaps even stimulate them to launch their own challenges to the old order" (O'Neil, 2010, p. 41). With this purpose in mind, choice of literature in the elementary classroom is key – literature that prompts students to learn how to confront beliefs unlike their own, participate in changing social orders, and negotiate rapidly changing global resources (O'Neil, 2010). This chapter reviews a genre that has come to be known as the "postmodern picture book" (PMPB) and its potential for introducing critical literary analysis to children as they prepare to be literate citizens in a world where communication and social discourse is rapidly changing. The literacy practices that are needed to engage in the world today may not even be recognizable in the near future. Therefore, rather than teaching our students the skills for reading today's text, literacy education for the 21st century must be focused on a stance where students interact with texts as critical designers and consumers.

NEW TIMES, NEW LITERACIES AND THE POSTMODERN PICTURE BOOK

Technologies of communication and the redistribution of wealth around the world due to ease of transportation and communication necessitate interaction among groups whose belief systems, values and cultural practices are very different. This increasingly globalized society brings into new relationships the diverse social narratives that shape cultural practices around the world. As in any social interaction, there exist power dynamics that define social positions and ways of operating in the world. These dynamics are communicated through texts consumed and produced not only in school but in everyday life. In order for children to fully participate in society now and in the future, they need to retain authority to both question and redesign the multiplicity of text forms encountered as part of a daily influx of information. Three related theoretical frameworks known as New Literacy Studies, Multiliteracies, and Critical Literac(ies) help us to reconceptualize this view (see New London Group, 1996; Lankshear & Knobel, 2003). In this chapter, the ideas found in these frames define how the term critical literacy is used. All three explain literacy in plural forms (i.e. literacies) indicating an expansion beyond what in modern education has been a text paradigm or a privileging of print-based communication. One key point is that print is only one of many semiotic (sign) systems that can be interrelated in order to create textual meaning (Unsworth, 2008). Today's texts are not only print-based but digital and usually include multimodal formats (e.g. a video game, a social media site, or an online newspaper article which includes video, animated data representations, and/or scrolling updates that compete with the main print article). Besides the reliance on printed text, a second key point challenges traditional assumptions that the message of a text is static and contained within the words. Instead, a critical literacies frame considers meaning as fluid and context-dependent where readers may make different choices about how to read a text and create meaning from the messages it communicates. Thus, a text may hold multiple meanings. Often the reader is also an author who inscribes the text further, choosing to identify with or challenge its meaning (e.g. engaging other readers using a comment area in a blog). Important to communication in contemporary society is the argument that there is "no reading or writing ... outside of social practice" (Lankshear & Knobel, 2006, p. 3). That is, the function of any text is defined according to the social context where it is produced or consumed. The New London Group (1996), anticipating the technological shifts and emerging global society of the 21st century, conceived a theory of "multiltieracies" or "literacy as design." Antsey (2002) explains that to be "multiliterate requires not only mastery of communication, but the ability to critically analyze, deconstruct, and reconstruct a range of texts and other representational forms" (p. 446).

A third key point is that literacy practices are to be used for social and economic justice. Anstey (2002) continues to argue that multiliteracy "also requires the ability to engage in the social responsibilities and interactions associated with these texts" (p. 446). This view of critical literacy emerged in relation to Paulo Freire's conception of literacy as power – to "read the word and the world" (Freire & Macedo, 2013). Critical literacy challenges the master narratives that are accepted within dominant society, not as natural truths but as constructions of specific power relationships that benefit some but not others (Janks, 2013). Learning to be aware of and to re-write these relationships in the interest of social and economic justice is a major focus of critical literacy pedagogy. Those representing marginalized positions assume power when they use critical literacy practices to improve their lives and those of their communities.

Thus, these related movements offer a framework for expanding understandings of literacy for social participation in these "New Times." Yet as others in this volume explain, these frameworks are still largely invisible within current school discourses. This is an issue of access to the power of full literacy practices, especially for schools in lesser resourced communities where it is common for teachers to be subject to standardization pressures (e.g. the test prep activity shared earlier), rather than supported in developing the types of literacy instruction where children learn to be active designers, rather than passive receptors, of meaning (Janks, 2013).

POSTMODERN PICTURE BOOKS FOR 21ST CENTURY ELEMENTARY CLASSROOMS

A genre of children's literature, the postmodern picture book (PMPB) (Goldstone & Labbe, 2004) lends itself to exploration of texts in ways that can enhance young readers' experiences of identity and agency as literacy practitioners within classroom instructional spaces. Traditional picture books are already multi-modal, and postmodern picture books build on (or some say disrupt) traditional relationships between image and story more extensively. Similar to digital texts, they invite interactions between the text and readers in ways that encourages the reader to shift from a role of passive recipient of the author's intended meaning to the role of active co-author. An early example is Maurice Sendack's *Where the Wild Things Are* appearing in 1963. The genre proliferated in the 1990's and early 2000's. Notable offerings often familiar to elementary librarians and teachers are bodies of work by Scieszka and Smith (e.g. *Stinky Cheese Man* and *Squids will be Squids*), Weisner (e.g. *Tuesday* and *The Three Pigs*) and Willems (e.g. *Don't Let the Pigeon Drive the Bus* and *Knuffle Bunny*). More recently, authors such as Shaun Tan (e.g. *Tales from Outer Suburbia* and *The Arrival*) continue to innovate with this genre. As will be repeated below, it is important to note that the relationship of the postmodern picture book and traditional picture books is not a binary – instead it is the constellation of linguistic and semiotic features of certain pictures books that reposition the act of reading which helps us select their use for a postmodern era.

WHY "POSTMODERN?"

The designation "postmodern" relates economically and politically to "New Times" – this is the era after WW II leading into subsequent decades of rapid cultural shifts driven by constantly emerging technologies. Postmodernism represents a contestation of the authority of universal truths or metanarratives that in the past were invisible arbiters of how power is distributed within society. Allan (2012) describes these to include metanarratives of progress, science and religion. A sociocultural critical literacy diverges from traditional literacy analyses. In the former, the goals are to enculture readers into these metanarratives. Instead, postmodern analysis is given over to "playfulness, pleasure, hyper-reality and image resulting in new metanarratives" (Allan, 2012, p. 3) which interrogate and reject the certainties which have naturalized life in Western cultures over the past two centuries. Postmodernism introduces skepticism toward: authority, received wisdom, and cultural and political customs. Allan shares an example of postmodern critical literacy where the reader takes on the metanarratives of consumerism that have become invisibly embedded within the range popular cultural texts consumed by both adults and children.

For young children, a purpose of traditional literature study has been to socialize them into the cultural values of the societies in which they live. Throughout history, folktales and fables have worked to teach important lessons about values and conduct necessary to interact successfully within a community. Critical literacy adds a dimension to this focus, by encouraging both recognition and questioning of societal norms. Although arguments have been made that such critical approaches to literacy are unsuitable for elementary-age children, there is evidence that young children are not only capable, but more flexible, in using literacy for social purposes (Goldstone & Labbe, 2004; O'Neil, 2010). Therefore, exploring postmodern texts can serve as a bridge for young students (and their teachers) to develop important critical literacy practices as part of their school experience.

POSTMODERN THOUGHT MEETS THE PICTURE BOOK

Teaching young children to be literate practitioners involves not only the skills that they need to decode text, but an invitation to see their roles as active meaning makers when they read and write, an identity that the New London Group (1996) terms "designers of meaning." Unfortunately in much of the prescriptive reading and writing curriculum provided to teachers in current classrooms the positioning of the reader is largely passive Rarely are teachers encouraged to teach elementary-aged children to analyze texts with a goal of rethinking or reworking the messages. As other teacher/authors in this volume explain, taking such a critical stance is usually invisible in the discourses of teachers' professional development. PMPBs, if included in text-sets used for literacy instruction, can be helpful tools for teachers who wish to re-center literacy identity and agency into their core curriculum.

Although conceived by some as a genre or sub-genre (see Goldstone & Labbe, 2004), the PMPB is less a text-type than a form of picture book which contains specific constellations of language features inviting the reader to develop relationships with text in new ways. Anstey's (2002) bulleted list, consolidated below, offers a concise summary of the understandings needed for a 21st century literacy curriculum:

> 21st century understandings include: all texts are consciously constructed and have particular social, economic, political and cultural purposes; texts come in a variety of representational forms incorporating a range of grammars and semiotic systems; the reader or viewer may need to draw upon several grammars and semiotic systems in order to process some texts; changes in society and technology will continue to challenge and change texts and their representational forms; there may be more than one way to view a text depending upon a range of contextual (social, economic, cultural, or political)

factors: there is a need to consider the possible meanings of a text and how it is constructing the reader and world of the reader. (pp. 446-447)

Picture books that offer opportunities to develop these understandings range from those with traditional structures or storylines to those whose message or structural features disrupt the expected. A picture book is considered postmodern if its features somehow offer the reader opportunities to think differently or divergently about the world and his/her place in that world (Allan, 2012). Goldstone and Labbe (2004) note that PMPBs have "different functions, formats, and semiotic codes" (p. 198) with some or all of the following characteristics: non-linearity in terms of story line (e.g. multiple storylines or multiple narrators), irony and contradiction, and/or exposure to the author/artist's creation of the text (e.g. "breaking the surface" where the characters leave the page or the story or the hand of the illustrator appears).

A favorite in my teacher education courses is the picture book, *Click, Clack, Moo: Cows That Type* (Cronin and Lewin, 2000). In contrast to other PMPBs, this resembles a traditional story with a clear setting, characters and linear plotline. However the plot revolves around a secondary text type, letters composed by personified farm animals. The plot is described in an editorial review on Amazon.com (Coulter, online) as follows:

> The literacy rate in Farmer Brown's barn goes up considerably once his cows find an old typewriter and begin typing. To the harassed farmer's dismay, his communicative cows quickly become contentious:
>
> Dear Farmer Brown,
> The barn is very cold at night. We'd like some electric blankets.
> Sincerely,
> The Cows
>
> When he refuses to comply with their demands, the cows take action. Farmer Brown finds another note on the barn door: "Sorry. We're closed. No milk today." Soon the striking cows and Farmer Brown are forced to reach a mutually agreeable compromise, with the help of an impartial party – the duck. But this poor, beleaguered farmer's "atypical" troubles are not over yet!
>
> This hilarious tale will give young rebels-in-the-making a taste of the power of peaceful protest and the satisfaction of cooperative give and take.

In this story, the image of literacy as a social practice is clearly conveyed as the characters create texts for a social purpose – to negotiate their labor for fair working conditions. The creation and exchange of texts is central to the plot. The reader follows a series of letters created using "typed" font to record the negotiation between animals and farmer. By centralizing the creation of texts (the letters), the author and illustrator demonstrate the act of reading and composing as purposeful. The reader sees the characters choosing both formal and informal

Figure 1. Example of a letter as a secondary text feature from Click Clack Moo: Cows that Type (Cronin & Lewin, 2000).

language, including the cows' own version of "moo" to redesign their workplace, or as New London Group (1996) describes, their "social futures."

Postmodern picture books, along with many other picture books, are often recommended for specific age ranges and yet the messages available reach across boundaries of age and interest. In fact, my pre-service teachers often question the suitability of picture books for older elementary readers and beyond. *Click, Clack, Moo: Cows that Type* is one example of how fluid boundaries can be when decisions are made about what counts as a suitable text and for whom. In a January 2014 official blog post, Carl Fillichio, Head of the U.S. Labor Department's Office of Public Affairs announced that this book had been recently added to the Department's list of "Books that Shaped Work in America." Support for this action, he explained, stemmed from a swell of public support for the value of its message, concluding:

> There is no doubt it is helping to shape an important aspect of work in America and I'm hopeful that it will continue for years to come. Because for work, workplaces, and workers to thrive (not just survive) in our nation or anywhere in the world, we need to continue to grow generations of leaders who understand labor-management relations ... and most importantly, who

will foster and utilize creative, "win-win" partnerships between labor and management. (online)

Recognizing that a range of ages is important to building social consciousness, Fillichio connects the use of this text to schools (providing an example of teacher, Jill Nicklas Rolle, who used it to explain a union strike to her second graders) but also relates its message to an adult forum, a White House summit where major corporations and the Labor Secretary explored collaboration towards common goals between labor and management. The lesson here is that the choices of texts that can be used as part of a basic reading curriculum (n.b. Fillichio explains that *Click Clack Moo* was used previously to "teach reading" by Ms. Rolle). His argument supports a critical literacy agenda; Classroom curriculum must also include messages that encourage young readers to question and construct big ideas important to their lives.

TEXTS OF PLEASURE VS. TEXT OF BLISS

How a text positions the reader is key when making choices of classroom literature. For example, teaching young children the workings of narrative texts provides them with tools to identify and question their own place in society through reading. Authors of fictional narratives, for example, invite the reader into the text using literary devices that allow him or her to enter the world of the characters and make sense of experiences important to their own lives. Escaping into the world of reading can and should be a practice that provides comfort and security for young readers living in a world of uncertainty and change (O'Neil, 2010). Yet, by also offering texts that are uncomfortable and invite readers to struggle with the unfamiliar, the authors/illustrators of PMPBs provide a second, important form of engagement with literature. Introducing both forms draws on Roland Barthes (1975) conception of texts of plaisir (pleasure) and texts of jouissance (bliss) as equally necessary types of engagement with literature. The former types of texts "content the reader and represent a familiar – and therefore comfortable – experience of reading" while the latter "are discomfiting because they represent a break with the familiar" (cited in McGuire, 2008, p. 205). In their research on reading PMPBs with third graders, McGuire et al. found that students became highly engaged in ways consistent with the latter. That is, their focal students "wrestled through the newness and ambiguity, playing, debating, flipping backwards and forwards, ventriloquizing characters, and voicing their own stories" (p. 205). The active involvement identified through McGuire et al.'s research is consistent with other studies of teachers who engaged their elementary age students with postmodern texts (see Hassett & Curwood, 2008; Pantaleo, 2004; 2006; Serafini, 2005). These classroom studies demonstrate how the genre affords young readers authority over texts important to their identities as critical literacy practitioners. This section of the chapter synthesizes characteristics of PMPBs including "metafictive" literary devices and a typology of features intended to help to elementary teachers interested in choosing such texts for their classrooms.

METAFICTIVE DEVICES

PMPB authors draw on specific "metafictive" literary devices to promote the types of interactions displayed by McGuire et al.'s (2008) young readers (e.g. playfulness, active co-construction of meaning through decision-making or filling intentionally left informational gaps). Metafictive writing "intentionally and systematically draws attention to its status in order to pose questions about the relationship between fiction and reality" (Pantaleo, 2006, p. 2 citing Waugh, 1984). Found in PMPBs, meta-fictive devices include:

- Intertextuality. In PMPBs the reader is asked to make "inter" textual connections with texts, illustrations and other cultural artifacts from his/her outside experiences as well as "intra" textual connections using multiple cues and lines within the text itself.
- Parody. Through satire or a comic take on original texts, PMPB authors show that rules can be broken while also providing a tribute to the original (Pantaleo, 2006).
- Irony/contradiction. PMPB readers face disruption of the expected in terms of competing styles within a text, or in the logic of the narrative. For example, illustrations may contradict what is said in the print, asking readers to decide how to use them (Goldstone & Labbe, 2004).
- Pastiche. In some PMPBs author's use pastiche or a compressing or interweaving of different tales in the same space (Pantaleo, 2006).

Many PMPBs often riff off of traditional fairy or folktales using these literary devices. A popular PMPB is David Wiesner's 2002 Caldecott winner, *The Three Pigs*. An analyses of PMPB by Goldstone and Labbe (2004), along with my own experiences with this text is synthesized below. In Wiesner's take on this classic fairy tale, the story begins with a traditional orientation. He introduces the characters using the expected text wording and a traditional illustration where the characters are center to the page (e.g. The wolf approaching the house of the first little pig requesting, "Little pig, little pig, let me come in." With the first little pig replying, "Not by the hair of my chinny, chin, chin"). Yet, when the wolf blows down the house of straw, the first pig is blown out of the text itself, appearing outside of the original page, and speaking to the readers directly. The illustration quality changes outside of the page, as the pig's figure appears more realistic, almost photographic in quality, and his speech is encased in a speech bubble similar to those found in cartoons. As the story progresses, the characters of the pigs take charge of their own fate. For example, the first pig invites the second out of the story to escape the wolf. Later, the three pigs are shown physically taking a page from the traditional tale and creating a paper airplane that they fly across several pages of the storybook. Wiesner breaks up and adds layers to the traditional story as the pigs travel between fairy tales visiting the nursery rhyme "Hey diddle diddle" and then rescuing a dragon about to be slain by a knight. Eventually two of the characters from these other tales, the dragon and the nursery rhyme cat, accompany the pigs back to the original story where the dragon successfully and permanently intimidates the wolf. Metafictive devices are visible as Wiesner presents the opportunity for intertextual connections to classic children's tales. The reader is also expected to make sense of contradictions between the printed text and what is communicated in the illustrations. For example, although the text continues to display the traditional verse, "The wolf huffed and puffed ... and ate the pig up," the reader sees the wolf looking confused and the second little pig having already escaped outside the parameters of the page). Finally the pastiche or interweaving of tales shows the reader that the rules of a fairy tale are able to be broken and demonstrates the power of the characters to make choices outside of traditional expectations.

Figure 2. Example of "Breaking the Surface" in Wiesner's (2001) The Three Pigs.

TYPOLOGY OF POSTMODERN PICTURE BOOK FEATURES

In addition to literary devices, PMBP authors also disrupt readers' expectations by manipulating features found in both fictional and non-fictional texts. In keeping with the postmodern intentions of this genre, PMPB authors present features that expose naturalized assumptions as well as offer readers opportunities to engage in reconstruction of assumed social realities. They do this by presenting texts that position and reposition the readers and his or her expectations. Readers are invited to witness the text creators' play with textual features and to play with these themselves. In doing so, readers fill gaps in meaning created through these disruptions. Thus, through their struggle to fill the gaps, McGuire et al.'s (2008) third graders actively made meaning by interacting with the texts and then collectively discussing and debating their meaning choices. Pantaleo (2004, 2006) organized a typology of features found in PMPBs using Dresang's (1999) characteristics of "Radical Change." These characteristics describe changes in children's literature in relation to "positive changes in the digital world" (Dresang, 1999, p. 14 as cited in Pantaleo, 2004). The three types of changes include: changing forms and formats, changing perspectives, and changing boundaries. These feature types necessarily overlap with each other as well as with metafictive devices, however, the typology helps refine our analysis by adding two additional lenses by which to explore: 1) the actual construction of the book and, 2) the boundaries between the producers, subjects, and consumers of the text. A summary of these features, using Dresang's/Pantaleo's organizational framework is shared in Table 1.

Table 1. Typology of characteristics of postmodern picture books.

Dresang's Typology (Pantaleo, 2004, 2006)	Examples from the Literature
Type One: Changing Form and Formats • Graphics in new forms • Words and pictures at new levels of synergy • Non-linear organization and format • Non-sequential organization and format	*Striking visuals* (e.g color shows meaning, words represent a sound, text imposed on a picture) (Pantaleo, 2004) *Typographic experimentation* (e.g. title upside down, readers prompted to insert their own names) (2006) *Symbols, fonts, sizes* chosen to convey meanings, color (Hassett & Curwood, 2009) "*Ontological meaning*" (e.g. structural changes to the text such as pathways to follow with parallel displays of information, cross referencing of elements, images that extend or replace the written word) (Lankshear & Knobel, 2003) *Contesting discourses* between illustrations and written text requires reader to consider alternative readings or meanings (Anstey, 2002) *Multiple narratives and narrators* require reader to bring "order" to the chaotic story (Goldstone & Labbe, 2004) *Non-traditional use of narrator voice, plot, character or setting* which disrupt expected authority of author,

	characters or reader (Anstey, 2004; O'Neil, 2010)
Type Two: Changing Perspectives • Multiple perspectives • Visual mixed with verbal • Previously unheard voices • Youth who speak for themselves	*Multiple voices* in one book or from many stories or books. Character(s) who speak from *range of life experiences.* Picture books with *multiple visual perspectives* (e.g. view from above or in the midst of action) (Pantaleo, 2004) *Distribution of power* from narrator to major or minor characters (Goldstone & Labbe, 2004) *Interactive narration* (e.g. direct address from characters to reader, over expectations to play with the book or contribute to story) (Hassett & Curwood, 2009; O'Neil, 2010) *Availability of multiple readings* and meanings for a variety of audiences (Anstey, 2002)
Type Three: Changing Boundaries • Subjects previously hidden • Settings previously overlooked • Characters portrayed in new and complex ways • New types of communities • Unresolved endings	Boundary crossing between author/illustrators and storyline (e.g. what is imaginary and *what is real*?) (Goldstone & Labbe, 2004) Reader should not expect to be immersed in "time and space" of story – instead *juxtaposed w/reality* (Goldstone & Labbe, 2004; McGuire et al., 2008) *Collapse of hierarchies* between high/low cultures (e.g. knowledge, taste, opinion) (Allan, 2012) *Exposing hidden or naturalized cultures* (e.g. making patriarchy visible in reconstructions of princess fairytales) (Allan, 2012) *Questioning of certainty* (Allan, 2012) *Difference co-exists* rather than resolves (Allan, 2012) *Disruption of the "peritext"* or how the book is made. *"Breaking the surface"* challenges to underlying structure and codes (e.g. "special planes" include: back, mid, front, off the page, space under or around individual pages) (Goldstone & Labbe, 2004; Pantaleo, 2006)

By its nature, however, the PMPB resists typification. The typology merely creates a tool for educators to dig more deeply into texts that challenge their own comfort levels before adding this to their instruction with students. For example, originally in my English Language Arts classes, I asked the pre-service elementary teachers to read a traditional version and then Wiesner's version of *The Three Pigs*.

When I asked, "What did you notice?" most students quickly gave up on the latter text, stating that they were confused by it and felt young children would be also. Interestingly, researcher Frank Serafini (2005) found a similar reaction from intermediate grade students who were initially reluctant to struggle with the complexity presented by books with metafictive characteristics. Yet, in keeping with McGuire et al.'s (2008) findings discussed above, and eventually in Serafini's project, when students struggled with complexity and negotiated meaning collectively, they became engaged, challenging their own thinking and that of their peers. Therefore, part of the teacher educator's and teacher's role is to provide entry points that challenge readers to dig deeper.

For example, analytical questions based on the typology shared here, may open a text that seems initially confusing and inaccessible to the reader. Examples are:
- Type One: How does the author/illustrator manipulate the graphics in this book and why?
- Type Two: Who is in charge of the story?
- Type Three: What is real in this story and what is make-believe?

In their analysis of *The Three Pigs*, Goldstone and Labbe (2004) share their thinking about the affordances of Wiesner's text in addressing the last question:

> What is real here? The book? The story? The reader's perceptions? In *The Three Pigs*, the pigs step out of the pages, knock over pages, and turn a page of the story into a paper airplane. On the last page, two pigs and their newfound friends, the cat and the dragon, sit down to dinner while the third pig is carefully placing letters to read 'and they all lived happily ever after' ... Postmodern picture books keep the reader aware of the physical world. True, these books invite the reader into the story, but they provide reminders to keep one foot grounded in reality. These books do not blanket the reader with their stories, rather they prod and tease the reader with questions ... By disclosing how the book is created ... [they remind] the reader that there is another world outside the narrative ... highlighting two significant aspects of the reading process: reading should connect directly with everyday life [and] the written word is not above questioning. (p. 201)

The literature contains examples of differing roles for teacher facilitators who challenged their students to develop habits of critical reading through PMPBs. A word of warning, however, is to keep in mind the intentions of teaching with PMPBs, which is, to diffuse power and authority over the text and its messages. The value of the PMPB is lost if the questioning becomes reified into close-ended, one right answer formats, that already render classrooms non-dialogic. In the classroom studies reviewed for this chapter, the purposes of active participation by students was achieved through contextually created instruction where power to create meaning was distributed across the student/teacher relationship, but those relationships did not always look the same.

TEACHING AND THE POSTMODERN PICTURE BOOK

Writing about the need for a 21st century pedagogy, Hassett and Curwood (2008) remind teachers that "if the world of communication is not standing still, why would our pedagogic practices?" (p. 281). Several of the classroom studies reviewed here included examples of teachers' pedagogy. In these, the teacher's role remained intact (instructor, teacher, model) but was reconceptualized with several new attributes. Of primary importance was ensuring increased student involvement as presenters and evaluators of ideas in ways that in traditional classrooms are often delineated solely by the teacher's interpretation. The teacher's role required active leadership in reminding students to hold one another accountable for listening as well as responding and ensuring that no voices were silenced, yet she remained a co-constructor of ideas "with" the students, realizing that "students sometimes know as much, if not more, about certain things" (p. 280). Instruction included teachers' monitoring and uptake of ideas in ways that continued to challenge the depth of students' thinking. McGuire et al.'s study suggests a "weaving of responses" and provides transcribed examples of teachers' questioning and prompting to show how they positioned students to "focus their gaze on the inquiry" without losing students' development of ownership in their ideas (p. 204).

In McGuire et al.'s (2008) research, they noticed teachers' roles as consistent with Aukerman's (2006 as cited in McGuire et al.) "Shared Evaluation Pedagogy." That is, the teacher invited students into conversations but actively refrained from "hypermediating" or forwarding their own ideas as primary. By facilitating multiple interpretations offered in the space of dialogue, teachers retain their authority as "knowers" but also position children also as "possible knowers" by weaving their responses into the conversation. In such conversations, children were positioned to grapple with the texts and with each other's ideas and teachers remained open to learning from student ideas. A sample question provided by the authors illustrates how a teacher maintained student Oumar's idea as central to the topic, while challenging him to think more deeply: "What do you think Oumar, do you have an answer to your own question?" (McGuire et al., 2008, p. 196).

Hassett and Curwood (2008) describe this type of dialogic literacy instruction as a combined space where "joy and laughter" between students and teacher exist along with explicit teaching of conceptual tools for text analysis. They describe how a teacher, Tess Theobold, served as "design consultant" as she incorporated PMPBs as mentor texts for writing. Through the use of analytic strategies such as "think alouds" Ms. Theobold engages students in dialogue with attention to specific text features over the course of several readings. For example, Keller's (2003) PMPB, *Arnie the Doughnut* served as a mentor for identifying author's tools. The protagonist, Arnie, is a personified doughnut, who sits in the bakery case watching as other doughnuts are chosen by customers, one by one, until he is finally sold to Mr. Bing. Hassett and Curwood's plot summary states,

POSTMODERN PICTURE BOOK

Figure 3. Cover of Arnie the Doughnut (Keller, 2003).

The book itself, in general terms, is about a doughnut that goes home with Mr. Bing, and then after some negotiations becomes his pet rather than being eaten. And yet, this brief summary of the plot does not describe the book at all ... Throughout the entire book, Keller writes and designs specific meanings into the story she wants to tell through words, images, and multiple perspectives. (p. 275)

The visual characteristics of this text lend itself as a great example to share "ontological meanings" (Lankshear & Knobel, 2003, as cited in Goldstone & Labbe, 2004, p. 271) through multiple, multimodal pathways. Communication includes: parallel displays of information, cross referencing of elements, and images that extend or replace the written word. For example, the cover epitomizes the graphic design incorporated throughout the book. It centers on a central graphic depicting Arnie, the multicolored pastry, with a speech bubble where he exclaims "That's ME!" In addition, multiple small figures are depicted across the cover, each with a comment nearby. Humor is communicated through the intersection of graphics and prints. For example, instead of the traditional "by" in front of the author's name, Keller substitutes "cooked up by" placing two figures of doughnuts nearby, referencing the author with the following comments, "I'm sorry, but that girl can NOT cook!" and the reply, "I know, I know – it's a

111

figure of speech." Throughout the book, the author uses multimodal graphics and texts (e.g. colored words, bold words, high levels of detailed pictures, words in different languages, sometimes things in order and sometimes order is all over the page, speech bubbles, thought bubbles and dialogue bubbles) through which choices of meaning are available to the readers (Hassett & Curwood, 2008, p. 275).

Ms. Theobold, by reading and thinking aloud in dialogue with her students, over multiple readings of the books, captured how Keller and authors of several more PMPBs utilized a variety of modalities and for what purpose. Eventually, for her students, the author's tools became their writer's tools as her own students chose from the variety of "available designs" to create their own story pages, examples of which are shared by Hassett and Curwood in their description.

CONCLUSION

Young children in today's society need experiences that position them as agents who understand how texts work and how to manipulate texts for a variety of social purposes – most importantly to practice literacy as social actors who contribute productively to the world in which they live. The field of critical literacy – defined in the socio-cultural scholarship by three related theories – New Literacy Studies, Multiliteracies, and Critical Literacies – provides a framework for teachers who wish to enhance their classroom teaching to promote literacy that prepares students for flexible, context-focused, and agentic relationships with a broad array of texts. The postmodern picture book provides a venue for classroom teachers to engage even the youngest of students as "designers" of texts which in turn invite them to become "designers of their social futures" (New London Group, 1996). PMPB authors present opportunities that blur the boundaries about what is held invisible and often unconditionally accepted constructions of reality. By doing so, they help circumvent the limits we set on children as complex thinkers. As we've seen above, readers of these books by necessity become co-authors of meaning. As one fifth-grader in a classroom study reviewed here stated, "I thought the book was like a movie that was never rehearsed" (as cited in Pantaleo, 2006, p. 285). That student recognized the text as fluid and open to adaption as it is performed – a potential inherent in all PMPBs. This student is developing a textual "author" ity (Hassett & Curwood, 2008) to claim a stake in the meaning, by assuming power to make choices as she engages in performing a role in her world.

CHILDREN'S BOOK REFERENCES

Cronin, D. (author), & Lewin, B. (illustrator). (2000). *Click, clack, moo: Cows that type*. New York, NY: Athaneum Books for Young Readers.
Keller, L. (2003). *Arnie the doughnut*. New York, NY: Scholastic.
Wiesner, D. (2001). *The three pigs*. New York, NY: Scholastic

REFERENCES

Allan, Cheri (2012). *Playing with picturebooks: Postmodernism and postmodernesque.* London, UK: Palgrave MacMillan.

Anstey, M. (2002). "It's not all black and white": Postmodern picture books and new literacies. *Journal of Adolescent & Adult Literacy, 45*(6), 444-457.

Barthes, R. (1975). *The pleasure of the text.* Translated by Richard Miller. New York, NY: Hill.

Bruner, J. (1996). *The culture of education.* Cambridge, MA: Harvard University Press.

Coulter, E. Review of *Click, Clack, Moo Cows That Type.* Amazon. Retrieved from: http://www.amazon.com/Click-Clack-Cows-That-Type/dp/0689832133/ref=tmm_hrd_swatch_0?_encoding=UTF8&sr=&qid=

Dresang, E. (1999). *Radical change: Books for youth in a digital age.* New York, NY: The H.W. Wilson Company.

Fillichio, C. (2014, January 2). Re: What typing cows teach us [Web log post]. Retrieved from: http://social.dol.gov/blog/what-typing-cows-teach-us/

Freire, P., & Macedo, D. (2013). *Literacy: Reading the word and the world.* New York, NY: Routledge.

Goldstone, B. P., & Labbe, L. D. (2004). The postmodern picture book: A new genre. *Language Arts, 81*(3), 196-204.

Janks, H. (2013). Critical literacy in teaching and research. *Education Inquiry, 4*(2), 225-242.

Lankshear, C., & Knobel, M. (2003). *New literacies: Changing knowledge and classroom learning.* Buckingham, UK: Open University Press.

Lankshear, C., & Knobel, M. (2006). *New literacies: Changing knowledge in the classroom* (2nd ed.). New York, NY: McGraw-Hill International.

O'Neil, K. (2010). Once upon today: Teaching for social justice with picture books. *Children's Literature in Education, 41,* 40-51.

New London Group (Cazden, C., Cope, B., Fairclough, N., Gee, J., Kalantzis, M., Kress, G., Luke, A., Luke, C., Michaels, S., & Nakata, M.). (1996). A pedagogy of multiliteracies: Designing social futures. *Harvard Educational Review, 66*(1), 60-92.

Pantaleo, S. (2004). Young children and radical change characteristics in picture books. *The Reading Teacher, 58*(2), 178-187.

Pantaleo, S. (2006). Scieska's *The Stinky Cheese Man*: A tossed salad of parodic re-versions. *Children's Literature in Education, 38,* 277-295.

Serafini, F. (2005). Voices in the park, voices in the classroom: Readers responding to postmodern picture books. *Reading Research and Instruction, 44*(3), 47-64.

Unsworth, L. (2008). Multiliteracies and metalanguage: Describing image/text relations as a resource for negotiating multimodal texts. In J. Coiro, M. Knobel, C. Lankshear, & D. Leu (Eds.), *Handbook of research on new literacies.* New York, NY: Routledge.

LESSON PLAN FOR PRE-SERVICE TEACHER EDUCATION
ENGLISH LANGUAGE ARTS METHODS COURSE

This is a lesson designed to introduce pre-service elementary teachers to the postmodern picture book.

Step One: Choose a picture book with postmodern features as described in Table 1. Several well known authors provide a body of work with some excellent choices to get started (see below for some authors who offer a body of work). Many of their texts are readily available in school and community libraries.

Provide groups of students (approximately five per group) with a copy of the text. Engage the whole class in a read-aloud making sure that everyone has full view of the illustrated text or ask each group to read the text together. Encourage students to respond freely to the first read. Did they enjoy the book? Why or why not? Listen for comments that you may want to explore further and facilitate a discussion if warranted. For example, in Tan's *The Arrival*, readers may share the strong emotion expressed despite the lack of words OR they may ask questions about who or where the story took place based on contradictory messages in the images (e.g. origami in what looks like a mid-20th century Eastern European family).

Step Two: Re-read with "Two Hats" – Hat #1: For your personal and group response. Hat #2: As a critical literacy teacher. Often I find in my courses that pre-service teachers jump to discuss the book in terms of their classroom teaching before they actually take time to engage as a reader themselves.

Hat #1. Personal and Group Response. Use the questions mentioned in the chapter as prompts. Find evidence in the text that support your opinion. Engage in a discussion about meanings in the book.

Prompt based on Radical Change Characteristics (Dresang, 1999)	Evidence (Table 1 from the chapter may be helpful for revising these questions to better fit the chosen text)
Type One: Does the author/illustrator manipulate the graphics in this book? How? Why?	
Type Two: Who is in charge of the story?	
Type Three: What is real in this story and what is make-believe?	

Hat #2. Critical Literacy Teacher. In what ways might a teacher facilitate a discussion around this book? What are some ideas for analyzing the features of this book? How might they engage in critical literacy practices to critique or reconstruct meanings from this book? What are some specific ways in which using this book can help young students expand their literacy practices?

Note: Interesting as well to check online to see what others have done with these stories. For example on You Tube, on the author's page, or … what else can you find?

Author	Web Page	Some Titles
Jon Sciezka and Colleagues	http://www.jsworldwide.com/	The Stinky Cheese Man Math Curse Squids will be Squids Baloney, Henry P. Battle Bunny The Real Story of the Three Pigs Time Warp Trio (Series)
Shaun Tan	http://www.shauntan.net/	Tales from Outer Suburbia, The Arrival, The Lost Thing, Eric The Red Tree
Chris Van Allsberg	http://www.chrisvanallsburg.com/home.html	Bad Day at Riverbend The Garden of Abdul Gasazai Jumanji The Mysteries of Harris Burdick The Polar Express Two Bad Ants The Wreck of the Zephyr
David Wiesner	http://www.davidwiesner.com	The Three Pigs Tuesday Flotsam Night of the Gargoyles The Loathsome Dragon
Mo Willems	www.mowillems.com/	Don't Let the Pigeon Drive the Bus (there are other Pigeon books) Knuffle Bunny We are in a Book!

KJERSTI VANSLYKE-BRIGGS & HEATHER MATTHEWS

7. A SOURCE OF SELF

Exploring Identity and Discourse in Young Adult Novels as Meaningful Text

ABSTRACT

Young adult literature can be utilized to assist young people as they search to develop identity and face many challenges of growing into an adult. The literature choices of young adults should be validated to encourage young people to continue to read and to seek out works that speak to their own developing Discourses. The use of YAL and an authentic narrative voice can help young people critique their lived world, but also to engage readers as the novels will resonate with reader's experiences. In addition, YAL is not just for pleasure reading and growth of a reader. When wise selections are made and the work is implemented in the classroom it can be used for critical analysis and growth toward important skills that are fostered in the English Language Arts. This chapter documents several contemporary realistic fiction selections that can be used in the classroom in an effort to engage with young readers in meaningful ways.

INTRODUCTION

Young adult (YA) literature speaks to student experience, and too often the adult world dismisses the genre without first considering the impact of this decision. Young adult literature addresses the contemporary concerns of teens as it is an authentic narrative voice that resonates with students' lived experiences. Although these texts are typically written by adults, it is the reading experience and the characters' voices that make it authentic. As students begin to sort out their own identities and their roles in this world, young adult literature can provide both a mirror to reflect back young peoples' experiences and also provide a window that can let young people look out into the worlds of other cultures and communities. This aspect of the use of YA fiction is particularly important because many young people wrap their lives within a veil of silence. Students are hesitant to share their personal experiences outside of their cadre and hesitant to speak about what often troubles them as they move toward adolescence. This literature speaks to the authentic lives of students and approaches with frank language the issues and concerns facing teens every day. Proponents of YA argue that the literature "assures teenagers that they are not alone in their experiences" (Enriquez, 2006,

p. 17). In this way, YA literature can often be viewed as an avenue for bibliotherapy, the use of literature to assist individuals as they sort out personal problems. Critical pedagogy can lend itself to the effective use of bibliotherapy as part of the reading process in that students explore identity construction. YA literature can help young people as they search for a developing identity and as they encounter the many challenges faced by teens.

While most people view young adult literature as simple pleasure reading, it also has a valuable place in the classroom as literature that can be read and appreciated with a critical analysis. For young adult novels to be quickly dismissed by adults posits the literature as worthless or foolish, and creates a similar thought process for the young person who enjoys it, making the reader feel similarly worthless or foolish. According to Crowe, "some teachers and parents believe that YAL is little more than cheap, pulp novels" (1998, p. 120). As educators, we need to move beyond this understanding and see the value that YA literature has to offer. YA literature reflects the same themes, motifs and figurative language found in most classic texts. Many YA novels are written with an author's craft that could rival the canon texts used for generations in the middle and high school classroom. The YA novel is a valuable text and can be used by the discerning teacher to act as a bridge between classic and contemporary works. It can also be layered as a text set with nonfiction or other multimodal sources in order to create a robust and rich classroom unit. For instance, the well-known YA text about the Holocaust *Number the Stars* by Lois Lowry can easily be paired with primary source documents from the time period and with film representations of related content. It can even be tied to stage performances and to other seminal texts such as *The Diary of Anne Frank*. Students engage in a multivocal, transliteracy experience as they explore multimodal literacies as connected to a central text. As evidenced by the Lowry example above, the multivocal experience of layering many narrators invites more students to the conversation.

Teachers and other adults in the lives of young people should validate the reading choices that young people make (Lesesne, 2006). These choices in reading selection, once validated, help young people share their own reading voices, develop their own discourses and help to avoid the alliteracy trend that is so common among young readers. Alliteracy, or the refusal to read by individuals that are capable of doing so, is on the rise with middle and high school students. The rise is occurring at younger and younger grade levels and researchers are finding the fastest rise in alliteracy is occurring with tweens – those students between the ages of 10 and 12 (Lesesne, 2006). In this age range, the students are rejecting the picture books they knew as children, but are also still resisting the longer chapter books assigned in classrooms. Carefully selected YA literature that is developmentally appropriate for the tween can help these students continue to evolve as readers as they develop reading skills and fluency. There is YA fiction available that specifically targets the discourse of this age group and should not be confused with the works that are more developmentally appropriate for teens. Not all young adult literature can be lumped into one all-inclusive category and there are subtle differences based on genre, target age range and stylistic approach just as there are subgenres within adult fiction. It is important to consider the needs of both tweens and teens as teachers select literature for the classroom.

When used appropriately in the classroom, young adult literature is interactive and transactive. Transactive reading is a process in which the readers are consistently encouraged to engage with the text making connections between text to text, text to self and text to world. The reading becomes both etic (viewing the text as from outside one's own culture and experience) and emic (viewing the text as reflected from within one's own culture and experience). The words on the page begin to have meaning once they pass through the eyes of the reader and the reader creates meaning as reflected by the reader's experiences. Rosenblatt's transactive theory of reading speaks directly to the etic and emic reading process. Moss summarizes the process of the theory as a focus on the nature of readers' responses to unfolding texts, and her transactional theory of reading provides a

> framework for exploring a reader's responses to literature. According to Rosenblatt, reading is a "transaction, a two-way process, involving a reader and a text at a particular time under particular circumstances" (1982, p. 268). The nature of this transaction is determined by the reader's stance or "mental set," which is related to a reader's expectations and the way he or she approaches the text. Rosenblatt uses the term aesthetic to refer to a stance that allows a reader to focus on the "lived through" experience of reading. She argues that the most effective way to read fiction and poetry is from an aesthetic stance. (2005, p. 4)

While many young adult novels are award winners, identifying a novel for the classroom should not hinge on this as a need for identifying quality literature. The best novels are a natural fit with the context of the classroom and school. The novel that meets the needs of the students and will engage students in essential questions about identity and the reader's lived worlds is the best option as it explores the spaces in which adolescents may experience dissonance and may struggle with conflicting discourses. Essential questions are open ended and broad questions that ask the students to look at the big picture. The book becomes the lens through which the world may be examined.

DISCOURSE, TRANSACTIONAL READING AND CRITICAL LITERACY

A large part of life as a tween (ages 10 to 12) or teen (13 to19) is the development of identity. Students are sorting out who they are and who they want to be. Their lives are marked by transitions and transience (Lesesne, 2006, p. 11). A large part of this identity formation can be guided through literature. Gee (2001), literacy specialist and critical literacy theorist argues that this identity formation creates Discourses, with a capital D – not to be confused with discourse (language use). Discourse, as he indicates, is a complete identity package. Individuals can have multiple Discourses and each one can be applied to different situations. A student can affirm or challenge one's personal Discourses through the reading of YA literature because the author's use of a teen protagonist voice in an authentic and plausible storyline will resonate with the lived worlds of tweens and teens. Pedagogy that is grounded in critical literacy theory builds an interaction with the reading in which the students examine what they have learned first about the self as the literature reaffirms or denies their lived experiences and then asks students to use this knowledge to examine the community and larger world. Critical literacy applications when coupled with YA literature asks students to examine the normative behaviors of society reflected in the novel and question their own role as they either are complicit with or resistant to those normative behaviors. It is this disruption of "normative readings" (Luke & Freebody, 1997) that requires students to examine the unwritten sociocultural rules of their world. A critical literacy framework for literature analysis requires that the goal be development of a critical consciousness. Cervetti, Pardales and Damico (2001) examine the differences between critical reading and critical literacy pointing out that as opposed to critical reading in which reality is knowable, in critical literacy reality is not definitively known in large part because each reader creates his or her own knowing based on the Discourse background brought to the current reading of the text. As Gee (1996) explains, "a text is meaningful only within the pattern (or social configuration) it forms at a specific time and place ... within a specific Discourse or at the intersection of several Discourses" (p. 149). It is important to note that not only does the space and time component change because of the reader's situatedness, but also the space in social time in which the text is read. As Wacquant (1992) notes Bourdieu's understanding of the social world posits that, "social laws are temporally and spatially bound regularities that hold as long as the institutional conditions that underpin them are allowed to endure" (Wacquant & Bourdieu, p. 52). If the normative rules change over time, so does the reading of the text by new readers of a new generation. Discourses are also shaped by the period of history in which they are developed. Once students understand those Discourses that ground their reading of text they can begin to disrupt the rules normativity which silence or marginalize.

Primary Discourses are those created and significantly defined in early childhood before the reader comes into contact with YA novels, as young adult novels typically aim for readers no younger than 12 years old. It can be explained to students as those Discourses which one does not always have a choice in participating. Primary Discourses include aspects such as religion, socioeconomic status, location (rural, urban) and so on. These are the Discourses of our circumstances. A Primary Discourse can easily be developed or strengthened through young adult literature as a means of youth exploration. These Discourses often are something as simple as "daughter," "friend" or "student," but often even these simple Discourses may be further developed through YA literature. A student reading the novel *Luna*, by Julie Anne Peters that explores a character transitioning from male to female, may find that he or she identifies with a gender that may not match their biological sex; a student reading *Speak*, by Laurie Halse Anderson may begin to understand the importance of a Primary Discourse of "daughter," as a defining role with expectations. In each case, these Discourses may be challenged or reaffirmed by the author's use of authentic voice.

Secondary Discourses are connected to the choices that individuals make. These would include peer groups, habits and those activities that may define identity. One single person may have multiple Secondary Discourses, which can be influenced dramatically by literature. For instance, a young person could have a Secondary Discourse (one that is created through later socialization as opposed to primary socialization which would occur in the early home). Literature that reflects back the lived experience validates the adolescent's chosen identity structure. Literature may also challenge this belief structure and ask students to question their belief systems. Students will be able to participate in "decentering the margins as spaces that offer the opportunity for other voices to be spoken and heard" (Giroux, 1993, p.376) including those not even present in the text as they are completely silent. A critical consciousness is developed in the student and students become active participants in reading their world through the lens of the literature.

This Discourse does not simply reflect a hobby such as skateboarding, but rather a larger more inclusive identity which would impact not only the hobby, but also dress, language use, how one carries the body such as mannerisms and even how one interacts with others. This student that now identifies as "skater" (skateboarder) may not use this Discourse at all times, but rather may be able to code switch to another Discourse more appropriate to each contextual situation. This border crossing allows the student to participate in multiple arenas while maintaining a spectrum of Discourses. In addition, multiple dimensions of identity can be developed and defined both "internally by self and externally by others" (Deaux as cited in Jones & McEwen, 2000, p. 406). Thus, the reflections that others impose on an individual must also be considered.

Each Discourse must be considered when reading any text. Because readers encounter texts through their own eyes, each reading becomes unique based on the lens of situatedness (Greene, 1988) at that time. The lens of situatedness considers every Discourse at play as well as all life events experienced by the reader. Thus, each reading becomes a new reading in many ways as individuals continue to grow and mature and as new life experiences change and shape how one views the world. The student then does not just bring in the Secondary Discourse to interpret the text, but also all other aspects of one's life. Returning to the Discourses of the "skater" student, when allowed the freedom to apply the multiple Discourses at play within one's construction, this student may find that the Primary Discourse of "rural" is more at play with a particular literature. Or perhaps, the student finds a multivocal reflection while bringing in an ethnic heritage and the "skater" understandings of music as text best help to interpret the novel.

Rosenblatt (2005) can be credited with developing a Reader Response, transactional view of interpreting text. As she states, "the literary work is a particular and personal event: the electric current of his mind and personality lighting up the pattern of symbols on the printed page. Or perhaps we should say that the symbols take meaning from the intellectual and emotional context the reader provides" (p. 63). Teachers of young adult literature can use this literature to speak to the life experiences of every student when structured well in a way that allows room for this connection to develop. Overly prescriptive analysis provided in a top down approach by teachers limits the use of the literature in the classroom and the ability for the literature to become transactional for students. This methodology can be a detriment to the reading experience as students engage with young adult literature. The reader should encounter the work without predetermined and limiting gates to knowledge and meaning making. By creating these limits, we as teachers do not allow students the ability to bring in multiple Discourses and they are limited to only those Discourses which the student views as most appropriate for school. Students by being victim to these superficial limits find that they "play school" rather than really experience literature. Young adult literature allows teachers the opportunity to guide students in developing their own meaning making without confining that interpretation to the most common responses. Young adult literature is not an exception to all other literature interpretations in that a top down approach to teaching limits the extent of student engagement.

The transactional view of interpreting text allows for each of the possibilities to play out and the possibilities will be a different configuration from day to day depending on the contextualized experiences of that student in that particular moment. In addition, this relationship between reader and text becomes reciprocal in that the meaning of the text is changed by the student's current interpretation and the text may impact the student's current view of self-identity. By allowing the reader to begin to define the critical interpretation of the text, the teacher opens the doors for much possibility in terms of analysis, but also allows for more potential growth as students engage with the text. The transactional use of young adult literature helps students develop their emic and etic understandings and may also help stave off alliteracy. A plurality develops in interpretation that can lead to engaging and robust classroom discussion as students in a safe environment explore the literature and relations to self.

The transactional view of interpreting text is beneficial when tied directly to critical literacy skills. All literacy is social and malleable. As socially constructed, literacy and literature analysis must consider the socially constructed normative behaviors that impact a readers' interpretation of text. As such, "all models of literacy are predicated on and prescriptive of particular social logics" (Luke & Freebody, 1997, p. 5). Each reading of text must also consider the sociocultural environment in which it is both written and read. Teachers must encourage students under this interpretive lens to ask questions such as *how am I being positioned as a reader, what is the author trying to "sell" me* and *who is being marginalized or silenced?* Often it is the adolescent voice which is ignored or discredited. It is important to note that all texts converse with the reader and are dialogic (Bakhtin, 1981). The readers brings all one's subjectivities to the text including thoughts, feelings, attitudes, memories, and social mores. Critical literacy allows the reader to both understand why a reading is interpreted in the personal and also how it can help the reader challenge the normative knowledge and rewrite the messages of the text. In this way, YA literature and the teen voice must be valued. An extension of this can be evidenced with the novel *Speak* for instance in that the narrator is both literally and figuratively silenced as she reacts to cultural norms surrounding rape.

She is first silenced by her attacker and then later selects to self silence as a rape survivor reflecting the silence projected by society on rape victims. Critical literacy interpretations can rewrite this message by putting focus on the act of gaining voice and reflecting on the social norms that reinforce a culture of silence and shame around rape incidents.

The "skater" student from earlier may come to a text asking questions about who is left out of the narrative and question why a particular population is marginalized by a text. That same student may see his or her own voice as missing and may question the authority of the text. Perhaps, the student as he or she is reading may notice that the Discourses of all the female characters are submissive and may reflect that interpretation back to the community in which the student lives. When examining the hegemonic discourse of a text, perhaps the student notices that the language of the text alienates or is inclusive of particular populations. Each reading may become multilayered once again. The possibilities become endless. Not only has the student now interacted with a text and made meaning, but that meaning is examined with a broader perspective related to social justice. Literacy and the reading of young adult novels becomes powerful in this context and, "literacy in this sense is not just a skill or knowledge, but an emerging act of consciousness and resistance" (Giroux, 1993, p. 367). While critical literacy can be applied to any text, often it is not applied to young adult literature because these novels are simply read on a surface level and not considered "serious" literature by adults. The interrogation of the text allows one to explore the voice of an adolescent as undervalued in contemporary culture.

Teachers may find it beneficial to first construct Discourse maps (see Figure 1 and following teaching plan) with students before applying the method of analysis to literature. In this way, students first come to know themselves and the different Discourses at play in their identity before examining a text. The Discourse maps (VanSlyke-Briggs, 2006, p. 44) begin with a brainstorming regarding labels that students may attribute to their identity. A guided brainstorming will allow students to begin to identify their Discourses. This could begin with showing students samples from popular contemporary films that display stereotyped Discourses. As students begin their own brainstorming these labels may begin simplistically with obvious selections such as *high school student, teen* or hobby linked activities such as *basketball player*. Once students explore these, the teacher can then guide students to a more inclusive examination by looking at other Discourses at play such as those that reflect upbringing, cultural impacts and community impacts. After brainstorming, students can select imagery to reflect the key Discourses and create a visual representation or map to help explain the grounding identities through which a textual interpretation will be filtered. Discourses can also reflect elements of a student's identity that they may not be comfortable sharing such as addictions, body image or aspects the student would prefer to keep hidden. While it is not in the best interest of the student to share these publically, a space should still be created to allow the students to take these into consideration as they will impact the reading of a text.

Figure 1. Student sample discourse map: front and back.

Discourse maps can be used not only to examine the Discourses at play within a student that would impact a reading, but also the Discourses that apply to characters within young adult literature and the overlaps between reader and character. These overlaps or areas in which there is a clear divide can be an entry point for analysis utilizing reader response theory and critical literacy applications. For instance, Melinda in the novel *Speak*, by Halse Anderson exhibits multiple Discourses. Within her Primary Discourses, those Discourses that she is born into, she can include daughter, young woman, student, middle class and white. Her Secondary Discourses or those that are shaped by experiences include rape survivor, developing artist, friend and high school student. A student's artistic portrayal of Melinda's Discourse map can be developed like a Venn diagram in order to display overlaps and differences with the character. It is this understanding of one's Discourses that allows a student to develop what Maxine Greene (1978) calls "wide-awakeness" and the ability to be active rather than passive as students view the world. She draws a connection between this to the idea of social imagination (Greene 1995), which is important in critical literacy. We must first understand ourselves, then become wide awake as we view the world before we imagine what can be done to resolve those places we find social injustice.

CONTEMPORARY REALISTIC FICTION AND AUTHENTIC LANGUAGE

Contemporary realistic fiction refers to texts that take place in a window of time within recent past or current time spans. The action within the novels, though fiction, are representations of "real world" events. For young adult novels, contemporary realistic fiction often has a focus on life events such as first loves, losses of family or friends, coming of age, and the discovery of personal identity, be it sexuality, gender, race, and so on. These profound moments in the teen experience are described throughout fiction in the range of bildungsroman (coming of age) texts over the course of generations and the theme has continued to be popular for contemporary young readers coming into their own identities. This genre of young adult fiction is "written with the purpose of connecting to their young readers by offering settings and events that are comparable to the ones that tweens and teens experience in the course of their daily lives" (Sprague & Keeling, 2007, p. 51). Several examples of this are discussed below and can include well known YA novels such as *Speak* by Halse Anderson, *House on Mango Street* by Cisneros and *The Perks of Being a Wallflower* by Chbosky.

Though young adult literature was not recognized until recently as a viable genre of literature, let alone a genre that can be used in a classroom, YA has potential classroom uses and applications for many students. Often, students are unable to connect to such characters as Willy Loman, a drunkard middle aged man with a wife and children, from *Death of a Salesman* by Arthur Miller, but have an easier time connecting to such characters as Melinda from *Speak*. This can be in part to multiple reasons, but mainly can be attributed to the fact that Melinda, unlike Willy Loman, is within the same life stage as the student reader. Whereas Loman may be dealing with the struggles of adult life, within *Speak* lies a world that the young reader can relate to on a personal level, be it the discovery of self, the competition within towns of the haves and the have-nots, or perhaps even just figuring out where one belongs in a family or social group in which all must have a specific role or set of roles to become important. Here is where the divide for young adult literature becomes apparent, and the need to be present in the classroom becomes stronger.

These qualifications for determining a young adult novel include the following: "the novel must be written for and marketed for young adult readers, contains a young adult protagonist, limited number of characters, a compressed time span, familiar settings, current slang, detailed descriptions of appearance and dress, positive resolution, few, if any, subplots, and a length of no more than 250 pages" (Niday, 2000, n.p.). These outlining factors do have a bit of flexibility, as some YA literature novels do run more than 250 pages or have a not-so-positive resolution, but on the whole, these are the specifics that all YA literature must meet. Therefore, using this criteria, it is easy to see how exactly these novels attract a different crowd of readers than for instance a traditional Russian existentialist novel.

Much of the young adult literature that is popular now can also be explored using sociocultural theory and situated learning as described by Vygotsky. The zone of proximal development as developed by Vygotsky has embedded within it "a 'cultural' interpretation [which] construes the zone of proximal development as the distance between the cultural knowledge provided by the sociohistorical context – usually made accessible through instruction – and the everyday experiences of the individuals (Lave & Wegner, 1991, p. 48). Rather than sorting through literature in an isolated context, for "neo-Vygotskians the construction of conceptual knowledge in students always appears as a guided construction" (Kozulin, 2003, p. 34). There can be guidance from a significant other, such as a teacher or a parent, or the guidance can come from literature, such as young adult novels. Young adults are drawn to novels that can guide them in one direction or another. Using their interests, identified gender, age, and other background information, young adults select novels that not only entertain, but also that guide this young person in the ways of life, and through the intimidating maze that is adolescence. In addition, this guidance is often also a form of communication that teens do not receive elsewhere (Scott & Palincsar, 2009, n.p.). Teachers can aid in that guidance as they suggest particular works that may act in a bibliotherapeutic manner for students and allow students to explore identity construction and textual interpretation through each new situated reading. As students develop their understanding of the text, the teacher can act as a guide to help students question the text and the sociocultural constructions reflected in the text. The use of transmediation (the process of moving meaning from one sign system to another) such as by having students create Discourse maps of characters can help students move beyond simplistic or initial interpretations and may help students begin to dig deeper in meaning making connected to critical literacy. It may also make students feel more confident in the role of someone who critiques dominant cultural norms. The act of the critique becomes an act of social resistance and the Discourse map becomes the foundation for the critique.

Realistic teen fiction speaks to many students that do not typically see themselves reflected in the curriculum. Students at risk, such as alliterate students, students that do not fully engage in schooling and those that are members of historically silenced populations, for instance may find that YA literature better connects to their own life experiences in contrast to the traditional novels of instruction found in schools. In addition, many young adults find YA fiction to be fiction that validates the tween and teen experience as being a young adult when life is confusing, and much of one's time is spent trying to not only figure out personal identity, but also how one fits into society as a whole especially when given the variety of constructs that may impact one's development such as instances of marginalization. Students need to draw on their social knowledge and personal experiences to make sense of text. A teacher driven, top down model as opposed to a transactive and critical model continues to "marginalize students as passive consumers of teacher-made interpretation" (Miller, 2003, p. 17) and closes off the opportunity to explore Discourse and identity development. Young adult literature addresses this gap in the standard curriculum of canon texts and teacher as filter for interpretation and allows students an outlet in literature in which they see themselves reflected in a way that is conducive to learning, as well as in a way that is safe to explore and learn as they critique their world. The sociocultural approach to analysis and the use of the teacher as a guide rather than an authority of only one interpretation allows for growth for the student. In his text, *Psychology of Art* (1971) Vygotsky applies this idea to the teaching of literature, "where he argues that the affects of literature excite the individual aesthetically" and that the teacher "must aim, further, to form reflective consciousness through 'intelligent social activity' that extends the 'narrow sphere of individual perception'" (Miller, 2003, p. 290). In this case, strategies such as literature circles and Socratic seminars based on open ended and multiple perspective essential questions generated by both teacher and student will guide students out of a single lens of interpretation, either by the self or the teacher and instead will capitalize on the group construction of knowledge and insight. Essential questions allow students to converse using not only textual evidence to support claims, but also connections to the self and other texts. The big questions are open ended to allow for multiple interpretations and for multiple access points for entry into that interpretation. It also allows for multiple truths to exist side by side. Each student can find empowerment through the discovery of their own subjective truths and exploration of how these interact with the truth other students experience. For instance, in reading *Speak*, an essential question could include, *who defines what it means to be an outsider and how does it impact voice?* There is no one set truth as each student is influenced by their lived experiences. This ties together Rosenblatt's Reader Response Theory with critical literacy analysis.

On the whole, much of what classifies a novel as being a young adult novel is that it pertains to the idea of identity and discovery of self for a tween or teen. The search for self is often constructed in a coming of age, bildungsroman framework as opposed to other adult novels that may engage in a discussion of identity, but is limited to adult protagonists. Many young adult novels do broach the topic of identity, either as the main theme or as a lesser focus that still plays an important side role in the development of the text. This aspect is also what draws many young readers to these books; the validation of experience that young people look for in each other, and that they crave to find. By seeking this validation in a novel where all things are possible, it allows the young person to experience life events by proxy, so that they may discover themselves.

WHAT TO READ?

While there are numerous quality reads to select from for the classroom, below are four sample novels that would be good instructional sources for the typical middle school or high school classroom. The field of YA literature grows at an extraordinary rate and a high number of new, high quality novels hits the market every year.

Playground by 50 Cent, 2011

Playground, by famed hiphop vocalist Curtis Jackson known as 50 Cent, is the very frank and honest book about 13 year old protagonist Butterball and his role as a bully. Butterball is the nickname given to and embraced by the central character, Burton. Butterball plays the role of a bully and attacks a peer on his playground. This role continues to follow him as he searches for his identity, enters mandated counseling in order to stay in school and explores the art of film making.

While this novel does include some graphic language, it is still aimed at young readers grades 7 to 9. Bullying is a topic that deserves consideration in the classroom and it is pervasive in schools beyond the watchful eyes of teachers and staff. In examining what makes a bully, the novel attempts to dismantle some of the myths around the archetype and the roles that students play as they attempt to shape an identity.

The language in this novel is authentic. The author writes from his own personal experiences and he is in a unique position as a person who is in touch with not only the current slang and cultural cache of teens, but as someone who helps to shape this culture as a music celebrity. Of particular note is the use of dysphemistic swearing, which serves to signal closeness or as a group marker for those looking to adopt the Discourse. As Butterball seeks inclusion with a peer group, his language shifts to a discourse that becomes appropriate for the situation. The peer group uses slang and discusses topics such as violence and posturing in a way that forces Butterball to play a part rather than stay true to his authentic self if he wishes to seek inclusion.

For instance, in one scene the young men are on the basketball court playing when they ask Butterball about his relationship with a young woman named Nia that he has a crush on. They discuss a party that they are all planning to attend and they expect another boy named Terrence to show up. Terrance is known for "stealing" a girl and the boys warn Butterball about him. Character Bobby states that he is glad Terrance isn't around because, "I'd kill that mofo dead if I had to see his face every day" (p. 59). As the scene progresses, the boys suggest that Butterball bring his batteries (loaded in a sock – the weapon he used in his original bullying act) to attack Terrance. Butterball is slow to acknowledge the violence and the use of language, but the chapter ends with him saying, "show her who's boss. Yeah, I get you" (p. 62). Butterball's language shifts throughout the novel to display the Discourse role he is currently participating in and shifts as his identity emerges.

Going Bovine by Libba Bray, 2009

Going Bovine (2010 ALA Printz Award Winner) tells the story of 16 year old high school student Cameron. Cameron begins to have hallucinations and after one public incident is sent to counseling for drugs. It is not his occasional marijuana use however that causes his hallucinations, but rather the "Mad Cow" disease which is slowly killing him. He is hospitalized as his health fails and his hallucinations become more and more a part of his daily life. The story takes a turn when he "escapes" from the hospital in search of a cure and along the way takes his hospital room mate, encounters a punk angel that serves as his guide and a talking lawn gnome.

Although a fanciful and bizarre tale, the novel is a quest story and mimics all of the literary analysis one would expect to find in any quest. While the novel borders the edge of classification as contemporary realistic fiction, it is his hallucinations which give the novel the fantasy element. Used as a plot device, the hallucinations provide a scene of instruction. These scenes of instruction can be used to examine the quest structure as Cameron's adventures to seek a cure parallel the key stages of a quest. Each element of a quest is evident in this novel including hero, sidekick, guide, the call to action, and the challenge. As students embark on the quest with Cameron, they can examine their own call to action and when they too may have explored a quest throughout the development of their many Discourses. In this way, the teen narrative becomes more authentic rather than a stale archetype.

The novel provides the opportunity to explore several essential questions with students. These questions when used in a Socratic seminar approach enable students the space to connect to the novels and their personal lives as well as to a critical literacy analysis. These can include questions such as:
– What is the value of life?
– What role does faith and religion play in our constructions of life?
– How does our society view illness?
– Who has a voice that is silenced or marginalized in this text?
– What Discourses are evident for the narrator? How do any of his Discourses rupture or get redefined throughout the course of the novel?
– How can the story be rewritten to respond to those experiences that should be challenged?

Crank by Ellen Hopkins, 2004

Crank, a poetic novel written in free verse, has won multiple awards. This novel tells the story of a young woman named Kristina, who quickly delves into drugs while on summer vacation to visit her father for three weeks. Kristina, in her drug usage, picks up other unhealthy habits, such as dealing drugs and wanton sex with next-to-strangers. In order to cope with the feelings she is having and her inability to manage her cognitive dissonance of being in essence two people in one body, she develops a personality that she names Bree. As Bree, Kristina is able to act and think how she wants, without fear of repercussion in her perfect Kristina life. However, as the novel progresses, Bree's choices begin to affect Kristina and her family, as soon she finds herself addicted to methamphetamine, in juvenile hall, and pregnant. Along with Adam (her new Reno boyfriend), Bree finds herself in situations that seem so outrageous that they could be true in alternative universe where teens run free to make bad decisions without any adult influence; the attempted suicide of Adam's *other* girlfriend, an attempted rape of Bree by three older biker men, and the constant usage of "crank" in the back room of the bowling alley where her father works.

Acting as a cautionary tale, *Crank* is an example of pointing young adult novels towards the grittier sides of adolescence that deal with drugs and sex. One such passage that uses an authentic adolescent voice in dealing with "adult" situations such as these is titled "I Wasn't Scared – Yet," and deals with the scene in which Kristina has been brought into custody for attempting to hitchhike (in a desperate attempt to score drugs). Kristina, desperate and unwilling to admit her secrets to her parents, calls up her new boyfriend Chase, and claims to be "Bree – your sister" (Hopkins, 2004, p. 456). Chase, however, is able to get her out of holding, as it must be the parents or guardian of the person in custody to bail her out. In this small vignette, Kristina comes face to face with the repercussions of her dealing with drugs and bad people. In holding, she shares a cell with three other women, all dangerous in their own rights and yet, Kristina is barely scared at all. In fact, one of the women who she meets in holding introduces her to a man who elevates Kristina to a drug dealer.

This scene is paralleled in many others within *Crank*; Bree constantly makes bad choices all in an effort to get high. She neglects family and friends, is abused multiple times by boys who she trusts, and ultimately ends up pregnant. However, as over-exaggerated as this novel may seem there are definite elements of truth within. However, these elements of truth are also those that isolate this novel to a specific audience; the mature content found within may stand to confuse or isolate younger readers; as it is, the topics may isolate some older readers, as many teens do not often experience hard drug addiction, rape and pregnancy. However, the novel allows older young adults a view through a window of Kristina's choices and her subsequent life events.

Jerk, California by Jonathan Friesen, 2008

This award winning novel delves into the adolescent world of abilities and inabilities that all young people deal with; in specific, the main character, Sam, who has Tourette's Syndrome. Sam also battles an abusive step-father, a dead biological father, and a mother who is mistreated. Suddenly, Sam's world is turned upside-down when he finds that his image of his father, the image instilled by his step-father, is completely wrong, and he embarks on a cross-country trip with the girl of his dreams to find his birthright. Sam and Naomi, his travel companion and maybe girlfriend, meet challenges of all sorts, mainly dealing with Sam's inability to control his most basic self and actions.

Jerk, California deals with the difficult world of physical and mental health issues for all young adults, mainly in Sam's Tourette's Syndrome. His journey and his tics seem to stem from the same issues. He faces issues that young adults can identify with on multiple levels, whether literal or metaphorical. As Sam, the reader is able jump into the skin of a young person against whom the odds are stacked, and yet who takes it upon him/her self to discover personal lineage, pride, and individuality as discovered, rather than being directly told who or what a person is. Sam finds out through his journey that his entire image of his biological father had been a lie, and in fact that he is much more similar to his father than he had ever hoped to be. He discovers who he is.

This novel also deals with the idea of inability, a world that many young adults have experienced, in one way or another. Sam is able to rise above these complicated issues, and allows the reader hope that they too may do the same. However, Sam is no perfect character. He is fallible, frustrated, angry and confused; in essence, a realistic young adult. The characters he meets, especially Naomi (or Nae), all seem to have their individual struggles as well. All of the characters have their individual battles, though many are not as visible as Sam's. Nae struggles to live up to her mother's ideals, George struggles with his health, and Sam's mother and step-father struggle to stay together for their baby Lane. No one character has the ability to be perfect, though they all strive to obtain this level.

Throughout the novel, Sam loses his cool, makes copious mistakes, lets his fear make decisions, and even uses a version of English that is closer to stream of consciousness than standard academic English. In one scene, Sam has a heart to heart conversation with an old friend of his father's, turned employer. This man, George, asks Sam what he knows about his father. In response, Sam says, "where to start. Dug ditches. Dumb and lazy. Ran off with some woman and wrapped his car around a telephone pole. Old Bill's told me more, but those are the lowlights" (Friesen, 2008, p. 133). Here, Sam begins to delve into the identity that he believes his father owned, and the identity that he feels he too will fall into. However, Sam soon begins to eclipse this idea and grows into a man who takes responsibility for himself, and begins to fashion an identity greater than he could have imagined. In essence, Sam is any young adult reader. They are beginning to grow into individual who are responsible for their actions, afraid of the world outside of what they know, and trying desperately to belong somewhere. Sam is able to challenge these ideas, and in a way, the reader too reaches a cathartic moment where he or she knows that the world is scary, but that it may also lead him or her to find where he or she truly belongs. In fact, a line that George says to Sam rings true as a definite theme of the novel; "Knowin' where you're from ain't just optional" (p. 133).

CLOSING

Young adult novels are a valuable aspect in all English education classrooms, and yet the genre is often one of the most neglected forms of literature by traditional education for its target age. Not only does YA prove to be a source of literature that attracts young readers due to the content and writing style, but it authenticates the young adult experience of growing up, or learning who one is, and of discovering what it means to be a person in society. YA novels allow the reader to delve into a parallel world where the reader can experiment and learn with the main character in a risk-free arena.

The windows and mirror application of literature is especially pertinent to young adult readers, who are in the midst of discovering their identities. By using these literary windows and mirrors, a youth is able to discover which roles and

Discourses he or she fits into, which they desire to reject, and how exactly a person is able to manage life in a way that is most fitting to the individual.

The novel selections above illustrate different identities and social contrasts allowing students to explore worlds both similar and different from their own lived experiences. Depending on the student and the sociocultural understanding the student brings to the novel, the novel may be seen as realistic or outlandish. The student can become engaged in critique of the Discourses and experiences of the characters in order to examine the larger world that the student may know in terms of power and identity. This exploration using both Reader Response and critical literacy allows students to challenge the status quo and teachers to help foster the social imagination of students so that they may engage in revisioning their worlds for change of social injustices.

REFERENCES

50 Cent, (2011). *Playground*. New York, NY: Razorbill, an imprint of Penguin Group, Inc.

Bahktin, M. (1981). *The dialogic imagination* (Ed. M. Holquist, Trans. C. Emerson & M. Holquist. Austin, TX: University of Austin Press.

Bray, L. (2009). *Going bovine*. New York, NY: Delacorte Press.

Cervetti, G., Pardales, M., & Damico, J. (2001). A tale of differences: Comparing the traditions, perspectives, and educational goals of critical reading and critical literacy. *Reading Online*. International Reading Association. Retrieved from http://www.readingonline.org/articles/cervetti/

Crowe, C. (1998). What is young adult literature? *English Journal, 88*(1), 120-122.

Enriquez, G. (2006). The reader speaks out: Adolescent reflections about controversial young adult literature. *The ALAN Review, 33*(2).

Friesen, J. (2008). *Jerk, California*. New York, NY: Speak, an imprint of Penguin Group, Inc.

Gee, J. (1996). *Social linguistics and literacies: Ideology in discourses* (2nd ed.). New York, NY: Routledge Falmer.

Gee, J. (2001). Literacy, discourse, and linguistics: Introduction and what is literacy?. In E. Cushman, E. Kintgen, B. Kroll, & M. Rose (Eds.), *Literacy: A critical sourcebook* (pp. 525-544). New York, NY: Bedford/St. Martin's.

Giroux, H. (1993). Literacy and the politics of difference. In C. Lankshear & P. McLaren (Eds.), *Critical literacy: Politics, praxis and the postmodern* (pp. 367-377). New York, NY: State University of New York Press.

Greene, M. (1978). *Landscapes of learning*. New York, NY: Teachers College Press.

Greene, M. (1988). *The dialectic of freedom*. New York, NY: Teachers College Press.

Greene, M. (1995). *Releasing the imagination: Essays on education, the arts and social change*. San Francisco, CA: Jossey-Bass.

Hopkins, E. (2004). *Crank*. New York, NY: Margaret K. McElderry Books.

Jones, S., & McEwen, M. (2000). A conceptual model of multiple dimensions of identity. *Journal of College Student Development, 41*(4), 405-414.

Kozulin, A. (2003). Psychological tools and mediated learning. In A. Kozulin, B. Gindis, V. Ageyev, & S. Miller (Eds.), *Vygotsky's educational theory in cultural context* (pp. 289-316). Cambridge, UK: Cambridge University Press.

Lave, J., & Wenger, E. (1991). *Situated learning: Legitimate peripheral participation*. Cambridge, UK: Cambridge University Press.

Lesesne, T. (2006). *Naked reading: Uncovering what tweens need to become lifelong readers*. Portland, ME: Stenhouse Publishers.

Luke, A., & Freebody, P. (1997). Critical literacy and the question of normativity: An introduction. In S. Muspratt, A. Luke, & P. Freebody (Eds.), *Constructing critical literacies: Teaching and learning textual practices* (pp. 1-18). Cresskill, NJ: Hampton Press,Inc.

Miller, S. (2003). How literature discussion shapes thinking: ZPSs for teaching/learning habits of the heart and mind. In A. Kozulin, B. Gindis, V. Ageyev, & S. Miller (Eds.), *Vygotsky's educational theory in cultural context* (pp. 289-316). Cambridge, UK: Cambridge University Press.

Moss, J. F. (2005). *Literature, literacy and comprehension strategies in the elementary school*. Urbana, IL: National Council of Teachers.

Niday, D. (2000). Young adult literature. Retrieved from http://www.public.iastate.edu/~dniday/394syllabuss99.html

Rosenblatt, L. (2005). The acid test for literature teaching. In *Making meaning with texts: Selected essays*. Portsmouth, NH: Heinemann.

Scott, S., & Palincsar, A. (2009, December 23). *Sociocultural theory*. Retrieved from http://www.education.com/reference/article/sociocultural-theory/

Sprague, M., & Keeling, K. (2007). *Discovering their voices: Engaging adolescent girls with young adult literature*. Newark, DE: International Reading Association.

VanSlyke-Briggs, K. (2006). Helping students explore personal identities. *Encounter: Education for Meaning and Social Justice, 19*(2), 43-46.

Wacquant, L., & Bourdieu, P. (1992). *An invitation to reflexive sociology*. Chicago: The University of Chicago Press.

TEACHING PLAN – DISCOURSE, IDENTITY AND YOUNG ADULT FICTION

Connecting students initially to a challenging concept such as Discourse can be difficult. The following lesson structure connects a writing activity with a Discourse analysis and is generic enough to be applied to the Young Adult novel of choice.

Objective	1. By the end of the lesson, the student will be able to identify those Discourses that apply to the self and to the main character of the novel. 2. Students will be able to explain how Discourse impacts decision making and will be able to examine the principal character of the novel through a Discourse analysis.
Anticipatory Set	Introduce students to a brief film clip from the film, *Mean Girls* or use the trailer to *Not Another Teen Movie*. While students are watching the brief clip(s) ask students to jot down stereotypes portrayed. At the conclusion of the clip ask students to pair/share what they wrote and to respond to the question, what do these stereotypes and expectations associated with them do to teen identity and how they complicate interpretations of the world. After a brief 5 min discussion, pull the class back together to discuss stereotype and identity formation. Note: *Not Another Teen Movie* trailer is not appropriate for younger students. http://www.youtube.com/watch?v=KAOmTMCtGkI http://www.youtube.com/watch?v=XdF6AfeBlH0

Input	Explain the concept of Discourse and normative behavior to students and examine a sample Discourse map. 10 mins
Model	Creating a Discourse analysis chart with the class, the teacher should outline several Discourses at play for the teacher. As a class, discuss how to represent those Discourses through imagery. 10 to 15 mins
Checks for Understanding	Ask the students to each select and share one Discourse at play in their identity. Share and check for understanding. 5 mins
Guided Practice	Have students develop and share their own Discourse maps. Discuss how these Discourses are shaped by society and how normative behavior expectations shape how students fulfill social roles. 15 mins.
Closure	Ask students to share one Discourse they see connected to the main character of the Young Adult novel. In small groups, students will discuss how this Discourse influences the character's actions. 10 min
Independent practice	Create a Discourse map for the main character of the novel. On the back of your page write 3 to 5 paragraphs explaining how these Discourses impact character behavior. Ask students to reflect on how these Discourses are silenced or enabled. Which voices have power and what is that power utilized for within the text? An extension question could be to ask students to reinvision the story line of the character in light of the Discourses examined in order to empower character to enact social change within the text.

MEGAN MARSHALL

8. WHAT MAINSTREAM CENTERS CANNOT HOLD

Growing Critical Literacy with Dystopian Fiction

ABSTRACT

This chapter examines how characteristics of contemporary Young Adult (YA) novels – specifically those within the popular dystopian genre – afford secondary level English/Language Arts (ELA) students the means to develop critical and analytic literacy skills. After contextualizing critical literacy and its marked absence in mainstream curricula, the chapter provides an overview of the genre of dystopian literature in both its canonical and contemporary forms, and demonstrates how certain elements of contemporary dystopic novels – in particular having to do with gender, class, and ethnic diversity – justify their use as supplementary texts in ELA classrooms for engaging students in critical reading and textual analysis. In addition, this chapter invites readers to consider how teaching with contemporary novels may be used to guide students towards a greater understanding of well-known canonical works by providing essential frameworks for meaningful, in-depth interactions with classic texts. The final section offers suggestions for ways students might take up themes addressed in dystopian novels and apply them towards innovative research projects and is followed by a brief reading list of contemporary dystopian novels annotated with themes and topics relevant to the chapter's discussions.

INTRODUCTION

In 2013, the January-February issue of *Academe* published Kenneth Bernstein's "Warnings from the Trenches." A quick Google search reveals how, in the days and weeks that followed, the piece was countlessly cited and reblogged by popular media outlets as well as shared via email and social media platforms. Framed as an open letter, Bernstein's warning to college professors (re)ignited a conversation about critical thinking that has consistently highlighted how students in the United States – both at the secondary and college level – all too often lack the capacity to think and write critically. And why? It seems as though this conversation regularly leans towards a common answer: national educational policy has become so focused on standardization and reform that students are no longer taking part in authentic learning and critical inquiry (McNeil, 2000; Stotsky, 2012). Simultaneously, those who have trained to serve as teachers in our nation's schools are becoming demoralized to the point of leaving the profession entirely (Nieto, 2009; Santoro, 2011).

It seems serendipitous that this chapter – one which links the weight of critical literacy to the extensive significant themes found in dystopian narratives – corresponds so well with certain dark views entertained by educational and/or critical theorists who view our educational system as a machine where teachers function as automatons, using rigid curricula in order to instil blind conformity and obedience in students (Hedges, 2011; Giroux, 2012; Whitehead, 2012). Personally, such indoctrination has never been my goal as an English teacher, and I have doubts that there are many practicing educators who actively seek to identify with cogs in a malevolent machine. However, I know that I am not the only teacher to have witnessed students resist inflexible curricula, balk at the prospect of multiple choice tests, and view much of the required reading and writing assignments in contemporary English Language Arts (ELA) classes as bland, uninspiring, and mired in hegemonic ideologies that have little connection to their actual worlds.

And how unfortunate is this last bit? The work done in ELA offers rich opportunities for critical literacy practices, all which can potentially occur within the current uniform frameworks that guide public education today. Yet, in order to be successful, certain notions regarding the best use of canonical "exemplary texts" as defined by the Common Core State Standards need to be reassessed, and genres of literature and writing that are often ignored in the typical classroom deserve a serious look.

This chapter will focus on how aspects of contemporary Young Adult (YA) novels, specifically those within the popular dystopian genre, are valuable tools for building/enhancing secondary (middle and high school) ELA curricula that encourages students to develop nuanced and analytical literacies. The first section of this chapter provides explanations for what critical literacy is and does, along with its absence in our nation's schools (McNeil, 2000; Giroux, 2012). The second discusses the dystopian genre, specifically its history and functions. The third segment seeks to demonstrate how contemporary dystopic novels can be used as supplementary texts for engaging students in a variety of critical literacy practices. Threaded throughout these sections will be thoughts regarding how the use of contemporary novels might lead to increased student understanding of canonical texts by providing essential frameworks for meaningful interactions.

Given the variety of themes and subjects to be found in YA dystopian novels, the preceding sections will, save for a few references to certain canonical novels, refrain from listing actual dystopian texts that can be used via the methods discussed. Instead, the concluding section of this chapter will be followed by a reading list of contemporary dystopian novels that will be annotated with themes and topics relevant to the previous sections' discussions.

CRITICAL LITERACY

Literacy as a Critical Action

Traditionally, gaining literacy has been seen as an autonomous act, one that involves reading and writing removed from any social construct (Street, 2003). However, this model ignores the import of cultural, and political influences (Friere, 1972) that shape how we use language for personal, academic and professional purposes (Gee, 1995). In this vein, student reading can also be seen as a practice that is personal and relational, especially to those who are coming into understanding their own agency within a variety of constructs, including school (Alvermann, 2009a).

It bears mentioning here that it is no secret that adolescents are oftentimes characterized as being impressionable and curious, and that they often apply these qualities in capable and creative ways when it comes to using texts to make sense of their worlds (Moje, 2010; Coates, 2011). Moreover, adolescents are normally desirous of exercising independence in their academic work (Alvermann, 2009b), just as they seek to share it with an audience. Therefore, critical literacy in a secondary (middle and high school) classroom potentially offers students a chance to examine the world(s) in which they participate (Alvermann, 2009b; Bruce, 2009).

Critical literacy also asks that students move their examinations beyond the personal and to challenge ideas that they may have previously accepted as the status quo. For instance, questioning what it means to be female, male, heterosexual or not, white or not, strong or less than, athletic, smart, rich, poor, religious, agnostic, political, apathetic, etc. gives students the chance to increase their awareness of perspectives apart from their own, while also emboldening them to realize an ethical commitment to work towards the implementation of social justice (Friere, 1972; Christensen, 2003).

Ultimately, critical pedagogies can lead to ideological literacies apart from the mainstream, dominant discourses that have historically framed students' experiences in virtually every aspect of their school-based lives (Street, 2003; Gorski, 2006). Additionally, by encouraging students to see how reading and writing are interpretive events (Behrman, 2006), literary authority becomes redistributed in the classroom, and allows for a move from the dominant discourse of education, and giving students the reign to "critique and question 'what ifs' and 'who benefits' as well as to hope and consider 'what if?'" (Short, 2011).

A Deficiency of Critical Literacy

It almost goes without saying that standardized tests have taken on new life since their inception in the 20th century. What used to be a (relatively) low-key event, generally administered once a year and with little fanfare, has become a perfect storm of acronyms (NCLB, AYP, NAEP, STAR, IASA, etc.[i]). Advocates for increased testing will likely point to the rising rates of high school graduates over the past decade (Layton, 2013); yet, research points to a bleaker story of adolescent disengagement (Henry, Knight, & Thornberry, 2012); students graduating without basic literacy skills (U.S. Department of Education, *Nations Report Card*, 2011); of 40% of entry-level college students enrolling in remedial English classes as freshmen (Cassidy & Loveless, 2011); of racial, gendered, and cultural bias (Strauss, 2011); and of an alarming lack of critical reading being done in secondary education, which leads to large numbers of students unprepared to succeed at the college level (Arum, 2011).

Considering that the content on most standardized tests is not geared towards assessing how students think critically, the emphasis on classroom instruction is steered away from creativity and curiosity, and towards rote "drill and kill" methods that teach students how to do well on tests without acknowledging how this information is applicable in the world (Strauss, 2011). Furthermore, while researchers have historically called for schools to become "critical spaces" (Dewey, 1933; Giroux, 1988; O'Brien et al., 2009), today's adolescents are not only being consistently tested, they are often being required to read and produce texts that are of no relevance to them in spite of the fact that they may be avid participants in a wide variety of literacies in meaningful contexts outside of the classroom. Yet, no matter what significant literacy work might be happening in students' lives, a substantial amount of time adolescents spend in school is dominated by "textbooks and titles from the literary canon that are read by an entire class in lockstep fashion" (O'Brien et al., 2009).

For this and other reasons, many stakeholders in public education across the United States – teachers and families, administrators and researchers – have begun to scrutinize the culture of our schools and the impact of standardized testing upon them (Santoro, 2011) while often moving into the arena of protest and opting out of tests and the curriculums that teach to test content (Hernandez & Baker, 2013). On one hand, these protests are valuable in that they raise awareness about our educational system; on the other hand, they might run the risk of being both misrepresented and misunderstood by the public. Some observers of the testing debate look at teacher strikes or students/families opting out of state-mandated testing as detrimental impediments to student learning and progress (Layton, 2013), whereas others believe these acts of protest are both justified and necessary (Giroux, 2012).

At any rate, the furor caused by these clashes of opinion often fill online Op-Ed comment sections of publications such as *The New York Times*, *Newsweek*, and *The Washington Post* with a variety of perspectives, many of which are often quite passionate and heated. Whether commenters blame teachers and teacher unions, parents, testing companies such as Pearson, the Obama administration, the Bush administration, Bill Gates, or some other entity, the rhetoric of these debates often reveals something akin to hysteria, as participants on all sides of these disputes seemingly offering up opinions and claims without ever considering the various perspectives of those with whom they engage. One might go so far as to imagine that such online discussions frequently demonstrate a significant lack of critical and dialogic thought, even as they endeavor to light upon a magic formula of sorts, one that will faultlessly educate and prepare our nation's children for living in a demanding world.

DYSTOPIA

Our understanding of dystopia requires working knowledge of its opposite: utopia, a term that is often used to describe situations of idyllic perfection, be it a wonderful day at the beach, a pristine neighborhood, or a teachers' lounge stocked with one's favorite baked goods. A more applicable (if broad) way to understand utopia is as an idealized society far removed from the various dilemmas of the world(s) we live and know (Claeys, 2013). In fact, in any definition of utopia (and there are many), societal constructs are necessary elements. This is to say, utopia cannot be merely individual; it must encompass a community, be it a nation, town, school, or some other functioning social group in which "humanity is a virtue" (Schaer, 2000) and the world has been made better.

Therefore, a dystopia (culled from Greek, meaning "bad place") must remain within this framework of society; but rather than exemplify a virtuous, honest, and "better" world, it is the anti-utopia, a place in which constraints are put on society in ways both malevolent and secretive (Parrinder, 2005). These communities are set in what Michael Foucault (1977) dubbed the "panoptical society," which, roughly translated, is a space in which authority may maintain continuous control over the population merely by the suggestions of the government's constant presence. Although this presence is often largely illusory, the citizenry is conditioned to believe they are under perpetual surveillance, and as such, they behave according to the norms placed upon them. In this way, discipline "functions like a piece of machinery...sustained by its own mechanism" (p. 177).

This is not to say that everyone is miserable within a dystopian society; in fact, well-known, classic dystopian texts (Huxley's *Brave New World* and Orwell's *1984* both come to mind, here) both demonstrate and provide models for narratives in which readers witness citizens who are operating under the illusion of perfect happiness, unconcerned by the structures in place that oppress them. In some instances, this is even true for the reader, in which case these stories could be regarded as "false-utopias" (White, 2008), where seeming perfection is eventually exposed as being sinister. Of course, even after the truth is exposed, there are often characters that refuse to acknowledge the reality of their situation, choosing instead to remain blissfully ignorant. Such characters are outlying elements of the antagonist (which is often the dystopian society as a whole) and foils for those characters "in the know" working to either subvert or escape the system. Perhaps most importantly, these acquiescent characters are symbolic of the questions dystopian narratives urge readers to ask: Might ignorance actually be bliss? What is there to be gained by knowing the truth? What makes access to the truth so important?

Dystopia Goes Young Adult

In literature, the move from conformity to individuality has been a fairly modern development, heralding the power of questioning, renaming, and challenging the dominant paradigms whether they be social, religious, political or artistic, at the same time alluding to the increasingly subjective and fragmented nature of reality (Harvey, 1990). This move is also evident in YA literature, which has evolved from its strictly didactic origins (Campbell, 2008) into realism, romance, angst, and finally, rebellion. The heroes and heroines of the contemporary YA novel are no longer content to remain fixed in the societal spaces that defined adolescent characters in the past, and they often engage with their worlds in positions that are often more defiant than submissive, challenging any and all efforts to be categorized by age, gender, or class.

This trend is highly evident in YA dystopian novels, a genre that is currently enjoying enormous popularity as a stroll through any children's section of a bookstore might attest. The reasons for this popularity are numerous and open to speculation, but one conjecture might be summed up with the apt metaphor made visually arresting in prime-time by Joss Whedon's *Buffy the Vampire* television series: adolescence is hell. Be it bullying, academic demands, endless standardized assessment, or social pressures, middle and/or high school might sometimes seem comparable to a dystopian nightmare taken from the pages of books like *The Hunger Games* (Collins, 2008) or *Divergent* (Roth, 2011). Another possibility might be that contemporary dystopias (especially those in YA literature) contain noticeable elements of hopefulness, even in the bleakest of scenarios. My own interpretations as a reader (both as a student and later a teacher) is that in some of the more canonical and widely taught, works of this genre (such as Bradbury's *Fahrenheit 451*, Huxley's *Brave New World*, and Vonnegut's novel *Player Piano* and oft-anthologized short story "Harrison Bergeron") are generally heavily pessimistic in both authorial voice and characterization; and in fact, hopeful endings are often largely absent in such texts.

Yet, even although contemporary texts might wax a bit more optimistic, the new crop of YA dystopian fiction closely mirrors classic dystopic texts in many critical ways – oppressive societies, secretive governments, panoptical illusions, and subdued/indoctrinated citizenry are all par for the course. However, just as society's problems have changed over time, so have the themes of dystopian novels. In addition, these novels serve as storied amplifications of the unique societal issues adolescents grapple with, such as gender/sexuality issues, racism and bias, classism, war, and environmental collapse. By placing these issues within a contemporary context that is familiar to readers despite any dystopian devices in place, these texts become more than mere novels/stories; they can be read as commentaries on the dangers of ideology and repressive societies, the sort that students may recognize from various aspects of their own lives.

Perhaps most significant is that the characters affecting change and subversion in these novels are often teenagers (or younger), which makes them both relatable and realistic. These fictional young characters overcome incredible obstacles as they come of age, which may prove validating for adolescent students who are in the process of negotiating their own difficulties while trying to navigate and understand their identities. In this way, these texts provide students with another compelling reason to keep reading, and more, to become invested enough to recognize instances of intertextuality and their own subjectivity while also thinking critically about the intentions of those within and outside of the pages.

CRITICAL PEDAGOGY VIA CONTEMPORARY DYSTOPIAN NOVELS

Though classic novels such as Bradbury's *Fahrenheit 451* (1953) and Orwell's *Animal Farm* (1946) are undoubtedly still staples of many ELA classrooms, they remain problematic for instructional purposes in that they were not deliberately written for an adolescent audience,[ii] nor do they place young people in key roles within their storylines. This is not to say that these particular texts (and many others like them) are not excellent, or that there is nothing to be gleaned from such novels in the typical high school English class. However, given the complex and abstract nature of many of these texts, certain novels in this "class" are often quicker to alienate readers than to draw them in, which means that opportunities for critical and resistant reading practices are often left unearthed, and the chance for nuanced and analytical thinking falls by the wayside.

That said: it would be difficult (if not impossible) to completely discount the standard, required, and canonical works that frame so much of what is done in ELA classes, and it is important to stress here that this chapter is not intended to be an argument against these texts. However, the use of YA dystopian novels can be extremely effective avenues towards critical literacy when incorporated into the classroom rather than being relegated as possible independent choices for student reading, even when this reading may lead to work done for an ELA class. Actual teacher-led integration, replete with in-depth and nuanced study – can open up these texts for deeper analysis than the typical secondary student might manage on her/his own. Such inclusion of these contemporary choices will potentially create a diverse array of applications that will promote and develop critical literacy practices in student work.

As Supplementary Texts

Canonical novels and mainstream textbooks do not always confront current issues that impact students' lives (Behrman, 2006). By using these YA novels as supplementary resources, teachers can deliver opportunities that involve students in dialogues about contemporary social concerns – such as technology, media, and gender/sexuality issues – that are usually not addressed in more mainstream, classic, and/or school-based texts. This allows students to critique themes and explore ideas in a context that they find accessible, while also giving them the means to apply these critical views to the topics and arguments that are presented in more traditional, required reading. The potential uses as supplementary texts are numerous, and possible examples are discussed below.

Gender issues. By looking at gender roles and expectations in a contemporary YA novel in comparison to those framed in a more classic dystopian work, students might consider the impact of generational differences, historical context, and authorial intent in relation to the manifestation of male/female dichotomies. Moreover, this same examination can lead to cross-curricular exploration, moving student inquiry into the topics covered in other classes, such as history/social studies or biology. Students might be asked to wonder: What are the historical underpinnings of gender expectations? What does it mean to be female, male, or something less definitive? How do my own views stem from my family, my culture, and my observations of those around me?

Media and technology. The proliferation and pervasive nature of mass media and technology is a recognizable theme in many YA dystopian novels. When placed against the conceptualized ideas presented in older novels/texts, students can draw correlations between what was expected and what has actually become. Questions driving inquiry might include: What did these canonical authors fear and what drove this fear? How much of these expectations have come to pass? What do present dystopian authors seem to fear? How might our current media-driven and technology dependent society be driving this fear?

As Counter Canonical

By considering the variety of ways that these contemporary works might operate in contrast (or in protest) to the themes and messages prevalent in classic/canonical texts, students can examine how contemporary texts might be arranged into counter canon. Furthermore, they can sort out the different elements and create categories that support this concept. For instance:

Who are the heroes? As discussed earlier, the protagonists of YA dystopian novels are young adults, which is a significant difference from canonical works. What is more, these new heroes embody a multitude of other characteristics that are a far cry from the white, male, able-bodied, heterosexual protagonist of the past. And even in the cases of male protagonists, readers will notice that they are less likely to fit the stereotypical embodiment of the classical hero. In fact, female characters often either surpass their male counterparts, or even reverse the roles that have traditionally occupied certain tropes, such as "the damsel in distress" scenario.

Who are the villains? It is worth mentioning that, save for fairy tales, classic texts don't often allow women the opportunity to inhabit spaces of power and control, which makes it a rare occurrence to find females occupying malevolent roles in the well-known canonical works taught in secondary schools. When contemporary YA novels place women in these positions, rendering them ruthless, cold, and decidedly un-nurturing, they not only redistribute power, but also dismantle notions of passivity historically attributed to "the weaker sex."

Who wrote the book? It is no secret that dead white men dominate the territory of canonical literature. Contemporary authors have flipped this trend on its head, with some of the most well known texts being written by women (Lois Lowry's The Giver and Susan Collins' The Hunger Games trilogy serves as notable examples of this). As of this writing, there are no real statistics relating to the ethnicities of YA dystopian authors; however, students can undertake their own research to create lists to this effect, which might lead to further avenues for criticism and analysis.

How was it written? In some cases, YA novels veer from the narrative and plot devices often found in traditional texts. Stylistic devices can speak to authorial intent in a variety of ways, which gives students a way to examine texts apart from characters and themes. How are words used? What is the writing like on the sentence level? How is the book arranged? What conventions might be altered and for what effect? Are writerly conventions disregarded or flipped on their heads? If so, what were my reactions to this, and why did I have them?

Towards Resistant Reading

The preceding point brings us to the concept of turning students into resistant readers of texts. The practice of reading from a resistant perspective requires that students attempt textual analysis and interpretation from a variety of viewpoints, especially those that deviate from the hegemonic, mainstream perspectives often found in typical school-based discourses and texts (Behrman, 2006).

In order for students to successfully apply these strategies to traditional works, it makes sense to start on familiar ground. Certainly, current YA novels in the dystopian genre contain more by the way of diversity – especially when it comes to gender roles – than might older texts. Yet, even considering the range of societal issues and ideologies found in contemporary dystopian narratives, students could still approach these from critical and resistant perspectives, asking themselves how people from different backgrounds might read these books. Do the ideologies in these texts speak to issues that might represent different notions of gender, race, sexual orientation, class, education and/or disability? Who is privileged and why? What might be missing? How are intentions both formed and framed? The process of answering these queries, and finding evidence (both within and outside of the texts in question) will be a valuable experience for students, serving to promote inquiry-based learning across the disciplines.

As Springboards for Independent Research

The themes and problems presented in YA dystopian novels are varied enough to lend themselves to significant and important student research. Such areas of inquiry might include (but are certainly not limited to) issues of sexuality, gender differences, environmental decay/collapse, war, poverty, the role of government, religion, and issues pertaining to social/class status. In addition, the selection process of choosing a focus will give students agency in selecting topics that are meaningful and relevant to their lives. When teachers encourage students to invest themselves in research focusing on subjects of their own choosing, they legitimize students' knowledge and interests, creating classroom cultures of empowerment (Marzano, Pickering, & Pollack, 2001).

Not only will student choice potentially lead to a diverse assortment of topics, but it will also create opportunities for students to engage in dialogue with one another as they open up to their classmates about their areas of inquiry. Such dialogue is an essential tool for practicing critical literacy, and is one of the primary means that students can demonstrate their growing questions about the world (Cervetti, Pardeles, & Damico, 2001). For instance, perhaps a student will start to consider how a peer's perspective on a subject differs from her or his own which will then lead to her/him viewing this topic with new eyes. No doubt, any initial exposure to new perspectives can lead to further investigations in which students can begin peeling back layers of social, cultural, and historical contexts they had never before considered in depth.

Research for Social Justice

Discussing the potential ways to go about implementing significant and positive change is a big part of critical literacy (Bomer & Bomer, 2001; Gorski, 2006). The themes addressed in YA dystopian novels can give students a starting point for valid research (as discussed) and provide a new lens for understanding the social worlds in which they live. The research process can lead students to participation with their topic outside of the classroom, which has the potential to create a meaningful and lasting impact (Behrman, 2006). Whether working individually, or in collaboration with their peers, possibilities beyond typical research papers include:

Letters to the editor and editorials. These acts of critical literacy are the proverbial stones with the power to take down more than one bird. Not only do students address issues that are meaningful to them; but they also send their ideas into a world outside of the classroom, thereby increasing their audience base. Additionally, these assignments guide students into critical writing for textual purposes, (which is always a school-required benchmark needing to be met) they provide students with the opportunity to be published, and to take pride in seeing their words in print.

Performative acts. Poetry and playwriting are two ways that students can address social issues using creativity and multimodality. Spoken-word and/or poetry slams are excellent vehicles for student expression, and once again, provide students with an audience beyond the teacher and classroom. The same hold true in cases when students choose to write plays/scripts and direct actors into performance, staged live or filmed and distributed in digital form via web platforms such as YouTube® or Vimeo®.

Artistic endeavors. Whether the medium is paint, clay, ink, found objects, or anything else one might dream up, there is an enormous capacity for students to create visual representations that convey their opinions and insight. As with the preceding ideas, art-based projects can provide students with the privilege of agency, while also allowing them the opportunity to put their ideas into the world in a way that is unique, thoughtful, and enduring. In addition, artistic projects invite feedback from peers, teachers, and others in one's community, creating a dialogue that spans generations, professions, and a variety of diverse perspectives.

Digital texts. Building websites, blogging, contributing to e-zines, and interacting within the frameworks of social media are literacy tasks in which adolescents typically invest their time and efforts (Alvermann, 2009a.) and are excellent examples of new/digital literacies and their place in student learning (Bergman & Sams, 2012). A search on YouTube can reveal many examples of student work in this vein (especially those that serve as responses to literature). Not only do these digitized spaces provide a place to situate ideas and/or projects, they also allow for relatively straightforward and efficient interaction and collaboration with others, which may potentially build a community around the students' area(s) of interest.

CONCLUDING THOUGHTS

In the spring of 2012, Lauren Oliver, the author of the popular *Delirium* trilogy, explained to me the reasons she chose to set her novels in familiar, present-day places (in which cities are written as they exist in reality, street names, neighborhoods and all).

> I wanted to set the book in a recognizable place because I thought it would be a closer commentary on the dangers of repressive societies and ideological movements; in other words, I didn't want it to read as sci fi. I wanted to show how absurd ideas actually become normalized; they take root on the main streets, in the post office, in the day-to-day lives of citizens.

Considering her goals, it is clear that Oliver's explanation demonstrates how her novels are, on their own, acts of critical literacy. Thus, the process of reading her novels (and others like them), grows the authorial act beyond its foundation, because as readers begin talking about these books, writing about them, sharing them with others, and mining their pages for topics to investigate in depth, the simple roots of critical examination give way to multiple branches of inquiry and thought.

One reason fans of dystopian fiction appreciate the genre (and here I choose to include myself as such a fan) is because these stories, by giving us vivid scenarios of bleak futures, illustrate the ways our current society might be actively considered (and reconsidered) to the extent that readers might be motivated to do all they can in order to prevent such developments from happening in our actual worlds. Like some of the characters in dystopian novels, we might be faced with situations that make us feel helpless, hopeless, uncomfortable, and fatalistic. Yet, if we are lucky, we are able to take more from fiction than the pleasures that entertainment provides: we make connections; develop insight and perspective; see our lives in different ways; ask new questions; embrace other points of view; and potentially grow our capacity to empathize with others. And, if we are thoughtful enough to take initiative, we could practice the fundamental aspects of critical literacy as we read these stories. We might take up ideas and do something with them, something about them.

In moving this discussion back to the classroom, I would like to reflect on the truth that one of the most essential tasks we have as teachers is to motivate our students towards substantial accomplishments – not just for a grade or a decent score on a test – but for reasons that matter to them. Therefore, practicing critical pedagogy in our classrooms is, arguably, the very best way to get this done; and, when used well, dystopian texts (contemporary and canonical) offer themselves up as excellent tools to reach this end. Perhaps the implications of dystopian narratives can be considered against this warning from Henry Giroux (2012) regarding our present educational establishment:

> Teachers will lose most of their rights, protections, and dignity and will be treated as clerks of the empire. And as more and more young people fail to graduate from high school, they will join the ranks of those disposable populations now filling up our prisons at a record pace.

This is a bleak vision. And yet, through some poetic quirk of fate, dystopian fiction has the power to see to it that Giroux's words remain an unrealized prophecy. Lucky us.

SUGGESTED READING LIST

The following list is hardly exhaustive, but contains titles with a wide-ranging scope of appeal (the tastes and interests of our students vary wildly, after all), and also offers a diverse assortment of themes and topics for students at the secondary level (6-12th grade). Please note: as certain themes/situations *might* be inappropriate for younger readers (such as those in early middle-school) it is always a good idea to familiarize oneself with the texts chosen for classroom use. Also, many of the popular YA dystopian novels being published currently are part of series; therefore, those that are marked with an asterisk (*) indicate the title is the first novel of such.

Each entry includes a brief list of evident themes and topics within each novel/series that have the potential to lend motivate students to take up critical inquiry, meaningful research, and to engage in dialogic discussion with teachers and peers, as well as others beyond their classrooms. However, just as the title list is limited, so are the possible approaches suggested towards critical reading, analysis, and action. Each student can bring unique perspectives to these (and other) texts. What follows is merely a starting point.

Invitation to the Game (Monica Hughes, 1990) technology; repressive government; unemployment and social welfare; drug use; gang violence; class struggles

The Giver* (Lois Lowry, 1993-2012): emotional repression; secretive government; memory; individuality; honesty; perfection vs. imperfection; disabilities

The Shadow Children* (Margaret Peterson Haddix, 1998-2006) population control; environmental decline; hunger/famine; militaristic government; identity confusion; class divisions

The Last Book in the Universe (Rodman Philbrick, 2000) genetic engineering; poverty; drug addiction; gang violence; class/social divisions; disability/epilepsy; disease; intellectual deterioration; environmental decline; rebellion

Feed (M.T. Anderson, 2002) human reliance on technology; corporate power; environmental collapse; social/class structures; privacy rights; decline of intellect/language; advertising and consumerism; conformity vs. individuality

How I Live Now (Rosoff, 2004) world war; terrorism; survival; anorexia/eating disorders; family; incest

Uglies* (Scott Westerfeld, 2005-2007) environmental collapse/global warming; totalitarian government; mind control; idealized notions of beauty; cosmetic surgery; conformity vs. rebellion; identity; free will; human reliance on technology

Little Brother[iii] (Corey Doctorow, 2007) terrorism; civil liberties; social activism; privacy violations; police state vs. democracy; technology; truth and freedom; civilian resistance

Un Lun Dun (China Mieville, 2007) environmental decay; governmental corruption; social hierarchies; choice vs. destiny; subversion of authority

The Hunger Games* (Suzanne Collins, 2008-2010) social hierarchies; panoptical societies; totalitarianism; violence as spectacle/entertainment; love and family; gender roles and expectations; sacrifice; war; rebellion

Forest of Hands and Teeth* (Carrie Ryan, 2009-2011) religion's role in civilization; knowledge as power; freedom; isolation; gender roles/expectations

The Maze Runner* (Philip Straub, 2009-ongoing) environmental collapse; civilization vs. savagery; secretive/controlling government; friendship and trust; memory; collaboration/teamwork

Delirium* (Lauren Oliver, 2011-2013) totalitarianism; panoptical societies; ideological movements; love; friendship; family; heteronormativity; censorship

Divergent* (Veronica Roth, 2011-ongoing) oppressive societies; segregation; class/social bias; identity; conformity vs. rebellion; family

Wither* (Lauren DeStefano, 2011-ongoing) genetic engineering; famine; class divisions; breakdown of society; gender inequality; child slavery and prostitution; polygamy

NOTES

[i] No Child Left Behind; Adequate Yearly Progress; National Assessment of Educational Progress; Standardized Testing and Reporting; Improving America's Schools Act.
[ii] Kurt Vonnegut's short story, "Harrison Bergeron" is a notable exception to this assertion, as the title character is a teenager.
[iii] This novel is available for free download on Doctorow's website under the specifications of a Creative Commons license.

REFERENCES

Alvermann, D.E. (2009a). Sociocultural constructions of adolescence and young people's literacies. In L. Christenbury, R. Bomer, & P. Smagorinsky (Eds.), *Handbook of adolescent literacy research* (pp. 14-28). New York, NY: Guilford Press.

Alvermann, D. E. (2009b). Reaching/teaching adolescents: Literacies with a history. In J. V. Hoffman & Y. M. Goodman (Eds.), *Changing literacies for changing times: An historical perspective on the future of reading research, public policy & classroom practices* (pp. 98-107). New York, NY: Routledge/Taylor & Francis Group.

Arum, R., & Roksa, J. (2011). *Academically adrift: Limited learning on college campuses.* Chicago, IL: University of Chicago Press.

Behrman, E. (2006). Teaching about language, power, and text: A review of classroom practices that support critical literacy. *Journal of Adolescent and Adult Literacy, 49,* 490-498.

Bergmann, J. & Sams, A. (2012). *Flip your classroom: Reach every student in every class every day.* Eugene, OR: International Society for Technology in Education.

Bradbury, R. (1953). *Fahrenheit 451.* New York, NY: Ballantine Books.

Bruce, D. R. (2009). Reading and writing video: Media literacy and adolescents. In L. Christenbury, R. Bomer, & P. Smagorinsky (Eds.), *Handbook of adolescent literacy research* (pp. 287-303). New York, NY: Guilford Press.

Campbell, P. (2008). Trends in young adult literature. In P. Cole (Ed.), *Young adult literature in the 21st century* (pp. 66-69). Boston, MA: McGraw-Hill.

Cervetti, G., Pardeles, M. J., & Damico, J. S. (2001, April). A tale of differences: Comparing the traditions, perspectives, and educational goals of critical reading and critical literacy. *Reading Online, 4.* Retrieved April 22, 2013 from http://www.readingonline.org/articles/cervetti/

Cassidy, J., & Loveless, D. J. (2011). Taking our pulse in a time of uncertainty: Results of the 2012 what's hot, what's not literacy survey. *Reading Today,* 16-21.

Christensen, L. (2003, March). *Acting for justice.* Paper presented at the Critical Literacy in Action Workshop, Bloomington, IN.

Claeys, G. (2013). News from somewhere: Enhanced sociability and the composite definition of utopia and dystopia. *History, 98*(330), 145-173.

Dewey, J. (1933). *How we think*. Chicago, IL: Henry Regnery Company.
Foucault, M. (1977). *Discipline and punish: The birth of the prison*. New York, NY: Random House.
Ford, Brian. (1993). Choosing the canon. *English Journal, 82*, 43-67.
Freire, P. (1972). *Pedagogy of the oppressed*. New York, NY: Herder & Herder.
Gee, J. P. (1996). *Social linguistics and literacies: Ideology in discourses*. London, UK: Routledge.
Gee, J. P. (2000). New literacy studies: From "socially situated" to the work of the school. In D. Barton, M. Hamilton, & R. Ivanic (Eds.), *Situated literacies: Reading and writing in context* (pp. 180-196). London, UK: Routledge.
Giroux, H. (1988). *Teachers as intellectuals: Toward a critical pedagogy of learning*. New York, NY: Bergen and Garvey.
Giroux, H. (2012, September 13). On the significance of the Chicago teachers strike: Challenging democracy's demise. *Truthout*. Retrieved from http://truth-out.org/opinion/item/11530-on-the-significance-of-the-chicago-teachers-strike-bearing-witness-to-and-challenging-democracys-demise
Harvey, D. (1990). *The condition of post modernity: An enquiry in the origins of cultural change*. Cambridge, UK: Blackwell.
Hedges, C. (2011). *Why the United States is destroying its education system*. Retrieved from www.truthdig.org.
Henry, K. L., Knight, K. E., & Thornberry, T. P. (2012). School disengagement as a predictor of dropout, delinquency, and problem substance use during adolescence and early adulthood. *Journal of Youth and Adolescence, 41*, 156-166.
Hernandez, J. C., & Baker, A. (2013, April 13). A tough new tests spurs protests and tears. *The New York Times*. Retrieved from http://www.nytimes.com/2013/04/19/education/common-core-testing-spurs-outrage-and-protest-among-parents.html
Huxely, A. (1946). *Brave new world*. New York, London: Harper & Brothers.
Layton, L. (2013, April 14). Bush, Obama focus on standardized testing leads to 'opt-out' parents' movement. *The Washington Post*. Retrieved from http://www.washingtonpost.com/local/education/bush-obama-focus-on-standardized-testing-leads-to-opt-out-parent-movement/2013/04/14/90b15a44-9d5c-11e2-a941-a19bce7af755_story.html
Luke, A., & Freebody, P. (1997). Shaping the social practices of reading. In S. Muspratt, A. Luke, & P. Freebody (Eds.), *Constructing critical literacies* (pp. 185-223). Cresskill, NJ: Hampton.
Marzano, R., Pickering, D., & Pollack, J. (2001). *Classroom instruction that works: Research based strategies for increasing student achievement*. Alexandria, VA: Association for Supervision and Curriculum Development.
National Center for Education Statistics (2011). The nation's report card: Reading 2011 (NCES 2012–457). National Center for Education Statistics, Institute of Education Sciences, U.S. Department of Education, Washington, D.C.
Nieto, S.. (2009). From surviving to thriving. *Educational Leadership, 66*, 8-13.
Oliver, L. (2012, April 24). Personal communication.
Orwell, G. (1946). *Animal farm*. New York, NY: Penguin.
Orwell, G. (1950). *1984*. New York, NY: Penguin.
Parrinder, P. (2005). Entering dystopia, Entering Erewhon. *Critical Survey, 17*, 6-21.
Santoro, D. (2011). Good teaching in difficult times: Demoralization in the pursuit of good work. *American Journal of Education, 118*, 1-23.
Schaer, R. (2000). Utopia: Space, time, history. In R. Schaer, G. Claeys, & L.T. Sargent (Eds.), *Utopia: The search for the ideal society in the western world* (pp. 3-7). New York, NY: Oxford University Press.
Stotsky, S. (2012) Common Core Standards' devastating impact on literary study and analytical thinking. *The Heritage Foundation Issue Brief, 3800*. Retrieved from http://www.heritage.org/research/reports/2012/12/questionable-quality-of-the-common-core-english-language-arts-standards
Street, B. (2003).What's "new" in new literacy studies: Critical approaches to literacy in theory and practice. *Current Issues in Comparative Education, 5*, 77-91.

Strauss, V. (2011, April 26). Unanswered questions about standardized tests. *The Washington Post*. Retrieved from http://www.washingtonpost.com/blogs/answer-sheet/post/unanswered-questions-about-standardized-tests/2011/04/26/AFNRPlmE_blog.html

Strauss, V. (2013, February 22). Massachusetts professors protest high-stakes standardized tests. *The Washington Post*. Retrieved from http://www.washingtonpost.com/blogs/answer-sheet/wp/2013/02/22/massachusetts-professors-protest-high-stakes-standardized-tests/

Vonnegut, K. (1952). *Player piano*. New York, NY: Avon Books.

White, R. (2008). George Orwell: Socialism and utopia. *Utopian Studies, 19*, 73-95.

LAURA RYCHLY & ROBERT LAKE

9. EXPLORING THE TENSIONS BETWEEN NARRATIVE IMAGINATION AND OFFICIAL KNOWLEDGE THROUGH THE *LIFE OF PI*

ABSTRACT

In this chapter we borrow the experiences had by the main character of Yann Martel's 2013 novel, *Life of Pi*, to show how imagination is a tool we use to help us survive. We explain that in many ways, because of the work involved to make sense out of new and unfamiliar things, children are surviving the hard work of growing up that is childhood. Drawing these two points together we make a case for children needing greater access to their imaginations than they currently have in their schooling experiences. Metaphorical thinking is one way we learn to think about new things; our imaginations help us to make connections between something we do know or understand and something new. The chapter ends with a few suggestions for ways teachers can give students access to this important survival tool which, as it did for Pi, will help them come to terms with that which would otherwise be too treacherous or frightening.

INTRODUCTION

What class of men would you expect to be most preoccupied with, and most hostile to, the idea of escape? ... jailers. (Tolkien quoted in Lewis & Hooper, 2002)

In the present day context of standards-driven classrooms, neither teachers nor students have much of a sense of freedom for thinking what to think and how to think about it. Given our standards-run teaching and learning environments, we believe it is of primary importance that students be allowed to continually cultivate imagination, that they be encouraged to handle new information in ways that empower them to make sense out of it, to puzzle over it, wonder about it, explain it, compare and contrast it, define it in terms of how it is and is not something else, imagine it. Permission to engage in this sort of imaginative thinking is important if students are to know themselves as powerful thinkers, as agents capable of constructing meaning. The consequences of students not learning of their own agency is that their active sense-making capacities wither and they become passive and inactive classroom participants. Educators all around know these students: they seem unmotivated, unwilling to try at all and definitely

P. Paugh et al. (eds.), *Teaching towards Democracy with Postmodern and Popular Culture Texts*, 151–164.
© 2014 Sense Publishers. All rights reserved.

unable to persist when the task at hand becomes "too hard." They seem to make few connections between their efforts, organization, preparedness, and their achievement but also, more important than achievement in the ways that we are measuring it currently, they fail to recognize the difference they could make in their own school experiences.

What our students can imagine about a topic under study, therefore, belongs in our teaching as much as the facts that we can help them memorize. This does not likely seem to be a revolutionary idea; there are probably not many people who would argue that children should be denied their imaginations during their schooling. But two pieces of evidence about the state of public education at present show how little consideration imagination is being given in this moment. The first is the fact that, despite exponential growth in the total number of books being published yearly on the topic of education, there has been a steady decline in the number of books published that discuss the importance or purpose of imagination for learning. The second is this: there are 35 elementary schools in the county in which Laura lives and works and in which my two daughters attend school. A quick internet search of their mission statements revealed the following language: the terms "productive citizens" and "lifelong learners" occurred the most (12 times), followed by "achievement" and "success" (8 times), and "responsible" and "safe" (seven times). The word "standards" occurred four times (one mission statement contained the word "standards" twice). None of the 35 schools' mission statements included the word, or any variation of the word, "imagination." The closest language I found to what might be considered acknowledgement of the importance of imagination is: "children must be recognized for their individuality."

We attest that the experiences of childhood are treacherous and can be threatening by nature. Children are constantly surrounded by that which they don't know; daily they encounter scenarios and phenomena that they never have before and have little to no prior knowledge of. In their "natural," or home environments, it is very common for children to engage in make-believe play or to tell themselves stories to help sort out this new and unfamiliar information. At present, school curriculum is dependent on there being one version of reality that can be cleanly taught, and students' memorization of which can be quickly assessed. In this context, children's natural inclinations toward imagination and/or metaphorical thinking are difficult for teachers to invite into their instruction. But, we argue, imagination and metaphor are essential kinds of thinking that children do naturally to help them survive a confusing and sometimes threatening world. Imagination helps us access otherwise inaccessible ideas, inaccessible because they are new, or intimidating because they challenge our present understanding, or scary even, because they are so foreign to the way(s) that we already know the world to be. Shortly we will explore some of the theories Bruno Bettelheim (1975) provides as explanations for the power of fairy tales in children's lives for helping them to make sense of unknown and frightening phenomena.

In this chapter, we suggest that in order to successfully navigate the treacherous experience(s) of childhood (treacherous by nature), children need ongoing opportunities to engage in imaginative thinking through metaphor. Children already formulate their own conceptualization of things and ideas with which they come into contact with or without adult intervention. The more random seeming, or less obvious, the connections are between concepts that children have discovered for themselves, the deeper or richer the thinking that connects the ideas. If school could give students permission to discover, access, elaborate on, or invent, their own metaphorical relationships between concepts, then students would form relationships with these new ideas, and this would help with the assimilation of new ways of knowing and being. In turn, this would help children develop knowledge of themselves as individuals capable of effecting change, which is the essence of personal agency. First we explain how metaphor serves as the language of imagination. Then we present three reasons why children need access to their imaginations, via metaphorical language, in order to benefit from the richest potential outcome of our system of public education: that our students will know their own agency.

The character Pi from the novel *Life of Pi* provides us with our own metaphor to illustrate the power and necessity of this metaphorical thinking. There is a question introduced at the end of the novel about whether or not the fantastic story we have just read is true. Did Pi survive a months-long journey in a life raft accompanied by a giant Bengal tiger? Or did he merely survive, and was the story his imagination helping him to endure the unimaginable situation with which he was faced? We use Pi's stories to show how important fantasy can be for children as they continually assert their own power over the incomprehensible. *Life of Pi* contradicts the possibility of there being only one version, and the popularity of the movie version of the book makes it an accessible example of why teachers should hold open plural versions of the "truth."

THE LIFE OF PI

> If we, citizens, do not support our artists, then we sacrifice our imagination on the altar of crude reality and we end up believing in nothing and having worthless dreams. (Martel, 2001, p. xi)

Yann Martel's (2001) book *Life of Pi* tells the story of a young boy's survival after the ship on which he and his family are sailing from India to Canada inexplicably sinks into the ocean. Besides Pi's family and the crew, the ship also was carrying an entire zoo's worth of animals, which were owned by Pi's family and being moved across the ocean to a new facility. The sinking of the ship leaves Pi stranded on the ocean, and the rest of the novel is his account of the events that take place until his rowboat reaches Mexico.

Until the end of the story the reader is unable to confidently doubt Pi's story. It becomes less and less believable, but we hold this in our minds the entire time that he is surviving something we have never had to, and this reduces our credibility as a critic. At the very end Pi is interviewed by investigators from the company that insured the ship. They are dissatisfied with his unbelievable story and tell him so. Pi responds by telling a different story, one more believable because it deals only with human beings and not with the zoo animals that comprise the character list in his first version. The investigators much prefer this version with which they can more readily relate. It is still gruesome and reveals many dark truths about the depths to which humans can descend in order to secure their own survival. It might be argued that the second story, the one about the humans, is more awful because the horrible things that happen are done to people by people, whereas in the first story the same horrible things occur between animals, and we already generally believe that animals are less worried about issues of morality or ethics when it comes to their own survival.

When the investigators reveal their satisfaction to Pi that results from his second, abbreviated, story and prepare to leave, Pi asks the men: "So tell me, since it makes no factual difference to you and you can't prove the question either way, which story do you prefer? Which is the better story, the story with animals or the story without animals?" (Martel, 2001, p. 398). The men agree that the story with animals is the "better" story, despite its being less believable. Pi uses his imagination to give himself power over his circumstances either as he survives the ordeal in an imaginary state (having substituted zoo animals for all of the humans surviving on the lifeboat) or as he tells the more believable story including only humans. This is evidence of his agency, his ability to act powerfully in and on the world. We lean on Pi's imagination throughout our chapter as a metaphor for the function of imagination on children's efforts to survive their own growth and development. As we more closely consider Pi's metaphorical journey, it is helpful to consider what metaphor is and how it might be considered a language of the imagination.

WHAT IS METAPHOR

> Isn't telling about something – using words, English or Japanese – already something of an invention? Isn't just looking upon this world already something of an invention? (Martel, 2001, p. 380)

The word metaphor comes from the combination of the Greek words meta, which means 'over,' and pherein, 'to carry' (Hawkes, 1972, p. 1). This "carrying over" describes the blending of the features of one concept to another, in a unique combination that results in a new shade of meaning. By this action, the creator of metaphor transcends walls of limited expression into personal sense making and identity. Richards (1936) astutely describes the structure of metaphor as "two thoughts of different things active together and supported by a single word, or phrase, whose meaning is a resultant of their interaction" (p. 93).

Lakoff and Johnson (1980) express this interaction as more than just the combination of the names of objects at the sentence level. Their emphasis is more on the conjoined meaning of concepts within the context of lived experience when they write that "the essence of metaphor is understanding and experiencing one kind of thing in terms of another" (p. 5).

To introduce the concept of metaphorical thinking to her teacher education students at both the graduate and undergraduate level, Laura does the following icebreaker activity at the beginning of every semester. As part of introductions, she asks each student to describe what kind of animal he or she is. The purpose of this exercise is to give students time to think in detail about his or her characteristics and how they are and are not like specific characteristics of animals. This is defining something (in this case, oneself) in terms of another (here, an animal). Usually after the first few people share someone will say "If I could choose to be any animal ..." which is a perfect opportunity for us to uncover what the original question asked – not about choosing (because the power of the comparison may be lost in the opportunity to choose which features to compare) but about what animal she already would be if she were an animal.

The traditional view of metaphor is that it is a form of figurative language that is used to dress up the literal usage of words and phrases. Many still view metaphor as fanciful or not really essential to basic communication. In the last half of the Twentieth century, this notion has been reexamined in the fields of psychology, neuroscience, philosophy, and linguistics. From these disciplines, a growing consensus suggests that metaphor is fundamental to the process of thinking and communicating. Lakoff and Johnson (1980) express the tenor of these views when they say that "our conceptual system is largely metaphorical" (p. 3). This view includes both conscious and subconscious thought expressed outwardly in words that tie concepts together into one expression.

For example, if we say "a tidal wave of weariness hit me yesterday afternoon," the person I am addressing gets a fuller picture than if we simply said, "I was very tired yesterday afternoon." By combining the image of a tidal wave with the condition of tiredness, a fuller and more personalized description emerges. Through metaphor, both conscious and subconscious thought are combined with past and present experience in defining moments that create personal meaning and signature.

Every person's inner landscape is unique. There is an infinitively wide range of sources of inner language emerging from the combined factors of nature and experience. Metaphor brings all these connections together in imagination. Indeed, metaphor is the very language of the imagination, or we should say, expresses the multiple languages of the imagination including visual, numerical, musical, somatic, and rhythmic expression as well as verbal discourse.

One of the reasons that metaphor contributes so much to personal sense making is because it can bring elements together that have no categorical relationship except in the experience of the creator of the metaphor. For example, what relationship does fog have to cats? In Carl Sandburg's mind, there is a very strong one.

> *Fog*
> *The fog comes*
> *on little cat feet.*
> *It sits looking*
> *over harbor and city*
> *on silent haunches*
> *and then moves on*
> (1916, p.71)

What would the information in this poem sound like without metaphor? You could not really capture it without the combination of fog and feline behavior. If it appeared in the weather forecast sans metaphor at the very best, the facts would describe a light fog eventually disappearing as the sun rose. No wonder students find learning facts so tedious and boring!

Literalism destroys the medium and the message and blocks the multiple dimensions of rich interpretation, robbing the imagination of its greatest power as a generative interpreter of experience. Black (1954-55) goes so far as to say that in some cases, metaphors create new meaning rather than just offering a means of expressing old ideas in a new way (pp. 273-294). Perhaps this is evident in the example of thinking of oneself as an animal. Characteristics that we normally define as they relate only to us suddenly take on an extra dimension as we weight them against what we know about something else. For example, if one were describe herself as 'shy,' we would immediately associate what we think about shy people with this person. But if she described herself as a fox, or a rabbit, because those animals are shy, we would apply a more imaginative understanding of "shy," to her description of herself. Also, she has access to a visual which may help to deepen the connection between herself and the characteristic she has identified.

CHILDHOOD AS TREACHEROUS

> And so, in that Greek letter that looks like a shack with a corrugated tin roof, in that elusive, irrational number with which scientists try to understand the universe, I found refuge. (Martel, 2001, p. 30)

Pi explains early in the novel that his given name, Piscine Molitor Patel, was his parents' way of honoring their memory of a swimming pool that had the same name. His teachers and classmates pronounced the first word as 'pissing,' which caused him great angst. This led to other jokes, and the young boy resolved to change the sound people used to identify him. One day at school he got up from his desk when the teacher reached his name on the roster, wrote his name on the board and underlined the first two letters, reintroducing himself to the class as Pi. His teacher accepted this nickname, and Pi's relief was substantial: "I was saved ... I could breathe ... a new beginning" (Martel, 2001, p. 29).

We have adopted a view that, metaphorically perhaps, childhood is a treacherous time and requires that children take action to ensure their survival. The above account from the novel is an example of such treachery. This is not to say that children are alone of course, though we do acknowledge the extent to which individual children are literally surviving varies with individual children. Our notion of metaphorical survival suggests that the work children must undertake to make sense out of the nonsensical is something like the work that Pi Patel undertook in order to arrive back on land after the ship he and his family are traveling on sinks (Martel, 2001). Pi is faced with the unthinkable – his family is lost at sea and he is wholly alone – and uses story to help himself navigate this treacherous reality. Fantasy is an important component for children's development. As children learn to negotiate relationships with others, and learn the ways in which their actions lead to consequences, they use fantasy as a safe space to play with ideas (Bettelheim, 1975). Bruno Bettelheim (1975) was a psychoanalyst who examined children's relationships with fairy tales. To adults, fairy tales may sometimes seem unnecessarily fantastical, or gruesome even, if reading the original texts as retold by the likes of the Grimm Brothers, Hans Christian Andersen, and other non-Western sources such as African or Native American Folktales. In the original Cinderella, for example, one of the evil stepsisters cuts off her toes to squeeze her foot into the glass slipper so that she will win her place as the prince's bride. In the slave narrative Little Eight John, retold by Virginia Hamilton (1985), Little Eight John is a terrible little boy who never minds his mother and is eventually turned into a greasy stain on his mother's kitchen table and wiped away: "And that was the end of Little Eight John. What happens to all little chil'ren who never mind" (p. 125). Bettelheim (1975) thought of this fantasy space as a kind of therapy for children: "The fairy tale is therapeutic because the [listener] finds his own solution, through contemplating what the story seems to imply about him and his inner conflicts at this moment in his life" (p. 25).

In a book review of *Once Upon a Time*, a recently published collection of Grimms' Brothers fairy tales, Joan Acocella (2012) explains how those who find fairy tales problematic for reasons such as that they are too violent, or portray women unfairly, may be coming from a place more rational and positivist than children naturally do. She quotes W. H. Auden as having "once described the Grimm-sanitizers as 'the Society for the Scientific Diet, the Association of Positivist Parents, the League for the promotion of Worthwhile Leisure, the Cooperative Camp of Prudent Progressives'" (p. 77). Consider this example of the different readings of *Snow White,* one of the most well-known fairy tales. Its heroine, recall, is the princess described as a 'good housekeeper.' She is so labeled by adults who misread the housework as being mindless tasks that are beneath her potential. Children, however, view Snow White's industriousness as an accomplishment, something above their current capabilities. Bettelheim (1975) explains the story of *Snow White* as a coming-of-age story in which Snow White moves through stages of infancy, pre-adolescence, adolescence, until finally reaching physical, emotional, and intellectual maturity. What some might criticize as a subservient nature, in Snow White's passive orientation toward the dwarfs and their household, is evidence of her growing up: "her behavior in restraining herself in eating and drinking, her resisting sleeping in a bed that is not just right for her…[show] that her ego too has matured, since now she works hard and well, and shares with others" (Bettelheim, 1975, p. 209). Here the mismatch between adult interpretation and the meaning ascribed to the stories by children becomes clear. Where adults blame Snow White for limiting the potential scope of a young woman's development, children see in her a role model for their social aspirations. Bettelheim (1975) references the fantasy elements of Snow White's "easy life with the dwarfs" in his summary of the purpose of the story to give children a space to think through "difficult and painful growing-up experiences which cannot be avoided" (p. 215). Children connect to Snow White as a metaphor for how things can, and ultimately, will be. This empowers them, provides therapy for the naturally treacherous endeavor that is growing up.

IMAGINATION-LESS SCHOOLS

When Mr. Kumar visited the zoo, it was to take the pulse of the universe, and his stethoscopic mind always confirmed to him that everything was in order, that everything was order. He left the zoo feeling scientifically refreshed. (Martel, 2001, p. 32)

Mr. Kumar is a character that we introduce here because he provides a great example of how compelling it can be to measure things in order to find them to be in order, and how refreshing it can be to have found this order. This belongs in our chapter two ways. First is the obvious parallel to the ways that we are measuring children almost daily to order them according to ability, or lack of ability, for example. The second is Mr. Kumar's example of searching for the known variable in order to find refreshment. He seeks confirmation of what is known, which is also what we are doing to students in classrooms when we convince them that the world is full of right answers.

It would be unreasonable to for us to claim that once-upon-a-time schools were full of imaginative experiences for children, and that children were encouraged to imagine their own explanations for new information. Traditionally American public schools have been places where teachers held the facts that students were required to memorize. Our current moment is no different or is arguably worse given our modern understanding of how important it is for students to connect with new ideas in ways that will help the information come alive inside of them. Our current high-stakes testing environment makes it so that teachers and students are convinced that 1) The universe is made up of questions that have one right answer, and of 2) the importance of knowing that one right answer. Unfortunately this situation is not only an inaccurate one but is also a depressing orientation to the universe.

Teaching as if there are only questions for each of which there is only one right answer is problematic because it disrupts what is a more natural state of being and definitely a natural state of being a child: that there are probably many more questions than answers. Paulo Freire (2010), in his book *Pedagogy of the Oppressed,* describes the problem of oppressors teaching the oppressed (his work regarded teachers of Brazilian peasants, but we can apply his observations and attestations metaphorically to our own public school classrooms). He observed that when teachers teach students in ways that require them to memorize someone else's ideas, "The teacher talks about reality as if it were motionless, static, compartmentalized, and predictable" (p. 71). A "motionless, static" reality is not one that encourages students to mess around with ideas until they can explain them in their own words, compare them to other things, prove and disprove 'truths' about them. But if learning is to be acts of assimilating ideas for the purpose of thinking our own thoughts, then teaching a static reality is not productive. Maxine Greene (2001) contributes that "to limit learners to single modes of seeing and interpreting, may be to frustrate their individual pursuits of meaning and, in consequence, their desires to come to know and learn" (p. 75). Learners' own sense-making capabilities are shunned, not invited to acts of assimilation which lead us to think our own thoughts.

OFFICIAL KNOWLEDGE AND LITERALISM

> I know what you want. You want a story that won't surprise you. That will confirm what you already know. That won't make you see higher or further or differently. You want a flat story. An immobile story. You want dry, yeastless factuality. (Martel, 2001, p. 336)

As Pi is lying in his hospital bed, recovering from his near-death ordeal on the lifeboat with the Bengal tiger, Richard Parker, the investigators ply him with questions about what caused the giant tanker that he and his family were traveling on to sink. Pi has no idea about the cause. He has shared instead the story of the hyena, orangutan, zebra, and tiger that initially made it onto the life raft with Pi, his many days lost at sea, his encounter on the man-eating island with its abundance of meerkats, and his eventual rescue. The investigators are unsatisfied with his tale, and Pi speaks the above words to them to confirm that they need a different, more believable story. "Dry, yeastless factuality" is a metaphor for the current circumstances in classrooms that we have been describing: teaching and learning as bread that does not change its shape, size, color, and aroma as it bakes, a bread-making process that yields a more static final product than a dynamic one.

The investigators want to hear a story that is more like one they have heard before. They desire the reassurance they get from things that are familiar and known to them. Teachers share this desire with the investigators. There is so much pressure to get every student to the same "right" answer so that they will recognize it to bubble in on their high-stakes tests that we are literally afraid of what our students will say if we ask them what they think. One reason we have discussed with teacher education students for why teachers struggle to give students time and space to let their imaginations run wild is the teachers' uncertainty with what "to do" with the crazy things their students might say.

The differences in these two stories – Pi's story containing the animals and the investigators' requested believable story – can be examined through the lens of Louise Rosenblatt's (1995) reader response theory. In her work Rosenblatt

(1995) describes two different kinds of engagement with literature, efferent and aesthetic. Efferent reading is when our reading is to fulfill an external purpose, such as writing a summary for a teacher to grade, or selecting a passage's main idea from a list of provided choices (Rosenblatt, 1995). Aesthetic reading, on the other hand, is the experience we have with a text when we experience it "with our senses fully alive" (Robinson, 2011). We bring "affective aspects ... [a] mixture of sensations, feelings, images, and ideas" to aesthetic reading and are able to experience personal connections and responses that are unavailable when we engage in efferent reading (Rosenblatt, 1995, p. 33). These two modes of engagement with text are not to be thought of as opposites, but as ends of a continuum on which readers move along based on the purpose of their reading (Rosenblatt, 1995).

The investigators ask for Pi's efferent experience. They wish to hear a story that is one they can retell themselves, more objective, and more real, real because it can be heard and understood by others. This availability to the public is a key to its efferent nature. Efferent means that two readers, or listeners, will answer the same question about the content the same way. Pi tells his aesthetic story, the one that is primarily a story of his own experiences and belongs to him in ways that it can never belong to anyone else. The investigators prove Pi's story is unavailable to them by not being able to engage with it as Pi is telling it; they look back and forth and mumble at one another during and after Pi's account. Its unfamiliarity makes it necessarily imagined, and to the investigators this makes it invalid, an unacceptable version of what might have happened were one to become stranded on a life boat with a number of animals and subsequently lost at sea.

The equivalence found here between a story being imagined and invalid is the current situation found in classrooms with regard to ways that children respond to their own reading experiences as well. Aesthetic reading is neglected in favor of reading that produces responses we can test: "teachers often forget that if students know that they will be tested primarily on factual aspects of the work (often by multiple-choice questions), a full aesthetic reading is prevented ..." (Rosenblatt, 1995, p. 293). On the continuum of reading responses, students are stranded at one end and are unable to access the more personal connections and interactions they would have with a text were they to read it without the expectation of having to make their reaction public. Not only do students expect to make their reactions public, they also are aware that their teachers are after a match to the "right" answers they hold in their minds as they ask their students to share, or grade student work. Such awareness discourages or even rejects students' agency.

This sort of a rejection is what we have all along claimed teaches students that they are not powerful meaning makers, and teaches them to passively wait to be "taught," and to endure unsatisfactory school experiences. Such school experiences are regarded as nothing short of "violence against children" by scholars such as Alan Block (2001) who write about the troubling state of "school culture [that] does not bode well for ... wildness that portends exploration and discovery" (p. 18). To take away a child's "wildness," his or her exploratory work of forming personal relationships with new concepts that he or she is just beginning to know (know not as in "know for the test," but know as one knows a friend) is a denial of the opportunity to form meaningful connections with all that human beings have to think about. Without these personal connections we are thinking thoughts that belong to others.

This dynamic troubles relationships between teachers and students as well. In our classroom environments where students are not excited to share their thinking that might be "wrong," teachers are in unfortunate positions as "authorities" over knowledge and thinking, and are expected to operate as judges of their students. These environments are not the safe spaces we know are conducive to the risks required for students to interact aesthetically with information. This positioning is also not satisfying to teachers who sense that their power inhibits their students. Block (2001) makes this point in an example of his daughter at play:

> I can correct her if I have the will, but then I have denied her play and creativity, given her an object with which she may not play, and I have myself become an object set in opposition and thereby threatening to her. When I tell her that the shirt on her head is only a shirt and not long flowing hair, I do more than end her game; I deny her. (p. 70)

Teachers "set in opposition" and "threatening" as they wait for the "right" answer that they need to hear from their students inhibit aesthetic engagement with text.

With so much emphasis placed on test scores and measuring student achievement (as we were writing this, the 2012 scores on the Program for Student Assessment that is administered by the Organizaton for Economic Cooperation and Development were released; the U.S. once again produced underwhelming results and students in Shanghai, China were performing on average an entire grade level above their counterparts) it may seem easy to wonder what point we are trying to make. Shouldn't we be emphasizing efferent reading if that is the kind of reading that will make American students mark the right answer on these tests? What are the consequences of neglecting aesthetic engagement with texts, of pretending that individual interaction and interpretation are not essential to a rich, meaningful human existence? Rosenblatt (1995) crisply suggests that our "stance toward the content of consciousness" (here we interject that "imagination" and "content of consciousness" are related concepts) will determine "the survival of the reading of literature as an active part of our American culture" (p. 293). The very idea that we would read at all depends on our being able to engage with texts in ways that bring our own sensations and experiences to the reading. If we insist on practicing as though there is only one way to read something and only one possible way to interpret, summarize, or respond to it, then we run the risk of eliminating a need to read at all.

TEACHING THROUGH METAPHOR

> The world isn't just the way it is. It is how we understand it, no? And in understanding something, we bring something to it, no? Doesn't that make life a story? (Martel, 2001, p. 380)

Children use metaphors to grasp abstract or invisible ideas. Metaphors make them visible, or concrete. For example, Laura's two young daughters recently started taking violin lessons. Most of what they are asked to do is invisible and inaccessible to them, especially because they have to make their bodies do things that they can't see. They have to command their outsides to pose in particular ways from inside. For example, their right arms, or "bow arms," are supposed to move mostly from the elbow with little to no shoulder movement. To help them "see" this, their teacher relies on two metaphors. One is to open the bow arm like a gate, with the elbow functioning as a hinge that allows the forearm to open and close. The second is to not move the shoulder like a jogger would: "you don't want a jogger's shoulder!"

Another way metaphor has been present in this violin learning is in acquiring a good bow hold. Each finger of the right hand belongs in a specific place on the bow and has to grip in a particular position. This is something string players can spend their lives on, tweaking the position of one finger to play with richer tone or to develop an advanced technique to produce a sophisticated response from the strings. My four- and six-year-old girls are at the very beginning of this immense learning! Their teacher uses metaphor to describe the role of each finger. The thumb, Mister Bumpy Thumb, is bent at the knuckle as if he is taking a bow. The index finger, "Stinky," leans on the stick and reaches away from the two middle fingers. These two are the "Hugger Brothers," and touch together and hang over the frog of the bow. "Pinky" stands up nice and rounded at the end of the stick. Their teacher explained this analogy once or twice as she modeled making her own bow hold, and quickly began referring to my girls' fingers with these terms. This is not a statement on whether or not children should be given false names for real things ("Stinky" vs. "index finger," for example). It is meant simply as proof that when we access what children already know by way of metaphor, we give them power to proceed.

One of the seventh-grade science standards in our state is: "Relate cell structures (cell membrane, nucleus, cytoplasm, chloroplasts, mitochondria) to basic cell functions." The parts and function of our human body cells are quite abstract concepts for middle school students to get their heads around. For one thing, cells are microscopic, and adolescents are, by their developmental natures, still on their way to being abstract thinkers. To not be able to see the "structures" that they are supposed to attribute "basic functions" to is its own challenge. Add the fact that these vocabulary terms are brand-new and not readily connected to other, already-known information, and it is not too hard to believe that we encounter teachers regularly who are frustrated with their job of teaching this standard. Understandable. But take Pi's words above, that in understanding life we bring something to it and in so doing make a story, and apply this to the task of teaching cell structure and function. Can we make a story out of this content by bringing something to it? What if we were to teach the parts and function of a cell as if the cell was a city? A city has several "structures" that serve specialized "functions" that keep daily life running smoothly. The cell membrane is a border, a river perhaps, or a road or, if imagining a medieval city maybe the membrane is a high wall. The nucleus could be a government building, perhaps city hall. The cytoplasm is the atmosphere that permeates the city. The mitochondria is a power plant that produces energy for the city. Teachers can give students just this much information and then release students to their imaginations. A modern city or a medieval one? A clean city or a polluted one? A bustling city or a quiet country town?

PEDAGOGICAL RECOMMENDATIONS

As the above example illustrates, we recommend giving students as many opportunities as possible to think in metaphors: "How is (something new) like (something known)?" This question prompts students to take hold of the new thing under study and compare it to something familiar. This sort of examination gives students freedom to discover for themselves the characteristics and components of the ideas, people, and objects that we find ourselves charged to teach.

Another example would be to have the students to retell a famously imaginative story or poem stripped of all the metaphors and symbolism like Pi's second story. Can you imagine how Frost's *The Road Not Taken* would look read without metaphor, or if fairy tales were written like newspaper accounts?

REFERENCES

Acocella, J. (2012). Once upon a time: The lure of the fairy tale. *The New Yorker*, July 23, 73-78.
Bettelheim, B. (1975). *The uses of enchantment: The meaning and importance of fairy tales.* New York, NY: Vintage Books.
Black, M. (1954/55). Metaphor. *Proceedings of the Aristotelian Society*, 55, 273-294.
Block. A. A. (2001). *I'm only bleeding: Education as the practice of social violence against children.* New York, NY: Peter Lang.
Freire, P. (2010). *Pedagogy of the oppressed.* New York, NY: Continuum.
Greene, M. (2001). *Variations on a blue guitar: The Lincoln Center Institute lectures on aesthetic education.* NewYork, NY: Teachers College Press.
Hamilton, V. (1985). *The people could fly: American black folktales.* New York, NY: Alfred A. Knopf.
Hawkes, T. (1972). *Metaphor.* London: Methuen & Co. Ltd.
Lakoff, G., & Johnson, M. (1980/2003). *Metaphors we live by.* Chicago, IL: Chicago University Press.
Lewis, C. S., & Hooper, W. (1982). *On stories, and other essays on literature.* New York, NY: Harcourt Brace Jovanovich.
Martel, Y. (2001). *Life of Pi: A novel.* New York, NY: Harcourt.
Richards, A. I. (1936). *The philosophy of rhetoric.* Oxford: Oxford University Press.

Robinson, K. (2011). *Out of our minds: Learning to be creative*. Chichester, West Sussex, UK: Capstone Publishing Ltd.
Rosenblatt, L. M. (1995). *Literature as exploration*. New York, NY: The Modern Language Association.
Sanburg, C. (1916). *Chicago poems*. New York, NY: Henry Holt.

TRICIA M. KRESS & PATRICIA PATRISSY

10. "CLANKERS," "DARWINISTS," AND CRITICALITY

Encouraging Sociological Imagination vis-à-vis Historicity with the Steampunk Novel Leviathan

ABSTRACT

This chapter explores the critical literacy potential of the steampunk literature genre by examining *Leviathan,* the young adult steampunk novel written by Scott Westerfeld. Often subsumed under the genres of science or speculative fiction, steampunk is a genre all its own that takes as its point of departure the Victorian era when steam technology ruled. By reinterpreting history, steampunk literature demonstrates that what we think, what we do, and how we act, right now in the present as in the past, matters and contributes to the creation of an unforeseen future. As critical literature steampunk fosters sociological imagination by confronting readers with long-lasting social issues that are just as pressing today as they were over a century ago. The authors demonstrate the potential of steampunk by showing how *Leviathan* raises numerous themes that are ripe for engaging students' critical and social imaginations. The book highlights gender roles and class struggle; it raises questions about nations' sense of exceptionalism, and it calls into question man's relationship with technology and man's relationship with nature as well. The chapter concludes with a lesson idea for encouraging students to write their own historical countertexts.

INTRODUCTION

What if history had played out differently? What if "the shot heard around the world" had left behind a possible heir? What if technology had developed differently as well? What if steam power had remained a dominant source of energy? And what if Darwin had the means to experiment with the species he studied, to create "the fittest,"" most useful creatures? These "what ifs ..." are a sample of the types of questions that arise from within the world of the young adult steampunk novel *Leviathan* by Scott Westerfeld. According to Thomas (2013), science fiction and speculative fiction (which includes the genre of steampunk), "are genres that 'move readers to imagine alternative ways of being alive'" (p. 4). Zigo and Moore (2004) explain, speculative fiction genres like steampunk can be thought of "as the metaphoric literature for social and cultural introspection and for inspiring multiple interpretive possibilities" (p. 85). And Bean and Moni (2003) make the case that young adult fiction is a useful tool for fostering critical literacy in teens because it deals with issues that are pertinent in their lives, allowing youth to better identify with the texts and their characters.

While we recognize there is no shortage of research on the above mentioned literature genres, steampunk is conspicuously absent from this conversation. Yet, as a genre of its own that is useful for cultivating critical literacy, it already has a longstanding history in the K-12 classroom via authors like Jules Verne and H.G. Wells. Furthermore, over the past 5 years, it has been increasing in popularity as both a literary genre and popular culture phenomenon, making its way into popular young adult fiction, movies and television. While steampunk could be located under the umbrella of speculative fiction, we believe that the unique properties of this genre, which are particularly relevant for discussions about critical literacy, are missed in doing so. It is our goal in this chapter via a discussion of *Leviathan* by Scott Westerfeld to familiarize our readers with steampunk, a literary genre that is "all about bravely breaking the rules" of society (Falksen, 2009, n.p.). In the sections that follow, we illustrate the ways in which the unique characteristics of this genre are especially appropriate for cultivating a critical literacy that goes beyond critique and fosters sociological imagination vis-à-vis historicity.

WHAT IS STEAMPUNK?

The term "steampunk" was coined in the 1980s to define a genre of fiction that was gaining popularity, but did not fit completely within science fiction (Rawlins, 2009). Combining technology from the Industrial age with historic time periods, steampunk provides an alternate view of the past and its resulting present and/or future (Falksen, 2009). Recently, steampunk has emerged in popular culture, expanding into movies, such as *Sky Captain and the World of Tomorrow* (Proyas, 2004), *Dark City* (Proyas, 1998), *The City of Lost Children* (Caro & Jeunet, 1995) and television shows, like Neil Gaimon's (1996) *Neverwhere* and the short lived *Firefly* (Whedon, 2002). In recent years, the young adult literature market has also seen an influx of steampunk titles by authors such as Scott Westerfeld, Dru Pagliassotti, and D.L. Mackenzie who are continuing in the tradition of H.G. Wells and Jules Verne. As a popular culture phenomenon, steampunk can be found in fashion, particularly in the U.K. where retailers such as Topshop and Asos have released steampunk inspired clothing lines. While steampunk has typically been on the periphery of mainstream popular culture conversations (if in the conversation at all), lately, it has been making its way into the mainstream public eye. For example, a number of magazines (e.g., Time; Forbes) and television shows (e.g., Oddities; America's Next Top Model; Project Runway: Under the Gunn) have featured various interpretations of the steampunk subculture; even in the world of home decor we see steampunk-like style, which is referred to as "industrial chic" (e.g., West Elm; Pottery Barn). As a subculture, steampunk values craftsmanship, imagination and re-invention. One notable example of the craftsmanship of steampunk that has been featured recently in a number of mainstream media outlets is The Neverwas Haul Traveling Academy of Unnatural Sciences, a Victorian house on wheels (Oatman-Stanford, 2012) that was designed and assembled by a community of steampunks who transport the museum (and its unusual artifacts like animal skeletons and rare antique photographs) to steampunk conventions in various parts of the United States. Just as the spirit of the genre is rooted in creation, blogs and fan fiction are also central to the rising culture. Simply typing "steampunk blog" into Google results in "About 25,400,000" results (to date).

Steampunk takes as its point of departure the Victorian era when steam technology ruled. Rather than assuming technological advancements occurred as they actually did during the century that followed, steampunk speculates what the world would look like today if steam technology had never been usurped by contemporary technologies. Steampunk stories are typically situated on the backdrop of urban industrial landscapes where steam-powered land, sea, air and subterranean machines and clockwork automatons are commonplace. Depending upon the story and whether it takes a utopian or dystopian leaning, steampunk often has a gritty, patinaed tone, as if century-old photographs had come to life. Storylines tend to capture a sense of adventure and invention, and technology is central to the experiences of the characters. Often, characters have special relationships with technology and they are featured tinkering with, modifying and caring for technology objects. The technology in steampunk is typically personified and may be described as coughing, sputtering, trembling or purring as human characters interact with them. We believe, as is the case with many popular culture trends, the recent interest in steampunk indicates a subconscious desire for a different present and future in the U.S. populace.

A number of researchers (e.g., Forlini, 2010; Perschon, 2013) note that in steampunk there seems to be a longing for "hope" and a desire to reclaim "humanity" in an alienated technological world. Forlini (2010) explains,

> First and foremost, steampunk is about things – and our relationships to them... In both its literary and material manifestations, steampunk is about learning to read all that is folded into any particular created thing – that is, learning to connect the source materials to particular cultural, technical, and environmental practices, skills, histories, and economies of meaning and value. (pp. 72-73)

Onion (2008) notes the potential of steampunk as a tool with which people can control technology rather than be controlled by it; as she explains, "steampunk domesticates a technology that has proven devastating to human life, reveling in its imaginary controlled power" (p. 150). Steampunk also has a productive edge in its propensity toward invention. Tanenbaum, Tanenbaum, and Wakkary (2012) explain, "although the genre celebrates an era in which mass production and assembly were coming of age, it resists traditional narratives of industrialization that prize uniformity and homogeneity" (p. 1590). In fact, steampunk as subculture and literary genre resists contemporary neoliberal narratives about progress and mass production.

Yet, aside from the theme of man's relationship with technology, steampunk offers a broad social critique in the very act of identifying a particular historical moment when society could have taken a different technological trajectory, thereby resulting in a different outcome. At the same time, in that historical moment, society is still quite recognizable for what it is today. As Nevins (2008) explains,

> More so than other historical periods, the 19th century, especially the Victorian era (1837-1901), is an excellent mirror for the modern period. The social, economic, and political structures of the Victorian era are essentially the same as our own, and their cultural dynamics – the way in which the culture reacts to various phenomena and stimuli – are quite similar to ours. This makes the Victorian era extremely useful for ideological stories on subjects such as feminism, imperialism, class issues, and religion, as well as commentary on contemporary issues such as serial murderers and overseas wars. Stories about the way in which women were treated in the Victorian era can easily be written to address how women are treated today, and without authorial straining of allegorical novels set in previous historical eras. (p. 8)

Pagliasotti (2013) and Tadeo (2013) both note this trend in contemporary steampunk novels' resistance to adhere to stereotypical female gender roles, and we see the same tendencies toward challenging issues like social class inequality and imperialism, as well. In fact, in *Leviathan* specifically, as we will discuss below, all of these issues are addressed in the various subplots of the book. In general, steampunk novels push back against social and cultural norms, and major story arcs are often tales of dissident and subversive characters intentionally breaking societal rules. By its very nature, steampunk is critical literature that fosters sociological imagination vis-à-vis historicity by confronting readers with long-lasting social issues that are just as pressing today as they were over a century ago.

CRITICAL LITERACY AND STEAMPUNK: IMAGINING THE WORLD OTHERWISE

Lankshear and McLaren (1993) assert that critical literacy is about "getting beyond the bland, surface talk of our cultural tradition and understanding how it got to be what it is by exploring seminal texts seen as constitutive of its nature and shape, and by reference to orthodox social and political histories" (p. 31). As texts that capture a particular historical moment that exemplifies the underlying ideologies that structure contemporary society, steampunk novels lead readers to dig beneath the surface of what is taken for granted as "commonsense" in the present. Not only can steampunk be used to address the priorities that are typical of the field of critical literacy (Behrman, 2006),[1] but it can help educators to take these goals further by tapping into students' sociological imaginations in order to move beyond critique toward envisioning social transformation. Here, we draw our definition of sociological imagination from Mills (1959) and Denzin (2003). According to Mills (1959) sociological imagination is the capacity to shift between perspectives such that the individual can see connections between broad social issues and individual circumstances of the self. He explains, "In the back of its use there is always the urge to know the social and historical meaning of the individual in the society and in the period in which he has his quality and his being" (p. 7). Denzin (2003) links sociological imagination explicitly to social justice in a concept he calls "critical imagination," which, as Kress (2011) explains, is a "disposition towards critiquing the social world by identifying oppression by being guided by a larger vision of how the world might be different" (p. 26). By rendering a different historical trajectory beginning at the Victorian era, it demonstrates, in the words of Freire (1985), "History has no power. As Marx said, history does not command us, history is made by us. History makes us while we make it" (p. 199). Steampunk novels suggest a different world and therefore illustrate that history as we know it was not inevitable; this casts the present social conditions as tentative and opens up a panoply of possible futures.

Thus, the genre of steampunk naturally engenders both a critique and a reimagining of the world. By altering the trajectory of history, the steampunk novel moves students beyond peeling back the veil of hegemony to using their sociological imaginations to envision and create a more humane world that "is not yet" (Greene, 1996). Fostering a critical literacy in this manner aligns with Luke's (2002) conceptualization of critical discourse analysis, which he argues "must be able to demonstrate what 'should be' as well as what is problematic with text and discourse in the world" (p. 105). Developing sociological imagination through critical literacy, "brings *depth* to analysis because it gets beneath the surface of prejudices and mystifies the ideologies and goes to the deeper level of structured relations and practices within which humans live their lives and their lives are shaped" (Lankshear & McLaren, 1993, p. 30). Steampunk is well positioned to foster sociological imagination by engaging students in a critical analysis of historical events, raising questions about social inequalities, and modeling how the world may have turned out differently if social conditions had emerged differently throughout the course of history. It offers students a platform for raising critical questions and encourages students to take the world into their own hands, following Freire's (1985) assertion that

> we attempt to emerge from this alienating daily routine that repeats itself. Let's try to understand life, not necessarily as the daily repetition of things, but as an effort to create and recreate, and as an effort to rebel, as well. Let's take our alienation into our own hands and ask, 'Why?' 'Does it have to be this way?' I do not think so. We need to be subjects of history, even if we cannot totally stop being objects of history, and to be subjects, we need unquestionably to claim history critically. As active participants and real subjects, we can make history only when we are continually critical of our very lives. (p. 199)

Steampunk is therefore not just a tool for decoding, it provides a reinterpretation of society that is underpinned by long-standing philosophical questions and a vision for a different future.

In this regard, even though the texts are situated in the Victorian era and are reflective of a past iteration of the world, they are also postmodern; historical events come to the forefront as not a particular logical story, but as coincidence, an alignment of particular people, ideas, and actions that resulted in a particular reality. Different circumstances could have produced a drastically different future, but social structures that reinscribe inequities still remain. The genre illuminates that "history itself is a quintessentially semiotic process ... It is *enacted* through the mediacy of the sign through which the mind structures its experiences of the real" (Lankshear & McLaren, 1993, p. 1). By reinterpreting history, steampunk literature demonstrates that what we think, what we do, and how we act, right now in the present as in the past, matters and contributes to the creation of an unforeseen future. In this regard, steampunk provides an example of critical literacy in both form and content. In the following section, we present an overview of the young adult steampunk novel *Leviathan*, followed by a breakdown of several themes that are useful for teaching critical literacy. We go in depth into the theme of technology and man's relationship with machines and nature and its ethical and power implications, pointing out opportunities for developing critical literacy and sociological imagination vis-à-vis historicity.

WESTERFELD'S ALTERNATE WORLD OF "CLANKERS" AND "DARWINISTS"

Leviathan is the first novel in Scott Westerfeld's young adult steampunk trilogy. Westerfeld creates an alternate history, rich with possible technologies. The Clanker "Central" Powers are devoted to the mechanical, steam-powered creations typical of the steampunk genre. While, the Darwinist "Allied" Nations have used the discoveries of their history's Darwin to fabricate organisms to serve their purposes. Westerfeld takes as his historical point of departure the assassination of Archduke Franz Ferdinand and his wife, Sophie Duchess of Hohenberg, which triggers the events leading to World War I. As the story opens, the reader is introduced to Aleksander Ferdinand, the son of Archduke Franz Ferdinand and secret heir to the Austro-Hungarian throne.[ii] Alek finds himself running for his life in the middle of the night with Count Volger (his fencing instructor), Otto Klopp (master of mechanics), and two loyal guards in a Stormwalker (a large steel Clanker combat robot). Alek's handlers were assigned to guide him to a secret fortress in the Swiss Alps upon his parents' death. As Alek flees to safety from Austria to Switzerland, Westerfeld turns our attention to a parallel storyline that begins in England.

Deryn Sharp is a teenage tomboy of Scottish descent whose dream is to fly and be free, though her mother and aunt try to force her to act like a proper lady. Deryn flees to London to live with her brother and dresses up like a boy so that she can take the Midshipman's exam and join the British Air Force. During her exam, disguised as Dylan Sharp, she finds herself stranded on a Huxley (a hot air balloon-like flying beast) in the middle of a thunderstorm. She is picked up by the Leviathan, the largest air beast in the British Air Force, and completes her training aboard the ship, where she becomes a Midshipman by outperforming all the young men she works with. While onboard the ship, Dylan/Deryn meets Dr. Barlow[iii] a lady "boffin" (scientist/engineer) who is transporting eggs of some genetically engineered species which will eventually hatch and be used as a weapon against the Clankers.

As the Leviathan flies over the Swiss Alps, transporting Dr. Barlow and the eggs to Constantinople, it is shot down by a Clanker war machine and crashes into the freezing mountain terrain. Alek, worried about the fate of the Leviathan's passengers, sneaks away from Count Volger and Otto Klopp and investigates the wreckage. He revives Deryn, who was unconscious from the crash, but when she is unconvinced that he a Swiss villager as he claims, she sounds the alarm and captures Alek. Soon, the Leviathan comes under attack again by Clankers, and Alek, Volger and Klopp help the crew of the Leviathan repair the ship by creating a beastie/clanker hybrid machine. Both groups then escape together. Although they are from warring nations and opposing backgrounds, throughout the course of the novel, Alek and Dylan/Deryn find in each other an unlikely alliance in a world where both must hide their true selves.

Themes for Critical Literacy

In addition to being a coming of age story that is typical of the young adult genre, *Leviathan* raises numerous themes that are ripe for engaging students' critical and social imaginations. The book highlights gender roles and class struggle prominently throughout, and it raises questions about imperial nations and their sense of exceptionalism. As is typical of steampunk novels, it calls into question man's relationship with technology, but it also raises questions about man's relationship with nature as well. The chart below outlines some of these subplots and the types of critical questioning that can emerge from them. Following this overview, we will present a detailed analysis of the theme of man's relationship with technology and nature to demonstrate how *Leviathan* is useful for encouraging social imagination vis-à-vis historicity.

Theme	*Context*	*Critical Questions*
Gender	Deryn and Dr. Barlow are two strong, clever females, both successful in their professions; yet, Dr. Barlow can openly be female and be highly respected, even powerful, while Deryn must hide her gender, not just her physical body, but also her emotions, voice and posture/walk.	In what ways do the expectations of profession, demeanor and appearance of male and female characters in *Leviathan* challenge traditional gender roles? In what ways do they uphold them? How does the treatment of gender in *Leviathan* reflect or differ from the present state of employment for women in U.S. society and globally?

		How are Deryn's and Dr. Barlow's experiences representational (or not) of contemporary trends in women in science and women in the military?
Class	Alek is an intelligent and refined youth who has been raised as an aristocrat to assume certain cultural dispositions and learn cultural norms and skills appropriate for being royalty. His demeanor, garnered from his upbringing, often reveals who he is even when he tries to hide it. There are numerous moments of conflict or misunderstanding between him and other characters (e.g., Count Volger, Deryn, the crew of the Leviathan, merchants in a marketplace) because of his social class.	How are characters of different social classes distinguished from each other in *Leviathan*? How do their language, skills, and demeanor indicate their membership in particular groups? How do wealth and status work together to provide Alek with advantages over other characters? When are Alek's wealth and status hindrances? In what ways do class distinctions and privileges as characterized in Leviathan reflect or challenge class distinctions in U.S. society and elsewhere?
Imperial Exceptionalism	Although imperial exceptionalism as plot is not at the forefront of the story of *Leviathan*, it is ever present in the context of the book, and is the catalyst for all events that take place. This is especially obvious in the disdain that "Clankers" and "Darwinists" have for each other and their cultures. At times, characters from opposing empires are compelled to cross borders and work together in order to survive, but their relationships are always marked by tension.	How does imperial exceptionalism drive the plot of *Leviathan* and compel the book's characters to act? In what ways does imperial exceptionalism create advantages and disadvantages for the characters individually and as a group? What techniques does Westerfeld use to challenge imperial exceptionalism? In what ways might characters be "let off the hook" for nationalistic hubris?

Man's Relationship with Technology and Nature: Issues of Ethics and Power

As demonstrated above, *Leviathan* is equipped with many themes that are ripe for critical analysis; however, in this chapter, we have opted to focus on the theme of man's relationships with technology and nature to demonstrate how this unique genre can be used to foster new ways of thinking about the course of history, particularly as it pertains to technology. We have chosen this theme because the role of technology is a common and significant theme within stempunk novels – the decline of the age of steam is after all where steampunk departs from history. Typically, steampunk disrupts the technological society without seeking to get rid of technology. It reconsiders the role of technology, and "argues for collaboration between the physicalities of human and machine, affording machinery more respect and dignity – a move that would, presumably, also re-humanise the human operators of machines" (Onion, 2008, p. 147). Westerfeld's books reflect this general trend, but also trouble this notion. By providing readers with the viewpoints of Alek the "Clanker" who favors man's use of machines and Deryn the "Darwinist" who favors man's use of genetically engineered organisms, he draws under scrutiny man's technological prowess and his ability to manipulate nature. Furthermore, the various ways in which different characters engage with technology afford opportunities for critical questioning around ethics and power relationships in man's relationship with the world and people's relationships with each other in society. In *Leviathan,* the borders between nations go beyond geographical points to having scientific and ethical meaning as illustrated through the main characters' relationships with technology and each other. The "Darwinist" Allies have turned to biological fabrication as the future. Based on the experiments of Charles Darwin, life threads (DNA) are used to create beasts that harness the natural defenses perfected in nature by evolution for the purposes of mankind. On the other side of the spectrum the "Clanker" Central Powers seek to improve their mechanical and electrical designs, scoffing the "godless Darwinists."

When Alek and Deryn's paths cross and Alek is taken aboard the Leviathan, the reader is introduced to the tensions between their cultural viewpoints. Alek is disgusted by the Darwinists' fabricated creatures: through his eyes, they are profoundly unnatural and grotesque. He describes them as disfigured, fleshy, veiny, ominous and unpredictable. Deryn, however, feels a kinship with the creatures, and she is sensitive to their emotions and needs as living beings. She works with them as partners in their endeavors. We see this in her adventure on the Huxley, the jellyfish-like flying beast, when she spoke to it soothingly in a moment of crisis and they emerged from the crisis together as partners. She does this with the Leviathan as well, often pressing her skin against the interior of the whale-like beast and feeling for its physiological state. Through Deryn's eyes, we see the beauty of a fabricated ecosystem interacting harmoniously within the Leviathan. Glowworms light the interior of the beast's corridors, fléchette bats protect the beast from threats, fabricated sniffing dogs patrol the beast's outer skin to ensure there are no perforations or hydrogen leaks that might imperil the ship and its inhabitants. On the flipside, Alek feels a kinship with the Clanker machines, while Deryn sees them as dirty, cold, loud and destructive. In a more classic view of technology as inanimate objects to be driven by man, Alek's Stormwalker, the mechanical combat robot in which he and his handles flee after his parents are murdered, is an extension of his body. Steering the machine is not like operating a car. The Stormwalker piloting controls are literally connected to Alek's limbs, and as he moves, so too does the Stormwalker like a marionette. For Alek, learning to control the Stormwalker has much to do with controlling himself and perfecting his ability to control the machine, technology does not function without man as the operator, and with technology, man is elevated – operating the Stormwalker makes Alek feel powerful.

Westerfeld's text can be interpreted as offering two opposing positions – one that privileges man's relationship with nature, while the other privileges man's relationship with machines. By presenting alternative viewpoints and then creating a situation where the Darwinists and Clankers must join technological forces, the text calls into question the superiority of either of these viewpoints. The debate that is raised through the intersections of the characters' different perspectives is a longstanding social debate that is evident in the controversies surrounding cloning, genetically engineered organisms, lab-grown replacement body parts, and stem cell research (among many other topics). Alek's disgust raises questions such as, "How entitled is man to manipulate nature?" "What are the benefits and drawbacks of experimenting with living organisms?" And at the same time, Deryn's harmonious relationship with the beasties also raises the question of whether genetic engineering might actually be a better way of living harmoniously with nature than is typical in a society that relies on mechanical technology. Similarly, Deryn's disdain for Clanker machines creates opportunities to question the ethics of man's use of mechanical technology, its role in war and destruction, and its impact on the environment. Topics such as industrial impact on the environment, global warming, consumption of natural resources, arms races throughout history and more. Questions that might emerge from this are: "How does man's use of mechanical technology impact the natural world?" "To what extent does mechanical technology contribute to the perpetuation of war and crisis?" Through their alternate perspectives Deryn and Alek allow for rich debates about man's use of technology and his relationship with the natural world.

When the above theme is looked at through the lenses of gender and class, even more critical questions arise. For instance, "Why is it that Deryn, who is female, has an empathetic relationship with the beasties, while Alek, who is male, feels kinship with machines? In what ways do these relationships reinforce stereotypical gender roles?" And, "Why is that Dr. Barlow's relationship with the beasties is different than Deryn's? What does it mean that Dr. Barlow, who comes from a more privileged social class, is the fabricator of the beasties and yet, she owns a pet thylacine, which is not fabricated and extremely rare?"[iv] In typical steampunk style, *Leviathan* "problematizes not only the dreams and ambitions of humankind, but humans' ability to maintain control over their environment, to fulfill their destiny, and to embody their national identity" (Miller & Van Riper, 2011, p. 91). When shot through with additional critical lenses of gender and class, "readers are encouraged to uncover implicit messages in texts and to examine all aspects of discourse" in the text (McDaniel, 2004, p. 475).

CONCLUSION: STEAMPUNK IN THE CLASSROOM

Through critical questioning described above, with a steampunk text as an object of analysis, teacher and students can make connections to pressing social issues that are just as relevant now as they were a century ago. This encourages social imagination vis-à-vis historicity because it forces yet another crucial question – "Why has society not changed all that much in regards to these themes?" By recognizing the past in the present, teachers and students can then begin asking questions about what needs to change. Critical literacy in this regard can accomplish what Behrman (2006) claims it should, that is, "encourage teachers and students to collaborate to understand how texts work, what texts intend to do to the world, and how social relations can be critiqued and reconstructed" (p. 491). Furthermore, as a tool for critical literacy, steampunk helps to demonstrate, in the words of Shor (1999)

> though language is fateful in teaching us what kind of people to become and what kind of society to make, discourse is not destiny. We can redefine ourselves and remake society, if we choose, through alternative rhetoric and dissident projects. This is where critical literacy begins, for questioning power relations, discourses, and identities in a world not yet finished, just, or humane. (n.p.)

As a next step, teachers and students might engage in creating what Behrman (2006) calls a "countertext" which could reinterpret the text from a non-mainstream perspective. In the lesson that follows, we offer one possibility for doing this in the classroom.

NOTES

[i] According to Behrman (2006), the field of critical literacy is characterized as addressing the following priorities:
  1. *domination*: language and symbols maintain social and political oppression
  2. *access*: literacy instruction should provide access to dominant discourse, while providing legitimacy for nondominant discourses
  3. *diversity*: language use contributes to the formation of social identities
  4. *design*: learners select from a range of signs and learn to use them strategically.
  In order to achieve social justice, he says, all of these must be integrated into pedagogical practice.

[ii] In reality, Archduke Ferdinande had three surviving children, none of whom were considered legitimate heirs to the throne because their mother was not of dynastic lineage. In the novels, Alek's father petitioned the pope to approve his marriage to his wife, a commoner, therefore entitling their child to assume the throne.

[iii] Nora Darwin Barlow was the actual granddaughter of Charles Darwin, but she was not a scientist.

[iv] A thylacine or "Tasmanian tiger" is a dog-like animal that was native to Australia, Tasmania and New Guinea and would have been alive during World War I but has since been hunted to extinction.

REFERENCES

Bean, T.W. & Moni, K. (2003). Developing students' critical literacy: Exploring identity construction in young adult fiction. *Journal of Adolescent & Adult Literacy, 46*(8), 638-648.
Behrman, E.H. (2006). Teaching about language, power, and text: A review of classroom practices that support critical literacy. *Journal of Adolescent & Adult Literacy, 49*(6), 490-498.
Caro, M. & Jeunet, J.-P. (Directors) (1995). *The city of lost children* [Motion Picture]. France: Union Générale Cinématographique.
Denzin, N. (2003). Performing [auto]ethnography politically. *The Review of Education, Pedagogy and Cultural Studies, 25*, 257-278.
Falksen, G. D. (2009). *Steampunk 101*. Macmillan, Tor.com. Retrieved from http://www.tor.com/blogs/2009/10/steampunk-101
Freire, P. (1985). *The politics of education: Culture, power, and liberation*. Westport, CT: Bergin & Garvey.
Gaimon, N. (Writer). (1996). *Neverwhere* [Television Series]. UK: British Broadcasting Company.
Kress, T. M. (2011). High achievement in an unaccredited, 'failing' school. *The Journal of the Imagination in Language Learning and Teaching, 9*, 23-29.
Lankshear, C. & McLaren, P. L. (1993). Introduction. In C. Lankshear & P. L. McLaren (Eds.), *Critical literacy: Politics, praxis and the postmodern* (pp. 1-56). Albany, NY: SUNY Press.
Luke, A. (2002). Beyond science and ideology critique: Development in critical discourse analysis. *Annual Review of Applied Linguistics, 22*, 96-110.
McDaniel, C. (2004). Critical literacy: A questioning stance and the possibility for change. *The Reading Teacher, 57*(5), 472-481.
Miller, C. J., & Van Riper, A. (2011). Blending genres, bending time: Steampunk on the Western frontier. *Journal of Popular Film & Television, 39*(2), 84-92.
Mills, C. W. (1959). *The sociological imagination*. Oxford, UK: Oxford University Press.
Nevins, J. (2008). Introduction: The 19th century roots of steampunk. In A. VanDermeer, J. R. Lansdale, I. R. MacLeod, M. Gentle, & M. Brown (Eds.), *Steampunk* (pp. 3-11). San Francisco, CA: Tachyon Publications.
Oatman-Stanford, H. (2012). There goes the neighborhood: Mobile Victorian house sets sail for the desert. *Collectors Weekly*. Retrieved from http://www.collectorsweekly.com/articles/there-goes-the-neighborhood-mobile-victorian-house-sets-sail-for-desert/
Onion, R. (2008). Reclaiming the machine: An introductory look at Steampunk in everyday practice. *Neo-Victorian Studies, 1*(1), 138-163.
Pagliassotti, D. (2013). Love and the machine: Technology and human relationships in steampunk romance and erotica. In J. A. Taddeo & C. J. Miller (Eds.), *Steaming into a Victorian future: A steampunk anthology* (pp. 65-88). Lanham, MD: Scarecrow Press.
Pershon, M. (2013). Useful troublemakers: Social Retrofuturism in the Steampunk novels of Gail Carriger and Cherie Priest. In J. A. Taddeo & C. J. Miller (Eds.), *Steaming into a Victorian future: A steampunk anthology* (pp. 21-41). Lanham, MD: Rowman & Littlefield.
Proyas, A. (Director). (2004). *Sky captain and the world of tomorrow* [Motion Picture]. USA: Paramount Pictures.
Proyas, A. (Director). (1998). *Dark city* [Motion Picture]. USA: New Line Cinema.
Rawlins, S. (2009). The next big thing: Steampunk. *The Hub*. Yalsa, 2009. Retrieved from http://www.yalsa.ala.org/thehub/2012/10/09/the-next-big-thing-steampunk/
Shor, I. (1999). What is critical literacy? *Journal for Pedagogy, Pluralism & Practice, 1*(4). Retrieved from: http://www.lesley.edu/journal-pedagogy-pluralism-practice/ira-shor/critical-literacy/
Taddeo, J. A. (2013). Corsets of steel: Steampunk's reimagining of Victorian femininity. In J. A. Taddeo & C. J. Miller (Eds.), *Steaming into a Victorian future: A steampunk anthology* (pp. 43-64). Lanham, MD: Scarecrow Press.

Tanenbaum, J., Tanenbaum, K., & Wakkary, R. (2012). Steampunk as design fiction. In *CHI '12: Proceedings of the SIGCHI Conference on Human Factors in Computing Systems* (pp. 1583-1592). New York, NY: AMC Digital Library.

Thomas, P. L. (2013). *Science fiction and speculative fiction: Challenging genres.* Rotterdam, The Netherlands: Sense.

Westerfeld, S. (2009). *Leviathan.* New York, NY: Simon Pulse.

Whedon, J. (Creator). (2002). *Firefly* [Television Series]. USA: 20th Century Fox.

Zigo, D., & Moore, M. T. (2004). Science fiction: Serious reading, critical reading. *The English Journal, 94*(2), 85-90.

JUSTIN PATCH

11. SCIENCE AND FICTION

A Polemic on the Role of Imaginative Fiction in Civics and the Economy of Innovation

ABSTRACT

In the wake of the recession and attendant conservatism, a pivot towards STEM educational initiatives and professional and pre-professional degrees poses serious challenges to sustaining the humanities. But to reduce the humanities is to silence critical thought and quell voices necessary for democratic and civic development. The humanities have contributed to the development of modernity and technical innovation, along with articulating society's most cogent critiques. They are essential in constructing a polity that is just, equitable, sustainable and humane. Science fiction and imaginative literature bridge the sciences and humanities in ways that teach young minds to think both expansively and ethically. Sci-fi can be a tool to teach STEM alongside ethical innovation, critical inquiry, and equitable policy, and can be a catalyst for trans-disciplinary cooperation and educational reform. The historical links between science fiction and invention are also a weapon against critics who would turn the academy into vocational training and eliminate critical thought from the curriculum. A humane future is dependent on the skills that both STEM and the humanities teach, and sci-fi can be a starting point for a holistic pedagogy in science and civics.

INTRODUCTION

The humanities are hurtling towards a vortex that places us on the wrong side of state and institutional budget cuts, political and economic rhetoric, and academic infighting. We are under assault from within and outside the academy, and in the teeth of public criticism that threatens our existence and questions our relevance. Among the humanities, our *raison d'etre* is disagreed upon: what does it mean to teach, produce and research culture, art, literature, history, thought, ideas and language? And what purposes – concrete, material and teleological, abstract and hypothetical – do these endeavors serve (Readings, 1996; Apple, 2001)? How do we balance concrete, quantifiable goals with civic concerns, scholarly production, and intellectual ideals? How do our teaching and scholarship simultaneously fit the rigors of the academic world and demonstrate our relevance to skeptical public and governmental spheres? In the greater university, the humanities are often underfunded, lines are closed, not renewed, or filled with adjuncts and lecturers, and budgets are reduced. Outside of the academy, state, local, and national governments are engaged in a re-prioritizing of educational monetary allocations, many of which are aimed at promoting science, technology, engineering and math (STEM) and professional degrees (medical, law, business, economics, etc.). The driving force behind these changes is overwhelmingly economic: the idea that STEM is what drives the economy, creates jobs and improves the conditions in which we live (although both Apple and Giroux make the case that these are equally ideological). With innovation on the minds of those whose task it is to produce increased return on investment, STEM and professional programs overshadow the creative, critical, contextual, and ethical complexities that are the strong suit of the humanities. In this politicized hand-wringing, where the concrete demands of economy, jobs, and growth reign supreme, the humanities are eclipsed by STEM, professional and entrepreneurial studies, and at times degraded as irrelevant and outdated, often by strategically referencing the most esoteric aspects of the humanities and ignoring relevant bits.

In the popular mind, the domains of innovation, invention and creation – and therefore job growth and economic prosperity – belong squarely to the empirical, technical, and entrepreneurial pursuits that STEM represents. This false dichotomy between the creativity, subjectivity, and playfulness of the humanities and the concreteness of STEM and entrepreneurship needs to be challenged. Critical, comprehensive, creative thought – the strength of the humanities – has a vigorous life outside of the mind, and is responsible for innovations that have transformed life as we know it. The humanities have provided cautionary tales and critical insight into both real and potential problems of technology, science, business, law, legislation, regulation, and a host of other material issues that we face daily. Humanistic study is absolutely necessary if the inventiveness that created modern marvels, sustains life, and improves the living conditions of so many is to continue into a more humane, equitable, and dignified future.

The humanities present a different model of learning and cognitive development from STEM (Arum & Roska, 2011), but that does not mean that we confine our argument to educational and developmental theories and vacate the public discourse concerning economic modernization, scientific development, and innovation. Nor should skills like advanced critical thinking and analysis, social theorizing and cultural criticism be sequestered from conversations concerning economics, innovation, and development. Contrary to much of the present public discourse, the humanities contribute a great deal to innovation and civic life, often in ways that are overlooked by both public and educational policy. Groundbreaking inventions, new economic models and cutting-edge re-purposing are as connected to fiction, creativity and the imagination as they are to the lab and workshop. Before everyday occurrences like wireless communication, aeronautical travel, invisibility, cybernetics, and organ transplant were realized, they were brought to life in fiction. They were the product of the creative mind journeying through both contemporary problems and those yet to be encountered, presciently presenting applications, solutions, pitfalls, and ethical quandaries. These flights of fancy are the province of the humanities, which among other things teach students to think with limitless possibility, beyond present boundaries and confines (how often have we heard the mandate to 'think outside the box'?).

Far from being childish, unchallenging, and unproductive, the humanities are now, more than ever, a necessity if we are to cultivate thinkers who will continue a path towards an intelligent, humane, equitable, responsible, and inclusive future. The criticality and critical pedagogy taught through the humanities is necessary to meet the challenges inherent in modernity – rapid demographic shifts, technological expanse, resource shortages, privacy in the internet age, new forms of terror and fear, surveillance in the drone age, new and previously unimagined social formations – in democratic, dialogic, polymorphic, and sustainable ways. Technology, innovation, economy and progress without criticality are potentially harmful, pernicious, unequal, dehumanizing and dangerous. In a similar fashion, the creativity inherent in scientific research methods – the formulation of incremental experiments to solve hypotheses or query results and methods – is often excluded from discussions about how scientists, engineers and entrepreneurs are educated and trained. The humanistic element necessary to STEM and professional education is often disregarded or minimized in these empirical, goal-oriented, industrial, and pragmatic endeavors. However, there is ample room for cross-communication, mutual understanding, and greater cooperation between qualitative-speculative and quantitative-analytical methods and practices in the pursuit of new ways to envision, construct and advance the future. The critical imagination opened up by science fiction is another dimension of critical pedagogy, one that extends critiques of institutions of systemic intolerance, injustice and oppression (Green, 1995; Rautins & Ibrahim, 2012) and can give careful critical considerations to formations on the near and far horizons of our contemporary moment.

In a compelling synthesis of thinkers as diverse as John Dewey, Emily Dickinson and Hannah Arendt, Maxine Greene (1995) theorizes that the imagination enables new beginnings that break with repetition, routine and conformity. It is a passageway into the genuinely new, what Frankfurt School theorist Herbert Marcuse considers an authentic, life: one that recognizes and realizes its potential, embraces embeddedness within social life, is free to become a Subject, and admits obligation to conscience and consciousness (Freire's *conscientizacao*). When placed in conjunction with Paulo Freire's notion of critical pedagogy – one that critiques the structures of injustice and speaks and enacts truth to power – science fiction as pedagogy creates a model for critique of myriad new beginnings brought forth daily. While Freire (as well as McLaren, Apple, Giroux and a host of others) rightly emphasizes a critique of the present – capitalism, neo-liberalism, centralized state control, dehumanizing educational policy, and fanaticism – in a world defined by speed (Virilio, 2006) and innovation, it behooves educators to also teach a critique of the future. Science fiction offers not only a lesson in new beginnings and the exercise of thinking beyond boundaries and conventions, but the opportunity for students to critically and non-ideologically contemplate institutions, inventions, and formations that do not yet exist. While critical pedagogy of the present and its maladies is an undeniable necessity, a critical pedagogy of the future can pre-emptively combat injustice before it becomes entrenched or bolstered by new creations, policies and potentialities. It can fuse the fierce momentum of STEM and entrepreneurship with the critical imagination of the humanities into dialogue towards responsible innovation, humane policy and deepening of civic awareness and inclusive process. Speculative fiction can also move towards normalizing the politics of refusal (Marcuse, 1991) and a critique of unreflective technological optimism.

To facilitate integration of the sciences and the humanities on both a secondary and post-secondary level three distinct tasks are needed. The first is to join the humanities and the sciences theoretically and provide a skeletal outline for the development of correlated curricula (in modules that join these methods in primary through secondary education, and trans-disciplinary course development for post-secondary and graduate education), university research clusters, and symposia for academics and professionals. The second is the development of a public discourse that promotes the existing educational research concerning the benefits of the humanities to critical thinking, civics, and ethical innovation. As Paulo Friere reminds us, ideologies in the absence of doubt, regardless of their intent, are dangerous (1970, p. 23). This extends to innovation, policy and even the creation of economy. Establishment of public discourse involves advocacy and transparent curricular experimentation that can be used for policy reform and public relations that emphasize civic benefit (see also Apple, 2001). The third is to turn these two ideas back towards the academy, proving that humanities education provides a social service and common good that meets the objectives of higher education – in short renewing our mission and mandate in light of current concerns about what an education must do for students and society as agents of social change and institutional reformation.[i] While a number of institutions emphasize ethical education, clarity is sometimes needed on what exactly this entails and how civics is or should be taught in their curriculum and as a lived practice.[ii]

One starting point for these three developments is science/speculative fiction, which inhabits the intersections of literature, imagination, criticality, science and technology. As a practice steeped in informed creative writing, critical and analytical thinking, and intense imagination, sci-fi is an opportunity for introducing young readers to speculative thinking about science and society, pairing ethics and innovation, breaking through conceptual barriers, and bridging disciplinary gaps.[iii] With its radical utopias and dark dystopias, sci-fi envisions the unbounded possibilities of technology and the human capacity deal with it, to use invention for common good or despotic destruction. Crucially, it puts the dynamics inherent in technological advancement into ethical dialogue with the human consequences. While priming the mind to think on un-striated planes, it also grounds thought in civic and communal life. Beyond personal morality, sci-fi places creativity into dialogue with the ethics of potentiality, contemplating how advancement – economic, scientific, and entrepreneurial – can both benefit and harm society. Science fiction has the potential to accomplish a great deal within curriculum: it can be used to sharpen technical, social, creative, and ethical minds. It can be the beginning for a pedagogy that simultaneously teaches innovation along with the democratic ideal of *e pluribus unum*. This is what Sandra Stotsky (1994) labels as civic literature, something that affects perception, performs real work in the world and serves a didactic purpose (in the largest meaning of the word). John Dewey saw art as opening up avenues and potentials first in the mind and then in action. Paulo Freire insists that reading as a cultural-political action moves outward – from the word to the world, from understanding the page to comprehending the social order and directing social action. I propose, following Dewey, Stotsky and Freire, that science fiction can serve to open avenues between the mind and materiality and into the future. It can 'release the imagination' (Greene, 1995) to a future that breaks the shackles of exclusion and exploitation and performs vital civic and cultural work.

In the remainder of this essay, I argue that science fiction can be included in secondary and post-secondary curricula to tie the sciences and the humanities together in the project of creating critically aware citizens while meeting an all-too-common rhetorical point of fostering innovative technological thinking and economic growth. On the secondary and post-secondary level it can foster the very effects that have eluded policy makers and are coveted by politicians, communities and nations: ethical innovation. It can also serve as a hub for interdisciplinary teaching and research on the collegiate level and foster the construction of cohesive curricula in primary and secondary education. By advancing our role in technological and economic development through external discourse and interaction with our peers, we can craft a cogent argument for reformed curriculum that appeals to a wider student body, preserves what is best about the humanities and cultivates our collective future, while maintaining a critical eye on the human implications of growth, development, progress, and society itself.

NEGATIVE PRESS

Unfortunate comments about the worthlessness of the humanities are well documented and have already fostered robust discussion, but it is important to contemplate the negative rhetoric so as to defend legitimate and necessary curricular changes and guard against unfounded dismissals. Many of these negative sentiments are based on erroneous assumptions and spurious anecdotes, and are done for cynical political gains. However, they represent an aspect of public opinion that haunts many polities, and one which is worthy of close analysis. Advocates for reformed, creative, cutting-edge, pluralistic educational practices can make cogent counter-arguments by understanding the roots of this negativity. As Apple (2001) reminds us, there is no such thing as neutral knowledge, or neutral pedagogy,[iv] and to advocate for a reformed curriculum is a cultural-political action that requires knowledge of the opposition's rhetoric and a well-crafted counter argument.

The proliferation of recent adverse sentiment is well represented in a series of comments made by high-profile politicians, most infamously Florida Governor Rick Scott and former presidential hopeful Rick Santorum. In a 2012 interview with radio talk show host Marc Bernier, then-governor Scott advocated for reorganizing the Florida higher education system in favor of what he deemed to be job-creating or job-ready fields. He characterized anthropology in particular as irrelevant to students and to the well-being of the state of Florida. In the interview, Scott states,

> They [Florida's college students] need education in areas where they can get jobs. [...] We don't need a lot more anthropologists in this state. It's a great degree if people want to get it, but we don't need them here. [...] That's what our kids need to focus their attention on [science, technology, engineering and math] so that when they get out of college they can get a job.[v]

Made in the context of talking about his plan for correcting Florida's ailing economy, Scott inferred that those with non-science, business, technical, or professional degrees do not create jobs, fix anything, or perform necessary services; they will not proceed directly from graduation to a job, and have no effect on the economy. They are therefore unnecessary. As steward of Florida's budget, it was incumbent upon Scott to be practical with hard-earned tax dollars, which necessitated streamlining higher education and eliminating waste, perceived or otherwise, anthropology included.

A more extreme example is Rick Santorum's rant against education as an elitist, liberal, brainwashing conspiracy. In comments made at an appearance at First Baptist Church in Naples, Florida, Santorum claimed that higher education was "indoctrinating kids into Left-wing ideology" and claimed that 62% of students who enter college with strong religious belief leave without it.[vi] I doubt that he was including physics, pre-med, accounting, and mechanical engineering in this salvo. He also accused Barack Obama of 'snobbery,' because Obama stated a desire for every student in the US to attend college.[vii]

While Scott and Santorum are not the only public figures with these convictions, and there are plenty with opposing opinions, they do serve as bellwethers for an influential segment of policy makers and the public.[viii] In the eyes of many, college exists on a continuum: on one extreme it is a meal ticket where one learns practical skills that lead to job placement, lucrative, secure careers and social advancement; on the other, a place where hedonism runs rampant and the lessons are esoteric and impractical, if done at all. On these opposing poles, STEM, and professional training reside in the former camp, creativity and free thought in the latter (area studies, philosophy, classics, gender studies), with fields like the arts, history, sociology and languages lingering somewhere in the middle. All too often, studies of liberation, valorization, ethics and civics are dismissed from their place in studies of science, technology, business and medicine. The vast connections between the humanities and the economic and social advancement of the community, state and nation are not even in the conversation. Neither is the role of the humanities in improving the human condition. For both Scott and Santorum, there is no relationship between creative, critical thought and skilled expression and betterment of the individual and society. What they blatantly ignore is the harm done by a robust economy that benefits only the few.

Attitudes like these have created smaller faculties, fewer classes and job opportunities, class sizes that hinder sustained critical and dialogical engagement, and a dearth of public figures ready and willing to understand creative education and defend its place in modern society. It also perpetuates the bland yet malignant repetition and reproduction of neo-liberalism, irresponsible consumerism, and privatization of both knowledge and access. While it is easy to bemoan these compounding events and their wide-reaching effects, lamentation is neither productive nor useful. A strategy is needed to provide humanists with the tools necessary to mount a concerted campaign to maintain our position as a vibrant part of our communities. A sustained and serious debate about our present and future that operates on multiple levels is necessary for the creative, critical elements in education to be presented, preserved and improved.[ix] Given the rumblings among educators about the lack of critical and ethical education in the classroom, and the tepid reception to overt social justice curriculum within some departments and institutions, perhaps it is time to re-inject the idea of civics by tying the critical strength inherent in our teaching to STEM and professional initiatives. In a pluralistic, postmodern age, the very question of ethics and civics is fraught, but an ethical education in the 21st century is necessarily different from the grand narratives of the past. It demands multi-disciplinary knowledge, and involves debate rather than dictate (Kincheloe and Steinberg). In this pursuit, the links between humanistic method and scientific knowledge become obvious, and the need for this debate extends many levels, from secondary education through graduate work. Humanistic method, when applied to the sciences, technology and business, provides a measure of ethical and civic consideration imperative for equitable innovation and progress.[x]

Although there is an irrefutable need to defend the role of the humanities, there must also be severe self assessment and reflection. Established procedures for research should be reconsidered, new scholarly priorities and methods identified, and unproductive distinctions erased.[xi] By critically reflecting on the past and present, we can begin to discuss exactly what we provide to our institutions, students and communities, now and in the future. The outcome of these debates should be multi-faceted, with theoretical and abstract elements (teaching critical thinking, civic engagement, and global perspective, which are part of many university mission statements) accompanied by material, ethical, and pragmatic concerns.[xii] As Apple (2001) tells us, we must present practical solutions to real world problems in conjunction with teaching as a political act.

To accomplish this, separate types of debate are required. First, we need a rhetoric that is fully prepared to be public – concise, to the point, jargon-free, persuasive, and able to exist and compete in the same air space as Scott, Santorum, and similar critics. Even if we chose not to compete with the unsubtle, uninformed negativism of Santorum, the economic concerns of Scott are understandably valid, even if we vehemently disagree with his solutions. There is credible evidence to refute Scott's oversimplification that business, science and technology equal jobs, but it needs to be communicated in straight talk through similar channels.[xiii] Thinkers like Henry Giroux and Jurgen Habermas have long been dedicated to public intellectualism and the maintenance of a public sphere where critical issues are examined.[xiv] On the issue of pedagogy, reform and advocacy, as well as discontent, there is no such thing as too much dialogue. If Jonathan Kozol's case study of East St. Louis and Robert Coles' analyses of students in Roxbury continue to speak to us today, then each voice can add critical dimension and offer insight to the debate. This debate can serve as guidance for experimental curricular developments that emphasize creative thinking and activities like science and robotics competitions accompanied by critical discussion and reflection on the potential uses, benefits and dangers of innovation. Questions of equitability, benefit, misuse, environmental impact and socio-cultural effect (in other words a consideration of the holistic totality social life) must be a part of any STEM oriented curriculum and praxis.

To compete in the court of public opinion, a clear, holistic and empirical argument for the creative humanistic curriculum must be presented in ways that speak in specific terms to the local, state-wide, national and global. This necessitates highlighting the practical, material affects of the humanities, and deeper participation in the critical conversation about the rat race of productivity, academic and economic. However, that is not all negative, and it is far from the total acquiescence claimed by academics who decry the corporatization of the university (Readings, 1997; Giroux, 2007).[xv] Being socially relevant, practical, or grounded is not automatically acquiescing to neo-liberalism, and can be integrated into our educational, institutional and personal ideologies. Striving to make concrete contributions to society requires an ethos not dissimilar to the hustle of productivity: self-sacrifice, punishingly long work weeks, intense attention to the work of colleagues (meaningful debates are often competitive), severe judgment and reassessment of methods and approaches, concrete proposals for further work, etc. Social justice is never easy work and requires a praxis that is out in the street, conscious of relevance rather than finality, and one that provides concrete proposals to real issues (Kress, 2011; Apple, 2001). We may not want to slavishly mimic STEM and professional curriculum in their procedure or expectation, but there are vital lessons to be gleaned from their techniques of survival and proliferation, especially in public perception.[xvi] If we continue to scoff at the thought of making our scholarship and purpose relevant and accessible to a greater public and our peers in empirical fields, loss of funding will become the least of our worries.

Second, we need to emphasize the intangible benefits of critical and creative thought that are provided by the humanities. While the material affects are persuasive in the realm of public policy, the idea of teaching civics, democracy and the ethics of living are the equivalent of soft power. The current economic situation, while having damaging financial and psychological effects, can also provide an opportunity to emphasize these necessary components of education. The humanities have both ethics and civics implicit and explicit within them, and a more overt effort must be made to overtly tether the benefits of these intellectual challenges to greater social benefits in innovation and humane development. It is time to discuss these ethics and the demands of a democratic society with immense power and impact. This concerns the kind of moral quagmires exhibited in works of fiction from the likes of Ayn Rand, Margret Atwood, Isaac Asimov, H. G. Wells, Philip K. Dick, and George Orwell. Their imagined inventions, potentials, and problems model the type of thinking that is essential in preparing students for the future: thinking beyond boundary and without restraint, but also with the mind turned towards the impact of change on society, utopia and dystopia. While civic and moral issues are deeply relevant to STEM, they are rarely included in STEM curricula, and should be. However, since the type of intellectual work required to model both mechanical and ethical quandaries requires differing methodologies, the humanities have an aperture to contribute significantly to thinking about the political economy of innovation and discussing its immense implications for society.

Third, we need a dialogue within the academy about defining our purpose and mission, and stating what students and colleagues gain from our scholarship and teaching at the intersection of economy, innovation and civic life.[xvii] It is assumed that the humanities are obligatory for a university to provide a complete education – one that nurtures the individual and community, instead of just skill and competency. The humanities are about far more than innovation and should be wary of being hijacked by neo-liberalism. However, discussion of new technology can benefit from discussion of *2001: A Space Odyssey* and *Jurassic Park*. In contemplating where and how the humanities proceed from here, it is essential that we develop a higher education-centered discourse that emphasizes the contributions – past, present and future – of the humanities. As business and politics teaches us, having talking points at the ready for given situations is never a bad idea. While the key points for English may be different from European Studies, African-American History, or Women and Gender Studies, it is essential that we prepare together, learn from dialogue across disciplinary lines and draw strength, inspiration and hope from expanding coalitions.

THINKING ABOUT THINKING

In the remainder of this essay, I will elaborate on three proposals for thinking and talking about the future of the humanities using sci-fi and speculative fiction as a model for revamping curriculum. In re-shaping ourselves, we can begin cultivating innovative paths forward in research, teaching and multi-disciplinary cooperation (Kress, 2011). The first proposal deals with public relations between the humanities and the population at large. This is largely anecdotal, and demonstrates three points. First, that some of the world's greatest innovators, from Leonardo Da Vinci to Steve Jobs, drew crucial inspiration from the arts, literature, and creative endeavors. Common narratives like these solidify the connection between the humanities and material progress, innovation and creation, justice and equality.

The second is what Frankfurt School philosopher Herbert Marcuse (1991 and 1978) theorizes: that the study of art – literary, visual, musical, choreographic – makes the impossible possible and in that endeavor expressive culture changes reality. Art opens up the imaginary dimension in ways that precede and direct the capacity of empirical and material reality and can play a critical role in directing social action and change. If not for Jules Verne, Isaac Asimov, Star Trek, Stanley Kubrick, or J. K. Rowling, what inventions and potentials might never have been conceived, let alone brought to fruition? The imagination, the playgrounds of the humanities, is as vital to innovative processes as testable hypotheses, flow charts, equations and formulae. By expanding the idea of creativity across the whole university and positioning the humanities as the first step in the process of experimentation, we perform due diligence to a history of free-thinkers who shaped our world. It is crucial that we maintain the space necessary for that process to continue with the added caveat that the ethical issues embedded in the arts are of utmost necessity.

The third proposal is for greater communication within the university between the imaginative pursuits and the empirical ones. In my encounters with university research scientists, many have been surprisingly candid about the importance of some facet of the humanities to their research and thinking (and dreaming), as well as to their sanity.[xviii] Some facet of the humanities lies at the inception of a number of scientific, mechanical, medical and entrepreneurial pursuits (a few key examples are discussed below). This provides an opening for dialogue, joint participation, and coordinated research and teaching that will combine the imaginative and empirical in fresh research and curricular pursuits. These can be as diverse as combining robotics, computer science and speculative fiction curricula, performance and cybernetics ethnography, the medical anthropology of alien autopsies, and social science fiction and ficto-criticism. By re-conceptualizing our role in the process of knowledge production, as well as pursuing multi-disciplinary studies to their fullest (in a modified Renaissance model), we maintain and enhance our role within the educational system, increase our potential to be forward-looking, and contribute to socially responsible future work of both materiality and imagination. Science fiction is an ideal place to start with this type of curricular redevelopment and disciplinary realignment because of the emphasis on technology in many institutions, sci-fi's myriad forms (film, TV, graphic novel, books, e-books, theater, dance and music), its appeal and obvious application to a wide array of disciplines, and its multiple levels (there are quality examples of sci-fi that are appropriate for nearly every reading level).

OPENING THE IMAGINATION

While there are a plethora of facets to the humanities and a humanistic education, science fiction will serve as my foil for educational reform. In sci-fi, the full range of human thought is exercised – material, imaginary, supernatural, theological, ethical, and psychological – and radical notions are realized. From fictitious expressive culture grows everything from wireless communication, inter-galactic and undersea travel, cybernetics, artificial intelligence, psychic manipulation, and corporeal regeneration. In it are the seeds of human kindness and scepters of inhuman wrath. More than simply depicting marvelous creations and situations, sci-fi also grapples with the ethical issues that they create, making space for dialogues that are not necessarily part of the curriculum otherwise, but are important for civic and democratic pedagogy. Many humanists include some aspect of fiction in our classrooms, making this aspect of cultural study and pedagogy widely applicable to a general argument about the vitality and potential inherent in alternate, popular forms of literature and their application to societal well-being.

Fiction is more than the wanderings of a singular imagination translated into idea, character, narrative, language, image and sound. It is a world unto itself, a universe of possibilities painstakingly hatched in the mind and shared, before it can become reality. It is in this exercise – in oral narrative, print and graphic novel, abstract expression, music, or film and digital creation – that we critique the present, see where our future might lead, and where our pasts illuminate paths and pitfalls. In teaching fiction in its many forms we demonstrate the most enduring figments of human creation, and exercise methods essential to envisioning and constructing the future.

Philosopher Herbert Marcuse viewed the study of art (he uses literature for his case study) as a necessity in progress, human liberation and the affirmation of life. For Marcuse, the imagination was the key to promoting the art of life: enjoyment, fulfillment, freedom and sensual experience.

> This [the novels of Samuel Beckett and Rolf Hochhut's *Der Stellvertreter*] is the setting in which the great human achievements in science, medicine, technology take place; the efforts to save and ameliorate life are the sole promise in the disaster. The willful play with fantastic possibilities, the ability to act with good conscience, *contra naturam*, to experiment with men and things, to convert illusion into reality and fiction into truth, testify the extent to which Imagination has become an instrument of progress. And it is one which, like others in the established societies, is methodologically abused. (Marcuse, 1964, pp. 247-248, italics in the original)

To Marcuse, the imagination, the internal creation of what is not yet existential, renders the new possible and actively alters the existing order. It is capable of transforming individuals from interpellated creations of one-dimensional society, caught in regimes of discipline, efficiency, and mechanization, into unique forms of subjectivity that are genuinely new. Literature that calls repression by its name and breeds the power of estrangement in the reader holds the immense potential to be revolutionary (given the myriad problems with the US electoral system, growing inequality, and social discontent, teaching classical democracy and the social contract is revolutionary). Pronouncing the revolutionary nature of the humanities is not necessarily a prime selling point in our current environment, but it is important to note three things. First that the idea of revolution is not roundly rejected by the establishment, as the digital revolution and the Arab Spring were both broadly welcomed. Much that is branded as a scientific revolution has a positive connotation, and one that infers at least a modicum of positive progress. A revolution that leads to humane concerns in science, business and technology might also receive such accolades. Second is what historian George Lipsitz calls "the long fetch of history" (2007, pp. vii-viii). Social and societal transformations are like waves; they begin as ripples and combine with myriad environmental factors thousands of miles from where we experience their arrival. The revolutionary nature of transforming curriculum to accommodate alternative literacies, experimental pedagogies, and inclusive ethics that embrace the proposal of improving life for everyone is necessarily a long-durational project. The radical hope of Freire, and Apple's idea of hope as a resource, point us in the direction of patience, persistence and tenacity in creating change without sacrificing expectance. Third, after the upheaval of the economic crisis and the rebirth of public scrutiny of capitalism and neo-liberalism, it is possible that revolution has overcome its Cold War stigma and is ready for rebirth.

By applying Marcuse's theories to the links between the creative mind and the material world, we come to the conclusion that progress happens in the imagination before the lab or the shop. Progress is a dream before it is a product, experiment, or policy. While art does not translate directly into material transformation, it makes the critical first step by retaining and expanding the dream of fulfillment and the ideology of human potential. The arduous work of writing, recording, animating, and depicting these visions is to be respected and nurtured, as is their study and perpetuation, for they present the future before it can be physically realized. In this pursuit, the works of Jules Verne, George Orwell, Martin Caidin, and Isaac Asimov stand as a few of the myriad examples of how sci-fi presaged actuality. Jules Verne's visions of the future, like submarine travel, are well known (in particular chronicled in the work of Arthur B. Evans). Scientists from biologist Jacques Cousteau to aerial pioneers Goddard and Sikorsky and engineer Marconi cite Verne as inspiration. Most recently, *The Economist* likened the difficulties with the ethics of robotics to Asimov's *Robot Chronicles* and suggested that scientists and politicians consider the issues that Asimov had grappled with decades earlier. Kubrick's robot run amok in *Space Odyssey 2001* performs much the same function, as does his critique of the arms race in the same film. Nobel Prize-winning Economist Paul Krugman cites Asimov for inspiring him to engage in math and economics. In an article in Smithsonian Magazine entitled '10 Inventions Inspired by Science Fiction,' Jules Verne, H.G. Wells and *Star Trek* feature prominently. Recently, breakthroughs in metamaterial use published in *Nature* were often glossed in the popular press, and even by the researchers themselves as the Harry Potter Invisibility Cloak. These visionary flights of fancy, existing in the mind and on paper, in sketches or narratives, are now what define our reality and future possibilities. The same might be said for the much-hyped Google glasses and eye-activated technology being the child of the visionary computer graphics and artistic design of the Terminator's vision in *Terminator 2*.[xix] Innovators in print, film, the plastic and performing arts have for centuries created reality before it was material.[xx]

For Marcuse, this is one of the essential aspects of the aesthetic dimension of life. The arts provide us tremendous pleasure, but beyond joy it has transformative effects that show us otherwise hidden or mystified truths, ideas so obvious they are constraining, and inchoate solutions to these problems. Science is indeed shaped by fiction, although the consequences of these actions – per Verne, Orwell, Bradbury and Atwood's examples – may take decades if not centuries to come to fruition. This makes an even more cogent argument for the maintenance of the humanities and the reform of literary curriculum for the sake of both STEM and civic education. If we fail to realize the potential of sci-fi (and other such alternative literatures) to education what version of the future will we eliminate? Are we to expect that the next great Nobel Laureate or inventor pick up science fiction on their own while being assigned the classics because they are deemed more challenging or appropriate? What improvements and cautionary tales (remember that Huxley, Orwell and Atwood have had an equally lasting impact for their ability to depict the horrors of humankind) would we be nipping at the bud? The act of knowing, studying and engaging with the imaginative is part of what makes innovation possible, and of ethically thinking through the ramifications of change and stasis. The forerunner of experimentation, sci-fi's place in education is in part to teach the kind of creative thought that aids civic ingenuity and innovation by refusing notions of 'just because,' 'the way it is,' tradition, and already-worn paths of possibility.

In seeking to foster these skills and values, we must be mindful that the jump between studying fictitious inventiveness and future innovation is not automatic. Standing in front of a class of sleep-deprived undergraduates or over-extended high school students extolling the meaning, form, style, and gravitas of novels, films and compositions does not inevitably manifest in unbound creativity, new ventures, patents, and technological breakthroughs. Translating the past into the future, particularly on the abstract level of the imagination, with the idea of morphing these fanciful, playful investigations into uniquely singular trains of thought, is a demanding pedagogical task. But it is precisely because of its difficulty that the humanities are valuable. Only the humanities study the imagination, past, present and future. If we are to be future-oriented, we must constantly change our approach to teaching and make concerted efforts to relate to contemporary concerns and prepare for future conflicts. Even while we are wading in the works of antiquity and before, we must be forward looking in our approach and emphasize their relevance to the present, even if it is a more goal-oriented, teleological model of teaching and research than we are comfortable with. The pedagogies of inventiveness coupled with civics, democracy, and the ethical mind are something that we should all enthusiastically support. This includes advocating for substantial curricular reform, including alternative and vernacular literatures, and disciplinary integration.

ON INTERDISCIPLINARY COMMUNICATION

The challenge of interdisciplinary research is to construct an object such that it cannot be understood without engaging multiple fields of knowledge. The intricacy and interdependency of the disciplines has been sturdily established by visionary scholars and educators who have painstakingly connected epistemologies across disciplines and opened our eyes to their necessity and potential (Klein, 1990). It is acknowledged that history cannot be understood without reference to literary style, literature without linguistics, music without political history, film without psychology. Research projects are simply far more complex and multi-faceted than the aging disciplinary boundaries that we work within allow for. This is not just a reason to embrace trans-disciplinary practice, but also an opportunity to reject ideological purity, outdated methods, and ideological barriers in breaking the cycle of destruction and domination that has defined modernity. Like the long fetch of history, curricular animation is an ongoing process that is constantly subject to the emergence of new becomings, mixed epistemologies, and nuanced understanding of information, transmission, reception and purpose (Kincheloe, 1998). Practical, holistic, real-world dialogues between disparate and seemingly dissimilar entities can be catalysts in creating new subjectivities, realities, and future possibilities. An essential part of this is productive engagement with our colleagues from across the university, not simply within the humanities and liberal arts, but also with STEM and professional fields. However, instead of framing this conjunction as the humanities modeling themselves on STEM, we must understand this as an expansion of knowledge production that circulates in multiple directions, not just from the STEM to the humanities, but vice versa and back and forth in dialogue. The effect of this move is to improve the method and scope of our research, and also transform pedagogical practices at the primary, secondary, post-secondary and graduate levels.

If we momentarily re-think the scientific method, decoupling knowledge from empiricism, we can reconstruct research methods in a way that spans the university (and the high school) and includes the specific role that the humanities have in the production of knowledge, particularly in the experimental and conceptual stages. This refiguring is less an ideology, or a bid to incorporate the humanities into the sciences, but a holistic view of knowledge production, which includes imaginative and ethical thought from across the humanities.[xxi]

The scientific method (admittedly over-simplified) looks something like this: established theory, hypothesis, experiment, result, analyses; repeat until new theories and hypotheses are formed. From a combination of proven theories, data, and an inquisitive mind, testable hypotheses are formed which lead to controlled experiments and verifiable results. If done well, properly authenticated, and re-tested, new theories are formed and the process starts over, spawning other experiments. If we are to embrace the interdisciplinary theory that knowledge of any object is more labyrinthine than a single experiment, theory, or method, and further reflect on the importance of the imagination to science, we find that the humanities play a key role in the initial phase of the method. We are the pre-theory creators who train, mold, and lend focus to inquisitive minds and boundless curiosities that animate experimentation. Ingenuity is not chthonic, an existential property, it has a social point of origin. That genesis lies in the study of everything from history to science fiction, fantasy, and ballet in conjunction with both empiricism and critical analysis. It is cultural critique, utopian idealism, dystopian terror, and dreams of superhuman potential that combine with innovation, experiment, and production in the Petri dish of the mind to erect the pathways of the future. Before we can think about formulas and equations and begin to ponder experiments that push existing boundaries, we must first meditate without borders. Before innovators tackle established theories, they must imagine the challenge, decide which assumed impossibility can be made possible, and locate the endpoint that can be transcended. This is done through the exact skills that humanists teach, the ability to utilize the imagination and critique practice. By staring into the abyss – utopia, tragedy, beauty, evil, life beyond death – ideas gain form, which are later harnessed in the form of testable hypotheses. The humanities can also serve as the post-test theorists, those who contemplate and discuss the applications, implication, and ethics of discovery, point to new possibilities and the potentials for both harm and humanity.

In this light, we see that trans-disciplinarity, a practical necessity in engaging the labyrinthine complexity of modern problems, covers the entirety of the university and beyond. It is not solely STEM and professional degrees that create and move humanity towards prosperity, self-actuation and dignity, it is a combination of many epistemologies, practices and methods. This particular conceptual model begins with the humanities and proceeds through the sciences before spreading outside of the academy and affecting collective creative life.

What shape might wireless technology have taken without the influence of Star Trek's visionary communication systems? Where would flight, aerospace, and ocean travel be without Jules Vern? Or artificial intelligence and robotics without Isaac Asimov? The infamous unrealized 1980s Anti-Ballistic Missile System borrowed so much from sci-fi it was nicknamed 'Star Wars.' For this extant synergy between sci-fi and innovation to be enhanced and perpetuated, there must be dialogic engagement across the educational system. However, we cannot let our place in knowledge production allow us to be solipsistic. Our research should be cognizant of the concerns, debates and theories of our colleagues. We should make every effort to work and dialogue across the university, learning from our colleagues, simultaneously advocating for our own work as it relates to theirs, particularly in the realm of civics and ethics. Without adding our voices to expansive, multidisciplinary discourse on current problems, not only are we all impoverished, but we lose opportunities to reinforce our relevance in solving contemporary economic and civic issues.

What I envision is an open exchange within educational policy and practice where the connections between the humanistic and the scientific disciplines feed educational and professional pursuits, and vice-versa. Because of the restrictions that primary and secondary educators currently face, the first curricular changes need to take place within higher education. With STEM on the mind of administrators and the public, the time is right to make the connection between sci-fi, creative education, and innovation. This can most easily be enacted by pairing humanities curricula with science curricula (biology, engineering, computer science, depending on the options available) in university education departments, designing projects for students to simultaneously engage with meaningful, challenging literature, and to translate questions raised by their reading into scientific theories, lectures, proposals, and policy papers. This in turn will foster new attitudes towards inter-disciplinary work at the collegiate level between departments outside of education. When young educators implement these changes, they will cultivate young thinkers who will continue a legacy of innovation and progress. It will also instill thinkers with the critical ability to conceptualize the implications of innovation and the potential impact on society, to see the potential for benefit as well as harm.

PUBLIC RELATIONS AND ADVOCACY

There are myriad examples of humanistic knowledge shaping modern innovations, both material and social. Space, air, and undersea travel, current work on tissue regeneration, cloning, gene therapy, and successful international marketing campaigns all bear the marks of creative humanistic thought. However, in matters that are strictly financial, as many decisions are, these histories are often forgotten. The fact that literature and generalized literacy is one of the key historical elements of human emancipation is rarely brought up as departments are culled and the number of faculty necessary to teach high-quality critical reading and writing skills diminishes. Likewise, the fact that Renaissance artists were among the first to uncompromisingly study human anatomy and physiology is rarely linked to the development of modern medicine. As humanists we know the stories of Leonardo Da Vinci, Michelangelo Buonarroti, Isaac Asimov, and Mary Wollstonecraft, whose lives and works changed society as we know it. But the complex relationships between what happened centuries ago and the lives we enjoy today are convoluted and difficult to convey in an age of short memories, brief attention spans, and the search for the next big thing. To confront this, better public relations and civic engagement are needed. These stories, as well as more modern anecdotes, should circulate more widely and serve as signposts towards education that consciously carries on this legacy.

A most compelling modern example is that of Steve Jobs, whose idea of design and aesthetic took a garage company and turned it into a global giant. When Jobs was in college he took a calligraphy class. Because of his experience with this highly refined Asian art form, Jobs came to take the appearance of his machines, inside and out, more seriously than his competitors, and ultimately created an instantly recognizable international brand that has defined the market for personal technology and lifestyle (Isaacson, 2011; Grossman & McCracken, 2011). An interesting discussion can also be raised by this example: that of Apple's questionable manufacturing practices with Foxconn. While the arts transformed Jobs' approach to design, marketing and manufacturing, what of the ethical implications of Apple's manufacturing practices? Could these have been done ethically? Perhaps the finest older example is Jules Verne, whose novels influenced a host of the twentieth century's greatest minds in flight, biology, engineering and exploration. These include Igor Sikorsky, inventor of the helicopter (Strauss, 2002), aerial pioneer Alberto Santos-Dumont (Griffith, 2012), and Robert Goddard, inventor of the liquid-fueled rocket (Wallace, 2007). Jacques Cousteau, biologist, explorer and man credited with turning generations of children and adults on to the wonders of the deep, was profoundly influenced by Verne as well

(Walter, 2001). In the sphere of economics, Nobel Laureate Paul Krugman credits Isaac Asimov's *Foundation Trilogy* with piquing his interest in economics, specifically the interface of mathematics and human behavior (Krugman, 2010). While we may not all agree on the ethics of Apple's corporate model, the uses of Goddard and Sikorsky's inventions, or Krugman and Cousteau's ethics, it is important to point out the ethical dimension of the latter two. This coupling of science with ethics is one of the unique contributions of sci-fi that both men represent. The imagination that pushed both of these men to effectively change the way we think – towards social justice and environmentalism respectively – makes the point that imagination (here stoked by sci-fi) is a vital resource. It is an entity that holds the nearly atomic potential to improve living conditions, mold humane policy, create sustainable futures, and enact meaningful democratic and civic reform.

These are more than anecdotes, they are an opportunity to examine the ways that the humanities, which teach different ways of thinking, feeling, and sensing, actively transform intellectual, economic, civic, ethical, and material life. Without the opportunity to study how the best and worst of human history were first conceived and articulated, we are at a lack to envision and sculpt a better future. Without the imagination and creativity, innovation is doomed to either lie materially unrealized or potentially trend towards monstrosity, and the bottom line will dictate technological and social change rather than a complex series of critical insights into the implications and potential of progress. This sort of discourse, in the form of making connections between the study of the humanities and significant material change, is needed to convince the public and legislatures that by losing the humanities, we lose the dynamism and creativity that has long defined the university and the private sector, and that the damage of short changing critical thinking outweighs the expense of sustaining quality humanistic education.

Pursuing these ends provides a practical tool – a direct response to the question: what do the humanities contribute? It seems obvious to those involved, but it is surprising how often there is only a whisper of an answer. The academy was built around humanistic study, and we take for granted that we will always be included. In crafting effective talking points for the public through anecdotal evidence, we can also prepare effective answers for the inevitable day when we are asked, *what do you contribute?* There is evidence that the reply to this query should be: innovation, creativity, ethics, and civics – in short, the future of democracy.

CONCLUSION

The global financial meltdown, economic crash and political shifts present educators with hidden opportunity, and a chance to reflect, reconstruct, reform, re-direct and rethink, albeit a painful one. As education on every level gets squeezed and pummeled, we should not miss this occasion to transform ourselves, attitudes and curricula, and learn vital lessons. This does not mean a complete break with the past, or slavish imitation of STEM and professional studies. This represents a moment where experiments can be realized, the fringes can be re-examined, multi-disciplinary scholarship can be taken seriously and new bridges built. It is also an opportunity to reconstruct our relationship with the general public, to reach out and include their material and social concerns in our discourse, and more convincingly advocate for our relevance to everyday lives and futures. By remapping our relationships with the public and our peers inside the academy and secondary education, and discursively expanding knowledge production to consciously account for the role that the imagination plays, we can re-craft the humanities to meet the specific mandates of the contemporary. Opportunity knocks, and it is imperative to fearlessly throw open the door if we expect not just to survive but to thrive.

Part of this process is curricular redesign with both creativity and pragmatism in mind. Contra to persistent critiques, new literatures are not lesser.[xxii] They represent the kind of innovation that is part of the legacy of higher education, and at times popular literatures incorporate modern intellectual and ethical dimensions more easily than older literatures. In the case of science fiction, students can exercise the creativity that is necessary for innovative thinking paired with the ethical concerns that many outstanding sci-fi novels introduce. By putting the concerns of intellectual ingenuity together with civic and ethical concerns, sci-fi literature in the curriculum contributes to a continued legacy of invention and democratic pedagogy that will affect our collective intellectual and material lives well into the future.

NOTES

[i] Kress, Tricia (2011). Stepping out of the academic brew: Using critical research to break down hierarchies of knowledge production. *International Journal of Qualitative Studies in Education*, 24(3).

[ii] While many MBA programs tout their alums who have become CEOs, how many have published whose graduates received TARP funds or were implicated in various unethical dealings in sub-prime loans?

[iii] Zigo and Moore present a pithy and compelling case for science/speculative fiction as a method for teaching critical thought and responses to contemporary issues like leadership, politics, meaning, and interpretation. Further, a volume edited by P.L. Thomas takes on similar issues in the application of science fiction in the classroom. Both are fundamentally aimed at teachers and teacher educators, but the wider implications are obvious.

[iv] There are a host of others who have written similar conclusions using a wide swath of case studies and methods. See McLaren and Giroux (1989), McLaren and Faramandpur (2005), and Provenzo (2005) for a few examples.

[v] http://www.marcberniershow.com/audio_archive.cfm Rick Scott's interview is #288. Also see Adam Weinstein's astute critique in *Mother Jones*, http://motherjones.com/mojo/2011/10/rick-scott-liberal-arts-majors-drop-dead-anthropology, accessed 5/9/2012.

[vi] Comments were made on January 25, 2012. A partial clip was published on youtube.com by CNN at: http://www.youtube.com/watch?v=20pjeeQ611s, accessed 5/9/2012.

[vii] Comments made February 25, 2012, which generated a great deal of press, forcing Santorum to apologize for them. http://www.youtube.com/watch?v=NkjbJOSwq3A, accessed 5/9/2012.

[viii] Henry Giroux has published lengthy online commentaries on the conservative educational agenda that concerns both of these men as exemplar of the (anti-)educational movement..

[ix] See Zigo and Moore and Thomas for readings specific to sci-fi in the English curriculum.

[x] The definition of progress is contingent and the term itself carries baggage. However, I would not shy away from using the term. After all, when Paolo Freire narrates the passage from oppression to liberation, he deems it to be progress; Marcuse considers the enabling of new Subjects to be progress. While this term has had pernicious effects, it is still relevant to educators as we work with our students.

[xi] As Tricia Kress (2011) points out, epistemological purity and hierarchy at its worst transforms researchers and pedagogues into oppressors. Stopped short of that, knowledge narrowly defined (often as dispassionate or empirical) is fundamentally exclusionary.

[xii] Cultural knowledge and language skills are increasingly needed as global firms set up shop in countries around the world. Doing business in developing countries (which account for the bulk of the world's population, see www.pbr.org) necessitates a host of cultural, gendered, sexual, and linguistic skills that are not taught in any other part of the curriculum. Historical analyses of previously endeavors, from colonization and mineral exploitation to legislation and economic experiments, are too complex for a non-specialist, in much the same way that computer and auto repair, and DNA amplification are left to experts.

[xiii] http://www.nytimes.com/roomfordebate/2011/03/20/career-counselor-bill-gates-or-steve-jobs/your-college-major-matter-less-over-time, accessed 5/9/2012 While this is a good argument, the *New York Times* does not reach the same people that Scott and Santorum do.

[xiv] Also see Apple (2001, pp. 212-218) for information about the Education Policy Project, which is dedicated to providing solutions against those proposed by those who oppose the project of critical public education.

[xv] In comments made to college board, Rick Santorum likens students and their parents as consumers, setting up a provider-consumer model, as opposed to the provider-recipient, interactive, enabling, or dialogic model. This has substantial ramifications, although to be fair, he Santorum was commenting on primary education, even though the interviewer was concerned with higher education. http://www.youtube.com/watch?v=kunV7U-NoAU&feature=related, accessed 5/9/2012

[xvi] See Apple, 2001, pgs. 227-8. As an educational reformer, he states that "we have much to learn from the right" in terms of messaging and advocating for our solutions to educational problems.

[xvii] The humanities are, obviously, much more than innovation. Arguments supporting the importance of critical though, writing, research methods and language skills have been made quite well. However, we also need to find ways to inject ourselves into ongoing debates on economy and innovation otherwise we risk crucial exclusions from the public sphere. Instead of hijacking the humanities to support naked neo-liberalism, we should hope that scientific research and technological development in the wake of intense discussions about *Jurassic Park* or *2001: A Space Odyssey* will be more humane and cautious, and less assuredly optimistic.

[xviii] In the summer workshop at the Center for Advanced Study of Behavioral Sciences at Stanford University I had the opportunities to speak in depth with some Stanford faculty members from Cognitive Science and Neurology. A number of them not only used literature in their teaching, but cited it as the starting point for their thinking processes. Likewise, interviews and conversations with colleagues in the sciences at Vassar College show that science fiction plays an influential and pasting part in many scientists' lives. Special thanks to colleagues Theresa and Chris Garrett (biology and computer programmer), Jenny Magnes (physics), Jennifer Walters (computer science), Tarik Elseewi (Media Studies) for making time to discuss their love and application of science fiction with me.

[xix] For an excellent laundry list of inventions inspired by science fiction, see Mark Strauss' excellent short 'Ten Inventions Inspired by Science Fiction.' http://www.smithsonianmag.com/science-nature/Ten-Inventions-Inspired-by-Science-Fiction.html?c=y&page=4&navigation=next#IMAGES, accessed July 27, 2013.

[xx] We should also be reminded, as C. J. Clover does (1992, in regard to horror films), that innovation often trickles up. In the world of speculative fiction films, ideas that are blockbusters are often taken from or experimented with first in low-budget B films.

[xxi] Henry Bauer (1994) makes a particularly cogent argument for STS (science, technology and society) as a replacement for 'scientific knowledge' in part because of the insight, perspective and application to liberal education. For Bauer, literacy is essential to modernity, more so than teaching pure scientific method, which is woefully incomplete and potentially hazardous in the early stages.

REFERENCES

Anthony, Sebastian. (March 26, 2013). *Researchers create ultra-thin and flexible Harry Potter-like invisbility cloak.* ExtremeTech.com. http://www.extremetech.com/extreme/151631-researchers-create-ultra-thin-and-flexible-harry-potter-like-invisibility-cloak

Apple, Michael W. (1991). *Educating the 'right' way: Markets, standards, God, and inequality.* New York, NY: RoutledgeFalmer.

Bauer, Henry H. (1994). *Scientific literacy and the myth of the scientific method.* Urbana-Champaign, IL: University of Illinois Press.

Butcher, William. (1983). *Jules Verne: A reappraisal.* http://www.ibiblio.org/julesverne/articles/prophetorpoet.htm

Clover, C. J. (1992). *Men, women and chainsaws: Gender in the modern horror film.* Princeton, NJ: Princeton University Press.

Coles, Robert. (1993). *A Robert Coles omnibus.* Iowa City, IA: University of Iowa Press.

Dewey, John. (1934). *Art as experience.* New York, NY: Minton, Balch and Co.

Evans, Arthur B. (1988). *Jules Verne rediscovered: Didacticism and the scientific novel.* Westport, CT: Greenwood Publishing Group.

Freire, Paulo. (1970). *Pedagogy of the oppressed* (Trans. Myra Bergman Ramos). New York, NY: Seabury Press.

Greene, Maxine. (1995). *Unleashing the imagination: Essays on education, the arts and social change.* San Francisco, CA: Jossey-Bass Publishers.

Giroux, Henry A. (2012, February 22). *Why teaching people to think for themselves is repugnant to religious zealots and Rick Santorum.* Truthout.org. http://www.truth-out.org/opinion/item/6812:why-teaching-people-to-think-for-themselves-is-repugnant-to-religious-zealots-and-rick-santorum

Giroux, Henry A. (2014, January 13). *Reclaiming the radical imagination: Challenging Casino capitalism's punishing factories.* Truthout.org. http://truth-out.org/opinion/item/21113-disimagination-machines-and-punishing-factories-in-the-age-of-casino-capitalism

Giroux, Henry A., & McLaren, Peter (Eds.). (1989). *Critical pedagogy: The state and cultural struggle.* Albany, NY: SUNY Press.

Griffith, Victoria. (2011). *The fabulous flying machines of Alberto Santos-Dumont.* New York, NY: Abram's Books.

Isaacson, Walter. (2011). *Steve Jobs.* New York, NY: Simon Schuster.

Kincheloe, Joe L. (1998). Pinar's Currere and identity in hyperreality: Grounding the post-formal notion of intrapersonal intelligence. In William F. Pinar (Ed.), *Curriculum: Toward new identities.* New York, NY: Routledge.

Kincheloe, Joe L., & Steinberg, Shirley R. (1993). A tentative description of post-formal thinking: The critical confrontation with cognitive theory. *Harvard Educational Review, 63*(6), 296-320.

Klein, Julie T. (1990). *Interdisciplinarity: History, theory and practice.* Detroit, MI: Wayne State University Press.

Kozol, Jonathan. (1991). *Savage inequalities.* New York, NY: Crown.

Kress, Tricia. (2011a). Stepping out of the academic brew: Using critical research to break down hierarchies of knowledge production. *International Journal of Qualitative Studies in Education, 24*(3), 267-283.

Kress, Tricia. (2011b). *Critical praxis research: Breathing new life into research methods for teachers.* New York, NY: Springer.

Krugman, Paul. (2010). Who are you calling dense? *New York Times*, August 30.
Lipsitz, George. (2007). *Footsteps in the dark: The hidden histories of popular music*. Minneapolis, MN: University of Minnesota Press.
Marcuse, Herbert. (1991). *One-dimensional man: Studies in the ideology of advanced industrial society* (2nd ed.). Boston, MA: Beacon Press.
Marcuse, Herbert. (1978). *The aesthetic dimension: Toward a critique of Marxist esthetics*. Boston, MA: Beacon Press.
Provenzo, Jr., Eugene, F. (2005) *Critical literacy: What every American ought to know*. Boulder, CO: Paradigm.
Rautins, Cara, & Ibrahim, Awad. (2011). Wide qwakeness: Towards a critical pedagogy of imagination, humanism, agency and becoming. *International Journal of Critical Pedagogy*, 3(3), 24-36.
Readings, Bill. (1997). *The university in ruins*. Cambridge, MA: Harvard University Press.
Stotsky, Sandra. (2012). *Death and resurrection of coherent literature curriculum: What secondary English teachers can do*. Lanham, MD: Rowan and Littlefield.
Strauss, Mark. (2012, March 16). Ten inventions inspired by science fiction. Smithsonian.com http://www.smithsonianmag.com/science-nature/Ten-Inventions-Inspired-by-Science-Fiction.html. *The Economist*, June 2-8, 15.
Thomas, P. L. (Ed.). (2013). *Science fiction and speculative fiction: Challenging genres*. Rotterdam/Boston/Taipei: Sense Publishers.
Wallace, Richard. (2007, September 13). *Tsiolkovsky, Goddard and Oberth – Three fathers of rocketry*. Museumofflight.org. http://www.museumofflight.org/education/tsiolkovsky-goddard-and-oberth-three-fathers-rocketry
Virilio, Paul. (2006). *Speed and politics* (Trans. Marc Polizzotti). New York, NY: Semiotext(e).
Walter, Fredrick Paul. (2007) Introduction to Verne, Jules *Twenty-thousand leagues under the sea*. http://jv.gilead.org.il/fpwalter/intro.html
Weinstein, Adam. (2011, October 11). *Rick Scott to liberal arts majors: Drop dead*. www.motherjones.com
Zigo, Diane, & Moore, Michael T. (2004, November). Science fiction: Serious reading and critical reading. *The English Journal*, 94(2), 85-90.

DENISE IVES & CARA CRANDALL

12. ENACTING A CRITICAL PEDAGOGY OF POPULAR CULTURE AT THE INTERSECTION OF STUDENT WRITING, POPULAR CULTURE, AND CRITICAL LITERACY

ABSTRACT

Popular culture – the body of movies, television programs, music, books, and clothing enjoyed by ordinary people – is ubiquitous. Despite the prevalence and accessibility of popular culture texts in our lives, however, educational researchers, policy makers, and classroom teachers continue to debate the usefulness of incorporating such "low culture" texts into English language arts curricula. Many literacy researchers, though, have shown that popular culture texts, whether or not they are acknowledged or sanctioned by teachers, do find their way into classrooms and can actually present rich opportunities to teach critical literacy practices such as deconstructing texts and reading resistantly – practices aimed at analyzing how language functions to reproduce and maintain unequal power relations in society. In this chapter the authors demonstrate how two texts composed by middle school students echoed other texts students had read, including popular culture texts. They argue that the students' written compositions, because they emulated other texts in multiple ways, introduced popular culture texts, and the values and messages in those texts, into their English language arts classrooms and in doing so created "openings" for enacting a critical pedagogy of popular culture.

INTRODUCTION

Pop culture is the elephant in the room, the presence that cannot ultimately be ignored by literacy teachers. (Newkirk, 2007)

Popular culture – the widely available and circulating body of movies, television programs, music, books, and clothing enjoyed by ordinary people – is ubiquitous. Most people have access to popular culture twenty-four hours a day, seven days a week via their television sets, their personal computers, and their smart phones. Popular culture is on the foods we buy, the clothes we wear, the advertisements we see, and the products we use every day. It is on the lips of politicians, news broadcasters, and late night comedians. It is part of the conversations we have with family, friends, and co-workers. It is present in our homes, at our jobs; and popular culture is in our schools and classrooms.

P. Paugh et al. (eds.), *Teaching towards Democracy with Postmodern and Popular Culture Texts*, 201–220.
© 2014 Sense Publishers. All rights reserved.

While some scholars and teachers insist popular, or low, culture has no place in the classroom and that becoming educated should entail becoming acquainted with high culture, others have argued that popular culture can and should play a larger role in academic learning, particularly in English language arts (ELA) classrooms. These researchers and educators agree that the inclusion of pop culture in the classroom curriculum has many potential educational benefits including fostering high levels of student engagement, bridging out-of-school and in-school learning experiences, and capitalizing on students' prior and on-going literacy learning. At the same time literacy researchers and teachers also acknowledge that utilizing popular culture in the ELA classroom has its challenges. For instance, many popular culture texts suffer from a lack of literary sophistication and feature mature or controversial subject matter and themes.

However, literacy researchers have shown that whether or not popular culture is introduced, acknowledged, or sanctioned by teachers, it finds its way into the classroom through both formal and informal channels. Additionally, many researchers have demonstrated that students employ their knowledge of popular culture when learning and producing academic content. These researchers have argued that school curricula and classroom teachers that do not take this reality into account risk missing opportunities to support and extend student learning, at best, and at worst, actually interfere with or interrupt academic learning. They contend, as the quote at the beginning of this chapter states that, "popular culture is the elephant in the [class]room ... that cannot [and should not] ultimately be ignored by literacy teachers" (p. 544).

One of the missed opportunities represented by a failure to acknowledge and respond to popular culture in classrooms is the possibility for teaching, learning, and enacting critical literacy practices. Critical literacy practices involve analyzing and critiquing texts in order to understand how language in texts functions to reproduce and maintain unequal power relations in society. It involves deconstructing texts in order to understand how they reflect certain values, beliefs, and messages about societal norms. Above all, though, critical literacy practices aim to disrupt dominant discourses about individuals and groups that contribute to relationships of dominance and oppression.

In this chapter we demonstrate how two texts composed by middle school students echoed other texts students had read including popular culture texts. We argue that their compositions effectively introduced those popular culture texts, and the values and messages in those texts, into their English language arts classrooms and in doing so opened up rich possibilities for enacting a critical pedagogy of popular culture.

BACKGROUND

In this section we present an overview of critical literacy theory, critical literacy classroom practices, and popular culture pedagogies. We begin by defining critical literacy and outlining important aims and basic tenets of critical literacy approaches to literacy education. Next, we detail specific classroom practices that reflect a critical approach to literacy and provide examples of scholars who have documented such practices in their work. Finally, we discuss students' engagement with popular culture and describe possibilities for utilizing popular culture as a vehicle for teaching and learning critical literacy.

CRITICAL LITERACY AND CLASSROOM PRACTICE

The term critical literacy refers to the use of the technologies of print and other media of communication to analyze, critique, and transform the norms, rule systems, and practices governing the social fields of everyday life (Luke, 2004). Critical literacies involve the consumption, production, and distribution of print and new media texts by, with, and on behalf of marginalized populations in the interests of naming, exposing, and destabilizing power relations; and promoting individual freedom and expression (Morrell, 2004). Critical literacy entails a process of naming and renaming the world, seeing its patterns, designs, and complexities, and developing the capacity to redesign and reshape it (New London Group, 1996). Luke (2000) referred to critical literacy as both a "theoretical and practical attitude" (p. 454). As a theory a critical literacy perspective posits that education can and should foster social justice by supporting students in understanding how language and power contribute to social relations.

Some of the primary aims of critical literacy education include teaching "students [to] examine the power relationships inherent in language use, understand that language is not neutral, and confront their own values in the production and reception of language" (Behrman, 2006, p. 490). Consequently, students are taught to interrogate texts – to analyze multiple forms of communication and expression in terms of the effects of capitalism, colonialism, and inequitable economic relations and to pose questions that problematize representations in texts and evoke thinking about issues of language, text and power. Ultimately, critical literacy educators aim to facilitate access to dominant institutions and dominant discourses for marginalized populations (Morrell, 2002) while at the same time honoring and valuing multiple ways of doing, saying, and thinking. In addition to enabling access to dominant forms and valuing diverse literacy practices, critical educators strive to prepare students with the capacity to use texts "to analyze social fields and their systems of exchange – with an eye to transforming social relations and material conditions" (Luke, 2012, p. 9). In fact, critical literacy approaches view language, texts, and their discourse structures as principal means for representing and reshaping possible worlds.

Critical literacy theory emphasizes the socially constructed nature of all texts. That is, it disrupts the notion that textual meaning is fixed and inherent in a text. Instead, authors of texts are understood to make choices from a range of possibilities as they produce texts – choices that reflect their purposes, interests, values, biases, motives and the like. Critical literacy theory assumes unequal and shifting power relations among social actors and that social actors, with different social identities and social locations, enact unequal power relations as they "do things" with and through language. Basic tenets of critical literacy include the following: all texts are constructions, all texts contain belief and value messages, each person interprets messages differently, texts serve different interests, and each medium develops its own language in order to position readers/viewers in certain ways. Essentially, determining whose values, texts, ideologies, and discourses are represented and reflecting on the nature of and implications those representations have for various groups is central. Critical literacy educators accomplish this by teaching students to identify multiple voices, dominant culture discourses, alternative readings, and sources of authority in texts and by engaging students in critiquing and producing a wide range of texts.

Janks (2000) described four orientations to literacy education each based on a different view of the relationship between language and power: domination, access, diversity, and design. Critical theorists working from a domination orientation view language as a powerful means of maintaining and reproducing relations of domination. From this perspective language functions to position readers in particular ways in order to wield power. The primary concern here is to deconstruct texts in order to make visible the choices made by authors in the construction of texts. An access orientation focuses on providing access to dominant literacy practices. This orientation wrestles with the "access paradox," (Lodge, 1997) that is, how to provide access to dominant forms and practices without maintaining the hegemony of dominant literacies. A diversity orientation emphasizes multiple ways with words including different ways of doing, saying, thinking, and valuing. The role of social identities in literacy practices is examined here. Finally, a design orientation refers to "the ability to harness the multiplicity of semiotic systems across diverse social locations to challenge and change existing Discourses" (p. 177). Emphasis is on transforming dominant social relations and literacy practices. Janks argues that each of these four orientations to literacy education are important in their own right as well as being "crucially interdependent" (p. 178).

Critical literacy educators currently employ a range of strategies and practices to help their students develop their critical literacy competencies. In a review of literature on critical literacy classroom practices at the upper elementary and secondary levels Behrman (2006) identified six broad categories of these classroom practices based on student task or activities: 1) reading supplementary texts, 2) reading multiple texts,3) reading from a resistant perspective, 4) producing countertexts, 5) conducting student-choice research projects, and 6) taking social action. In these classrooms, students practiced reading texts from different viewpoints, or alternative frames of reference (Alford, 2001), and peeling layers of meaning from a text to explore how the same reader might approach a text from different identities based on race, ethnicity, class, gender, language, sexuality, and religion (Foss, 2002). Additionally, students were supported in examining their own values and considering how those values influence their interpretations. They analyzed texts to understand how text features functioned to position readers in various ways, how authors' motives and ideologies were reflected in their authorial choices, and how what was excluded in a text often communicated as much as what was included. They were encouraged to produce countertexts that presented a topic from a nonmainstream perspective and to use literacy as a tool for social change. This process of textual analysis centered on asking questions of texts. Such questions included: Who constructed the text? When, where, for whom and for what purpose was the text written? What values are being promoted in this text? Whose values are they?

One challenge teachers often cite as a reason for not employing critical literacy approaches in their classroom is a lack of space in the curriculum to include extra content, that is, content beyond the scope of school, district, state, and federal content expectations, curriculum frameworks, pacing guides and the like. Many teachers feel enormous and increasing pressure to focus exclusively on preparing students to be successful on high-stakes standardized texts. Indeed, in far too many instances teachers' jobs are quite literally on the line. Yet, critical literacy instruction can and should be woven seamlessly into existing curricula. As Luke and Freebody (1999) suggest, "critical literacies – in all their varied print and multimedia, practical and theoretical, cultural and political forms – refer to openings in the curriculum that enable teachers, students, and communities to explore alternative ways of structuring practices around texts to address new cultural and economic contexts and new forms of practice and identity. So the term marks out a space for development and exploration of a new set of active, agent-oriented, denaturalizing, and counter-ideological textual practices" (Drawing on History section, para. 10).

A CRITICAL PEDAGOGY OF POPULAR CULTURE

Morrell (2007) argues that such "openings" are frequently created when popular culture texts are imported into classrooms – either by teachers or students. He writes, "By honoring and drawing upon local literacy practices and the everyday culture of youth, educators can prepare curricula that simultaneously increase academic literacies while also reaching into the worlds of students, facilitating empowered identities among these students, and making connections between their local practices and global concepts of educational and social justice" (Morrell, 2007, p. 11). Morrell calls this approach to teaching a *pedagogy of youth popular culture*. According to Morrell, such a pedagogy must involve examining the everyday language and literacy practices of students to make connections with classroom practices. What he has advocated for and investigated in his work is "a critical approach to urban adolescent literacy instruction that fosters access while at the same time developing the language of social critique and spaces for transformative action" (p. 238).

Popular culture encompasses print and non-print formats such as books, films, television, music, and multi-media. Youth are avid consumers of popular culture in its various forms. A robust body of literature has documented student engagement with popular culture texts (Jewitt, 2008) including the literacy practices they engage in as they view, create, and respond to such texts (Alvermann, 2001). Much of that literature documents practices students engage in outside of formal classrooms. However, there is also research that showcases how students regularly engage with or draw on popular culture texts as they read, write, and make sense in school settings (Obidah & Marsh, 2006; Tatum, 2006). Some of that literature presents ideas for how teachers can plan curricula that draw on their students' experiences with popular culture in order to support them in making connections to the "official curriculum." An example of this is Morrell's (2007) work describing how he used popular culture in conjunction with canonical texts to teach argumentation in an urban English classroom.

Though teachers can (and in our opinion should) plan to incorporate popular culture in their teaching plans, students frequently import popular culture texts and their understandings from such texts into classrooms of their own volition (Dyson, 1997, 2003, 2008; Ives, 2012). For example, in a study of middle school students' meaning making of social studies content, Hall (2011/2012) showed how middle schoolers drew on understandings gleaned from popular culture texts to inform their meaning making of academic texts in ways that both supported and limited their learning. She reported that the students uncritically accepted popular culture texts, including cartoons and video games, as authoritative over social studies texts. Ives and Crandall (2014) also demonstrate how middle school students model multiple aspects of their written compositions after popular culture texts as they attempt to write for the kind of audience they are accustomed to being themselves. Newkirk (2002), whose research has focused on gender and literacy, found that boys' literacy practices, though varied, most often take up popular culture that allows them to play with ideas about identity, power, and masculinity, but in ways that often disturb teachers not only because of concerns about the value of popular culture but also the themes often found in popular culture including violence.

Often students' literacy practices, especially those that draw on popular culture texts including comics, cartoons, sitcoms, movies, video games, are marginalized in classrooms. Unfortunately, opportunities students' use of popular culture present for teaching and engaging in critical literacy practices are often missed entirely in classrooms. Sometimes this is because teachers fail to see what their students are doing (occasionally because students are actively hiding it from them [see Finders, 1997; Ives, 2011]). More often, though, such openings are missed because teachers (or other decision makers) view students' engagement with popular culture as irrelevant, extracurricular, or inappropriate. Such engagements are viewed as "kids' business" – unrelated to the academic goals of formal schooling.

National, state, and district standards include the teaching of critical thinking and literary analysis and effective teachers already teach critical thinking within their curricula, encouraging students to analyze, synthesize, and evaluate the texts presented to them. That critical thinking extends beyond the ability to restate and reconstruct a situation; it encompasses higher-level thinking that involves the ability to analyze or *deconstruct* and then to examine all of the ramifications. Yet students are not always taught to extend the critical practices they apply to canonical texts to the everyday messages they receive beyond the classroom walls. A critical popular culture pedagogy focuses on just that: helping learners apply critical thinking about the everyday messages conveyed in advertising, movies, television programs, music, radio talk shows, newspapers, magazines, books, posters, clothing, and the Internet (Summers, 2000). This approach, Morrell (2002) argues, helps students to uncover social and political meanings within texts, consider how texts are attempting to position readers, and question the ideas being presented. Such a pedagogy promises not only to develop students' abilities to become critical consumers of school-sanctioned as well as popular cultural texts, but also to actively participate in re-imagining and re-structuring textual practices and social relations toward a more just future.

SITUATING THE TEXTS

Herein, we feature the compositions of two girls – a play composed by Kristina, an African American sixth grader and a short story written by Charlotte, a European American eighth grader. The texts described in this chapter were collected during two different ethnographic studies both conducted in middle school English language arts (ELA) classrooms separately by the authors. Study One, conducted by Author One, aimed to document the literacy practices of African American students in an urban middle school ELA classroom. Study Two, conducted by Author Two in her own suburban English language arts classroom, sought to examine the narrating practices of middle school writers. Both studies employed ethnographic methods including participant observation and field note writing, interview, and artifact collection.

The site of Study One was Ms. Wagner's ELA classroom at Hoyt Middle School (HMS). HMS is one of four middle schools in a school district located in a midsized Midwestern city. The student body at Hoyt Middle is composed almost entirely of African American students from poor and working-class homes. At the time the study was conducted, Hoyt was in its fifth consecutive year of failure to meet adequate yearly progress (AYP) as defined by the federal No Child Left Behind Act. Not surprisingly, concern about preparing students to take and pass the state assessments, called LEAP tests, was an ever-present and highly visible pressure in the lives of Hoyt administrators and teachers including Ms. Wagner, the focal teacher in this study. Ms. Wagner is a middle-class, European American woman, who at the time of the study had taught at Hoyt her entire 12-year teaching career. Ms. Wagner described herself as an avid reader and reported that she "tried to always use best practices" in her teaching and worked hard to stay abreast of and align her instruction with current federal, state, and district curricular expectations for sixth grade language arts.

The site of Study Two was Author Two's own ELA classroom at Garden Grove Middle School, one of two middle schools in a small suburban town located in the Northeastern United States. This school, with a student population of 434, is comprised largely of young people who are European American and come from middle, upper-middle class, and wealthy homes. The school provides not only the core content classes during the school day but also offers classes through an extensive music program. Most students participate in one or more athletic leagues outside of school. While school personnel were sensitive to the school's status as a Level 2 school, teachers at Garden Grove were given wide latitude in determining curriculum and assessments. While the state-mandated test, MCAS, informed the work of the classroom, teachers, like Author Two, made final decisions about what to teach and how to teach. Author Two is a middle class European American woman who was new to the school during the time of Study Two. Although Author Two had been teaching for nearly twenty years at the time, this was her first year at Garden Grove. At the time of the study, students had worked with her for approximately six weeks.

A TALE OF TWO TEXTS

In what follows we present Kristina and Charlotte's texts in turn. For each we describe the content and character of the text and how the text was introduced and integrated into the classroom. Then, we analyze how each girl drew on various features of popular culture texts they consumed in order to write into being desired worlds. We begin with Kristina's text, *Ghetto Family*.

Kristina's Ghetto Family

The first text, written by Kristina, was a play titled, *Ghetto Family*. Kristina's play consisted of several sheets of three-hole punched, lined notebook paper filled from edge to edge on both sides with the balloon-like print characteristic of many middle school girls. In the top margin of the first page was a cast of characters including the narrator, Tamika, MJ, Grandma Cookie, TaNesha, Ra Tonya, Shonda, Tonya, La'Tonya, Re'Lonya, and Doctor. The play began with the narrator speaking to the audience. "Yo, yo, yo. What's [the] dealio? Well this play is about a ghetto rich family. They is ghetto about everythang. Then MJ gets shot." In essence the play is about a family, a ghetto family to be precise – that is made up of parents, Tamika and MJ, Tamika's mother, Grandma Cookie, five teenaged girls, and a two year old. In the play the characters chided, squabbled, teased, and tried to get each other into trouble. They also did homework, attended school (where Ta'Nesha got into a fight over a boyfriend), and held down jobs.

Throughout the first part of the play, the reader comes to understand that something is bothering MJ, but when Tamika tries to find out what's wrong by asking him if he got somebody pregnant, he hits her and accuses her of not helping out. She reminds him that she cooks, cleans, and takes care of the children during the day and then goes to work at night. The following day Cookie and Tamika discuss what happened, and Cookie says he doesn't have the right to put his hands on her. Tamika says she knows but what can she do, she loves him. Before Tamika and MJ have a chance to address the situation, the narrator informs the audience MJ has been shot by his work partner. MJ is taken to the hospital where he dies from his wounds. The narrator declares an unhappy ending, but teases readers with the promise of an upcoming *Ghetto Family, Part II*.

Kristina wrote *Ghetto Family* on her own outside of the classroom. It was not a school assignment. However, the text made its way into the ELA classroom when Kristina brought it to school in order to ask her English teacher, Ms. Wagner, if she would type it up for her. Kristina brought *Ghetto Family* to class on the first day of a novel study unit featuring *Hatchet,* an adventure story about a young boy stranded alone in the wilderness written by Gary Paulsen. During the novel study unit planned by Ms. Wagner, students would read the novel in whole and small group configurations, learn about story elements and literary devices, answer discussion questions, complete literature circle role sheets, and compose several texts of their own including an informative essay on survival and a descriptive essay analyzing a fictional character. Through these assignments, Ms. Wagner planned to address the following state Grade Level Content Expectations in writing: set a purpose, consider audience, exhibit individual style to enhance the written message, use writing style conventions, and be enthusiastic about writing.

Author One was introduced to Kristina's play by Ms. Wagner. Ms. Wagner said she thought to show Kristina's piece to Author One because it was written in African American Language (AAL), which she knew from previous conversations was a research interest of Author One's. Author One was indeed interested. In fact, later that same day after reading the play she approached Kristina to talk to her about it. Author One asked Kristina if she could take the play and make a copy. Kristina agreed. Several days later when Author One returned Kristina's play to her (She had made a copy for herself and was returning the original to her.), it became clear from the crest fallen look on her face, that this was not exactly what she had wanted. Author One asked Kristina if she had wanted her to make enough copies so that the play could actually be performed. That was indeed what Kristina had wanted.

So, Author One delivered multiple copies of the play to Kristina and approached Ms. Wagner about allowing Kristina to perform the play. However, Ms. Wagner said she did not "feel like there [was] time" to let Kristina perform the play. She explained that there was "just too much [external] pressure" to devote time to anything that did not address the Grade Level Content Expectations or directly prepare students for the state LEAP test. Still, Kristina was eager to do the play and Author One wanted to find a way to give her the opportunity so she suggested to Ms. Wagner that perhaps the play could be performed during the lunch hour. Ms. Wagner agreed to let Kristina choose a group of actors who could practice and perform the play during the lunch break. Kristina was given time in class to select her actors and pass out scripts, and Ms. Wagner wrote out hall passes so those actors could return to the classroom during lunch to enact *Ghetto Family*.

Kristina frequently read and wrote texts of her own choosing on her own time. The texts Kristina read, wrote, and viewed reflected an affinity for African American characters, language, and themes that mirrored her African American, working-class, adolescent, and female identities. In fact, the majority of the texts Kristina both read and wrote in class, especially on her own, featured Black characters and/or African American Language (AAL). For instance, during the twice-daily independent silent reading time, Author One often observed Kristina reading books about African Americans. Once, over the course of several class periods, she read a biography about Marian Anderson, the first Black singer to perform at the White House and the Metropolitan Opera. On another occasion she read *Player Haters,* a book by Black author Carl Weber (2004) about the "bickering, beautiful Duncan family," three African American, adult siblings.

In addition to reading books about African Americans, Kristina also frequently produced texts featuring Black characters and language. For instance, I spotted Kristina composing, in stolen moments during class, several poems and songs, and once over the course of several days, she authored, on the backs of folders and worksheets, an entire series of comic strips about the exploits of three teenaged African American girls. For the final writing assignment of the novel unit, when Kristina was asked to write an essay about a fictional character she admired, she wrote about Major Payne, a Marine Corps Special Forces killing machine, played in the 1995 movie by Black actor Damon Wayans, who is forced to find new work as the commander of a junior ROTC military academy. Kristina wrote in her essay that she and Major Payne were a lot alike because they were both bossy and liked yelling at people.

The texts Kristina most often selected to read featured Black language, characters, and themes. In those texts the characters were Black, multi-aged, or adults; families were large and extended; relationships were contentious; dialogue was fast-paced, sardonic, and irreverent; and the tone was humorous. In addition, love relationships were central, typically between adults, and characterized by problems like abuse, infidelity, and unplanned pregnancy. For instance, another book that Kristina told me she had read also by Carl Weber, titled *Baby Momma Drama,* revolved around the problems of Jasmine who was trying to stay faithful to her "lying, drug-dealing hustler" (Weber, 2003) boyfriend while he did time in prison despite the fact that when she came to visit him she found him in the arms of his baby's momma.

Kristina's play shared many features with the books by Carl Weber she had been observed reading in class as well as the movie, *Major Payne,* that was the subject of her essay. One of the most obvious was that Kristina's text was populated by Black characters who, like the characters in *Player Haters, Baby Momma Drama,* and *Major Payne,* negotiated life's problems with a distinct style. As was the case in the other texts, characters in *Ghetto Family* bickered, bossed, got into trouble, and were unapologetic about who they were. Kristina's play, like these other exemplars, adopted a playful, almost slapstick, tone in the face of serious problems. For the Duncans, in *Player Haters,* those problems included surviving the death of a parent and negotiating tumultuous love relationships. For Jasmine in *Baby Momma Drama,* conflict stemmed from infidelity and romantic relationships complicated by men with a string of baby mommas. For Kristina's characters, troubles included weathering domestic abuse and losing a partner to gun violence. Despite the seriousness of the issues experienced by the characters, though, all the texts seem to be designed to entertain their audiences with humor, fast-paced dialogue, and indomitable spirit.

Charlotte's Emerald Eyes

Charlotte's text, *Emerald Eyes*, was written outside of the classroom for a required assignment in her eighth grade English class. Students were asked to write a 5-page, double-spaced short story as part of a curriculum unit on the short story. The assignment fell midway in the unit so students had spent time reading the works of published authors such as Jamaica Kinkaid, Langston Hughes, Shirley Jackson, and John Cheever, and discussing narrative and literary techniques specific to the genre. These lessons and activities focused on the uses and development of conflict and characterization, the importance of details for making writing vivid for a reader, and audience as the final arbiter for an author in making a story successful. This assignment also preceded their final term project, an analytic essay constructing arguments about character motivation and choice. Author Two, Charlotte's ELA teacher, viewed the short story assignment as a way to move students from their position as consumers of a text to the producers of such texts in order to develop an insider's perspective on how stories are constructed. Class discussions, free writes, and partner writing activities were utilized for students to practice with the idea of how one can transform writing for the self into a piece that can resonate with another person.

As per the assignment requirements, Charlotte handed in her completed short story typed using Times New Roman font. The length of her story surpassed both the assignment expectations and the length of nearly every other story submitted by her peers. Charlotte's story includes a two-voiced narrative, which allows her to tell the main story of a kingdom ruled by a cruel tyrant through the voice of his daughter, Evelyn, and the commoner she is secretly in love with, Rowan. These characters describe their resistance to the king, their plot to prevent Evelyn's arranged marriage to a man like her father, and their burgeoning love for one another. Minor characters include the king; Frederick, the evil suitor; Galen, a palace worker Evelyn sees as a surrogate father but who will betray her; Matilda, the "castle seamstress," who is a surrogate mother; and the members of Rowan's family, who suffer in poverty due to the king's reign. Other characters include various guards at the castle and villagers in the kingdom.

Charlotte's story begins with Evelyn's wedding, but rather than continue the scene, Charlotte halts that scene as she uses several pages to explain Evelyn's family situation, life as a princess, and the social and political conditions of the kingdom. Rowan, who has been her best friend since childhood despite the forbidden nature of their relationship, is introduced. When Evelyn and Rowan sneak out of the castle in order to bring food to the starving inhabitants of the village (including his family) they are caught by palace guards. Rowan is imprisoned while Evelyn is told she will marry Frederick. At the same time, her father presents her with the choice to have Rowan killed or allow him to live but as a slave. While she makes the choice, she also hatches a plan to rescue him. He is released from prison and rouses for revolution sympathetic villagers and later guards who begin to see their ruler's treachery. While Evelyn prepares for her wedding day, Rowan and his allies prepare for revolt and rescue. As the story moves to its conclusion, Charlotte brings her readers back to the initial scene. Evelyn is rescued as her father, Frederick, and even Galen die in the midst of the battle that breaks out in the castle hall. Evelyn and Rowan are free as are the subjects of the kingdom. For the two main characters, they are also freed to love one another.

While Kristina was seeking an audience beyond herself (and her teacher), Charlotte was reluctant to share her writing with others. She composed her short story at the behest of her English teacher and expected that as an assignment it would be read and evaluated by her English teacher. She also knew from experience that she could expect to receive written feedback from her teacher on her text. Charlotte's teacher had also explained that after their short stories had been returned to them, they would have the opportunity to share their short stories with their classmates either reading aloud to them herself or having the teacher read the story aloud. Charlotte, though, declined to share or have her stored shared with her class.

In addition, the only process of review and revision for this writing assignment was with the teacher; peer conferencing was not included largely because all of the students had some initial trepidation around themselves as creative writers. For Charlotte, who also refused to show her story to any friends or her parents, the only real-world audiences she was willing to consider were herself and her teacher. Imagined audiences, though, could have included any of those people she refused to let see her writing, but perhaps wished she could show them: peers, family, and the best friend in her English class that she had romantic feelings for.

Charlotte also had a lot of experience being the audience of other writers. The texts Charlotte read feature youthful characters and strong female characters who are engaged in violent struggles of good versus evil. They also feature romantic relationships between star-crossed lovers and fractured families that allow for emancipated characters. Main characters are White, though class boundaries are often crossed. The endings are generally happy and the tone serious.

She shared in personal discussions with Author Two her love of reading and even showed Author Two a photograph of herself reading one of the Harry Potter series books at age two. She described herself as a voracious reader who enjoyed complex texts and read them with ease. Her interest in reading led her to such texts as the popular series books of Harry Potter, *Twilight*, and *The Hunger Games*. She preferred to read stories that had fantastical elements, though not necessarily the fantasy genre, and strong female characters who were active participants in the fictional situations in which they were involved but who also were negotiating love and heterosexual gender relationships.

In all sorts of ways, Charlotte creates a fictional world, not unlike the fictional world she has inhabited as a reader, that allows a girl not only options for agency, but the drive to act and in acting the ability to create the kind of world she imagines. Her main character is the sort of hero popular fiction offers to young adult readers today, and Charlotte is an avid reader of such books. Like Bella of the *Twilight* series, Hermoine in the Harry Potter saga, and Katniss in *The Hunger Games* trilogy, Charlotte can, in the machinations of Evelyn, live outside of her

ENACTING A CRITICAL PEDAGOGY

boundaries, rescue others, and declare her feelings of love–all in public ways Charlotte might not access for herself. Her story fuses imagination with action to provide her audience with a happy ending and perhaps offers her audience the belief that such things are possible in real life as well. Charlotte has written what she knows, both in the literary symbols she chooses and the narrative structure she creates, but also she writes about what would matter most for an early adolescent girl: the ability to fulfill her desire for love and power in equal measures.

DISCUSSION

In this chapter we have described how the compositions produced by two middle school students reflected the popular culture texts they consumed. We have shown how the students drew on popular culture texts in order to write into being desired worlds. Additionally, we argued that the girls' texts, essentially imported popular culture, along with its values and messages, into the students' English classrooms. Here, we discuss how the students' writing created openings, or possibilities, in the curriculum for their teachers to enact a critical pedagogy of popular culture.

Domination and Deconstructing Texts

As explained by Janks (2000), a domination orientation to language and power emphasizes deconstructing texts in order to uncover how language functions to maintain and reproduce relations of domination. Both girls' compositions presented opportunities to engage students in discussions about the constructed nature of texts and about authorial decision-making. As authors of their own texts, the girls could be guided to answer a number of critical questions about their texts such as: Who is the text about? What is the race, gender, and class of the characters? How are those aspects of identity communicated to readers? What is the nature of the relationships between characters of various identities? Who is empowered/disempowered in the text? What do you, the author, want readers to believe or feel about certain characters? How does this reflect your own feelings or beliefs? How is your text attempting to question or disrupt notions of race, class, or gender? What it is your purpose in doing so? Asking critical questions such as these of their own texts can help support students in understanding their beliefs and values about language and power as well as how dominant discourses about social relations are re-produced and maintained, often unwittingly, through an author's language choices.

Charlotte and Kristina could also be encouraged to reflect on how their texts mirror the messages and values present in other texts they consumed, both inside and outside of the classroom. By identifying the kinds of texts they read and viewed and then interrogating the messages in those texts, the girls could begin to make connections between the messages in their texts and broadly circulating dominant discourses. Through this process, Charlotte and Kristina might discover how their texts inadvertently re-produce oppressive discourses they may (or may not) think they are disrupting. For instance, Kristina's *Ghetto Family* is in many ways reflective of negative stereotypes about ghetto culture. Her play re-produces dominant narratives about ghetto life that center around violence, misogyny, and promiscuity. Charlotte, too, re-creates a world where a female character's life revolves around pain inflicted by male characters – by her cruel father on the one hand or her longing for a forbidden lover on the other. Kristina and Charlotte have both re-created all too common female characters who suffer at the hands of the men in their lives and yet continue to love them and depend on them for their happiness.

Access and Reading Multiple Texts

Ensuring access to dominant discourses is an important aim of critical literacy education. The two teachers featured in this chapter had both carefully planned curricula for their students following the frameworks, pacing guides, and content expectations of their respective states and school districts. The girls' texts both showcased the girls' competencies in relation to the official curriculum and dominant literacy practices as well as created opportunities for providing access to the official curriculum. Charlotte, in fact, produced her text as part of the broader short story unit her teacher had planned. Her teacher had prepared her to write her story by exposing her to a number of canonical exemplars, and the assignment was created in order to further the students' understanding of the genre of the short story. In writing her story, Charlotte demonstrated her command of the literary genre through her uses of literary devices such as flashback, dialogue, and two-voiced narration. Similarly, Kristina's play also showcased her competencies, but in the writing of a dramatic work. She employed the conventions of drama, including a narrator and stage directions to advance the story she wanted to tell. Both authors demonstrated an understanding of the role of conflict in plot and character development, and both authors utilized language that showed their enthusiasm for their piece as well as incorporating a writing style that furthered their own understanding of thematic aspirations of each piece. For both authors, a consideration of audience – who they wrote for, why they wrote for that audience, and how they wrote for that audience would provide further ways to consider the story they wanted to tell as well as the authorial choices they made to advance that story.

Even though Kristina's text wasn't written as an assignment it could have been read in relationship to *Hatchet,* which her classroom teacher used as an anchor text. Like the novel's central theme of survival against numerous odds, Kristina's play offered another example of how an author writes about universal themes such as survival. In *Hatchet,* a young man's survival is predicated on his ability to face internal and external conflicts related to his parents' divorce and his plight in the midst of a wilderness following a plane crash. While the novel appears on one level to be a traditional story of man versus nature, it also provides young readers with existential questions on the individual, anger, redemption and forgiveness. In Kristina's play, questions of survival despite the odds are again taken up despite her setting of an urban home life versus Brian's wilderness environment. In providing a female, working-class, Black protagonist, how does Kristina's text take up these thematic questions raised in the novel she has recently read as part of a literary canon and approved curriculum while also asking her readers to consider how race, class, and gender take up such themes in new ways. Additionally, how do violence and sex work across both the texts? Both texts embed examples of violence, infidelity, and marital discord. But how has one text been sanctioned and other text been marginalized by the classroom teacher and to what affects for Kristina as read and potential author? If Kristina's play reflects themes she has recently addressed as a reader, how does her text not only disrupt but further these themes by considering them from her subject position as poor, Black, and female? In Charlotte's case, her short story takes up the themes and literary devices of works she has read both within and outside of her classroom and seems to complement rather than disrupt them. Her position as White, middle class, and female places her work closer to the texts she and her classmates read as part of the sanctioned curriculum. However, her text also attempts to reconsider a fundamental aspect of fairy tales: female power. Both authors then are attempting to take up and work against the literature that surrounds them.

Diversity and Reading Resistantly

A critical literacy approach balances the need for providing access to dominant forms of literacy with providing opportunities to relativize, resist, and reinvent those dominant forms. Dominant literacy forms and practices are relativized, or made aware of competing ways, through the inclusion of other ways of saying, doing, thinking, and being. This means reading and writing from multiple points of view, which both authors have attempted to do in the production of their own literature. Charlotte and Kristina both produced very different texts, under different conditions, for different purposes and different audiences. Both students also have different social identities. Kristina was an African American female, living in a poor, working-class urban area while Charlotte was a European American girl residing in a suburban, affluent area. Kristina spoke AAL as well as Standard American English (SAE), and Charlotte infused her SAE with youth language as did most of her peers. Yet, reading and writing resistantly allows students like these to bring their vernacular literacy practices into conversation with school-based, dominant literacy practices. It allows them to read and write from multiple subject positions. This approach rests on both an understanding of and an interrogation of whose voices, beliefs, language, and problems are included and whose are excluded in the texts one consumes – and, in the case of these two authors, the texts one produces. For instance, Kristina commented that she had never read Black books in school, and she later clarified by saying that these were books that felt real to her. She explained this lack of diversity was because books with Black people were inappropriate (due to the inclusion of violence, language, or specific content). Further, she understood her language to be inappropriate, too.

For Charlotte reading and writing resistantly might have included examining the roles available for females in the stories she read as well as the story she had written. In an interview, Charlotte explained that she imagined her story because of her own interest in fairy tales and a desire for a time when life was simpler and easier than it is in her life. She added, though, that this desire ends when she considers the limitations placed on women in the past. For her, female power was an issue that was present in her reading of texts and in the text she had written. Additionally, Charlotte hoped to position her female protagonist as someone who fought not only for her own empowerment but also for those less fortunate than she. But how had Charlotte represented the poor in her story, largely the townspeople who suffer at the hand of her father the king? How has Charlotte's understanding of various class backgrounds constrained her ability to consider how her text takes up and reifies notions of gender and class?

In similar ways, these young authors have produced literary works that embed the sanctioned practices both have come to know and understand as readers and students. At the same time, both authors have purposefully created texts that work to engage with and interrogate notions of gender, class, and the appropriateness of behavior and life choices and by doing so provide both young women with a platform to consider how these notions construct meaning in their lives but how these notions might be questioned and resisted.

Design and Taking Social Action

In a design orientation the power of critical literacies is harnessed in order to rewrite the world. Alternative scripts are produced which both challenge dominant, hegemonic narratives but also demonstrate new possibilities for thought and action. One way of doing this is by producing countertexts. Countertexts challenge dominant discourses. In a sense both girls' texts were countertexts. Kristina's text flipped the script related to discourses surrounding "ghetto." Rather than ghetto being something negative, Kristina's text celebrated and embraced ghetto. The family was ghetto rich, making ghetto a resource. The characters were not just irreverent and violent; they were also sage, resilient, and witty. Charlotte's character was motivated by love, but she was a princess of power who rebelled against a cruel father, took risks, and acted on her own.

Both girls could have been supported in engaging in social action. Both wrote into being desired worlds reflecting interests, identities, longings all pieced together with the materials of the textual lives they lived as readers. Both authors wrote from a position of hunger: hunger for texts that reflected not only their interests but who they are as young woman and what is meaningful in their lives. For Kristina, she produced *Ghetto Family* in part because she craved more stories about Black folks doing Black things. She and her classmates did not read Black books in school, and she explained that there were not enough Black books in her classroom, school, or community library. What books she had found or were provided with were not always age-appropriate and part of a sanctioned curriculum that privileged White, middle class texts that advanced agendas considered important by adults and educators. Kristina needed help in locating and selecting texts that had features she craved. Additionally, since Kristina was clear in her understanding that the texts she sought were somehow not good enough, she needed to feel empowered to ask for what she wanted in order to find and read more diverse representations of Black characters and by doing so, not only have reading experiences that engaged her with texts she found meaningful but also see the texts she appreciated most valued as representations of meaningful and respected life experiences.

Charlotte, too, needed to take social action. In her school, issues of gender, power, and sexuality were constantly simmering barely below the surface. In fact, that year Author Two and another teacher began a Girls' Group to help support the middle school girls in dealing with issues of sexual harassment and bullying that were happening at the school. Charlotte was well aware of these issues and reported that a male classmate had purposefully stroked her breast during a field trip without her permission. Charlotte, who is now a high school junior, visited Author Two recently and shared that she hoped to double major in college in psychology and Women's studies. Like Kristina, Charlotte's interests as reader and writer echo her own attempt to make meaning in her life around issues of gender and power and by doing so find not only texts but life experiences that help her to resist what she has experienced and known.

As Janks argues, none of these orientations, or their associated pedagogical practices, alone are enough. Instead, they are critically interdependent. Together they create productive tensions, which must be continuously navigated and negotiated. They reveal the constructed nature of texts. Together they represent a critical approach to ALL texts – canonical and popular culture, print and media texts, school-based and vernacular.

CONCLUSION

Everyday, students are absorbing and learning from the popular culture they encounter in their daily lives. What they learn finds its way into school classrooms via a number of routes. One of the ways it makes its way into the English language arts classroom is through students' writing, both required and not. In this sense, students are not only consumers of such texts they are also (re)producers of the values and messages they find there. We have argued that students' compositions that echo the popular culture texts students consume are rich sites for teaching critical literacy practices.

Students' reading and writing practices in the classroom can provide a starting point for teachers who wish to support students in learning to critically examine the messages in popular culture texts and the myriad ways those messages shape their texts and their worlds. Teachers can begin by making space and time in the classroom for the popular culture texts in students' lives. This can be done by selecting popular culture texts to bring into the classroom, but it can also be accomplished by being on the lookout for opportunities to build on the practices students are engaging in in the classroom. For example, students' compositions can act as the jumping off point for discussion about popular culture texts. Students can be guided to trace the threads of their texts, and their peers' text, back to other texts.

Centering students' texts and building on what they bring to the classroom will require teachers to be learners. They will need to be open to learning from their students about the popular culture texts their students value. They may need to do some homework of their own such as listening to rap music, viewing popular teen sitcoms, reading anime, or playing a hot new video game to get up to speed. Teachers, who have not had the opportunity to learn about critical literacy or critical media approaches, will need to educate themselves. They will need to seek out resources and wisdom from more experienced others. They will also need to prepare themselves to navigate ideologically complicated conversations that will likely include topics such as race, class, gender roles, sexuality, profanity, violence, and the like.

Debates rage on about the role popular culture should play in formal English classrooms; ultimately though, it is teachers who will decide if and how they will respond to the popular culture. They can choose to ignore what Newkirk (2007) has described as "the elephant in the room," that is, the profound influence of pop culture in their students' lives both inside and outside the classroom. Failing to acknowledge popular culture, however, does not mean it isn't there; it just means its effects go unexamined and unchallenged. Alternatively, teachers could adopt a critical pedagogy of popular culture in which they commit to helping their students learn to critically analyze the messages embedded in popular culture texts. If teachers wish to prepare students who are truly literate, they must support them in learning to read not only canonical texts, but also the popular culture texts that shape their worlds, their lives, and their choices as authors of texts and desired worlds. Teachers, and other adults, need to stand with kids in processing the messages embedded in popular culture texts, including messages about race, class, gender and in exploring the possibilities for re-reading and re-writing their world. If not, our children will be left to themselves to make sense of it on their own.

LESSON IDEA

Set aside a regular day and time in the classroom dedicated to critically examining the texts students consume and produce in their daily lives. Invite students to bring in texts they consume or have produced (i.e., books, movies, television shows, video games, text messages, etc.) for the class to discuss during this time.

Using the key concepts of critical literacy as a framework, model for students how to introduce texts, pose questions, and facilitate a discussion with their classmates. Key concepts of critical literacy include: 1) All texts are constructions. 2) All texts contain belief and value statements. 3) Each person interprets messages differently. 4) Texts serve different interests. 5) Each medium develops its own "language" in order to position readers/viewers in certain ways.

Support students in analyzing and deconstructing the messages in the focal texts and comparing those messages to other texts including texts authored by students, other popular culture texts, and canonical texts.

REFERENCES

Alford, J. (2001). Learning language and critical literacy: Adolescent ESL students. *Journal of Adolescent and Adult Literacy, 45*, 238-242.

Alvermann, D. E. (2001, May). Reading adolescents' reading identities: Looking back to see ahead. *Journal of Adolescent & Adult Literacy, 44*(8), 676-690.

Behrman, E. H. (2006). Teaching about language, power, and text: A review of classroom practices that support critical literacy. *Journal of Adolescent and Adult Literacy, 49*(6), 490-498.

Dyson, A. (1997). *Writing superheroes: Contemporary childhood, popular culture, and classroom literacy.* New York, NY: Teachers College Press.

Dyson, A. (2003). *The brothers and sisters learn to write: Popular literacies in childhood and school cultures.* New York, NY: Teachers College Press.

Dyson, A. (2008). Staying in the (curricular) lines: Practice constraints and possibilities in childhood writing. *Written Communication, 25*, 119-160.

Finders, M. J. (1997). *Just girls: Hidden literacies and life in junior high.* New York, NY: Teachers College Press.

Foss, A. (2002). Peeling the onion: Teaching critical literacy with students of privilege. *Language Arts, 79*, 393-403.

Frankenberg, R. (1993). *White women, race matters: The social construction of whiteness.* Minneapolis, MN: University of Minneapolis Press.

Freebody, P., & Luke, A. (1990). Literacies programs: Debates and demands in cultural context. *Prospect: Australian Journal of TESOL, 5*(7), 7-16.

Hall, L. (2011/2012). How popular culture texts inform and shape students' discussions of social studies texts. *Journal of Adolescent and Adult Literacy, 55*(4), 296-305.

Ives, D. (2011). Spotting foolbirds literacies hiding in plain sight in an urban English language arts classroom. *Journal of Literacy Research, 43*(3), 250-274.

Ives, D. (2012). Kristina's "Ghetto family": Tensions and possibilities at the intersection of teacher and student literacy agendas. *Research in the Teaching of English, 47*(1), 39-63.

Ives, D., & Crandall, C. (2014). Writing for the audience that fires the imagination: Implications for teaching writing. *Teaching/Writing: The Journal of Writing Teacher Education,* Winter/Spring, *47*-56.

Janks, H. (2000). Domination, access, diversity, and design: A synthesis for critical literacy education. *Educational Review, 52*(2), 175-186.

Jewitt, C. (2008). Multimodality and literacy in school classrooms. *Review of Research in Education, 32*(1), 241-267.

Lodge, H. (1997). *Providing access to academic literacy in the Arts Foundation Programme at the University of Witwatersrand in 1996 – The theory behind the practice.* Unpublished draft of Master's Research Report, University of Witwatersrand, Johannesburg, South Africa.

Luke, A. (2000). Critical literacy in Australia: A matter of context and standpoint. *Journal of Adolescent & Adult Literacy, 43*, 448-461.

Luke, A. (2004). Foreword. In M. McLaughlin & G. Devoogd, (Eds.), *Critical literacy: Enhancing students' comprehension of text* (pp. 4-5). New York, NY: Scholastic.

Luke, A. (2012). Critical literacy: Foundational notes. *Theory into Practice, 51*(1), 4-11.

Luke, A., & Freebody, P. (1999). Further notes on the four resources model. Retrieved from http://www.readingonline.org/research/lukefreebody.html.

Morrell, E. (2002). Toward a critical pedagogy of popular culture: Literacy development among urban youth. *Journal of Adolescent & Adult Literacy, 46*(1), 72-76.

Morrell, E. (2004). *Linking literacy and popular culture: Finding connections for lifelong learning.* Norwood, MA: Christopher-Gordon.

Morrell, E. (2007). Critical literacy and popular culture in urban education: Toward a pedagogy of access and dissent. In C. Clark & M. Blackburn (Eds.), *Literacy research for political action and social change* (pp. 235-255). New York, NY: Peter Lang.

Newkirk, T. (2000). Misreading masculinity: Speculations on the great gender gap in writing. *Language Arts, 77*(4), 294-300.

Newkirk, T. (2007, July). Popular culture and writing development. *Language Arts, 84*(6), 539-548.

New London Group. (1996). A pedagogy of multiliteracies: Designing social futures. *Harvard Educational Review, 61*, 60-92.

Obidah, J. E., & Marsh, T. E. J. (2006). Utilizing students'cultural capital in the teaching and learning process: "As if" learning communities and African-American students' literate currency. In D. E. Alvermann, K. A. Hinchman, D. W. Moore, S. E. Phelps, & D. R. Waff (Eds.), *Reconceptualizing the literacies in adolescents' lives* (2nd ed., pp. 107-128). Mahwah, NJ: Erlbaum.

Smitherman, G. (1999). *Talkin that talk.* New York, NY: Routledge.

Summers, S. (2000, October). Get 'em thinking! Using the "3 Rs" of media literacy. *Reading Online, 4*(4). Retrieved from: http://www.readingonline.org/newliteracies/lit_index.asp?HREF=/newliteracies/summers/index.html

Tatum, A. (2006). Adolescents' multiple identities and teacher professional development. In D. E. Alvermann, K. A. Hinchman, D. W. Moore, S. E. Phelps, & D. R. Waff (Eds.), *Reconceptualizing the literacies in adolescents' lives* (2nd ed., pp. 65-82). Mahwah, NJ: Erlbaum.

CHRISTOPHER ANDREW BRKICH, TIM BARKO &
KATIE LYNN BRKICH

13. SHADOWS OF THE PAST

Historical Interpretation, Propaganda, and the Story of Ender Wiggin

ABSTRACT

Popular science fiction provides classroom teachers multiple rich opportunities to adopt a critical lens in examining the ways in which governments and their people interact. Given the highly contested nature of both the social and natural sciences presently in the schools – particularly because of the ways in which these subject areas impact the political arena at the local, regional, and national levels – these serve as excellent fora in which to use popular science fiction to teach about and around socioscientific issues (SSI) and controversial public issues (CPI). In this chapter, we examine specifically the ways in which popular science fiction – Orson Scott Card's (1985/1994) *Ender's Game* in particular – is useful in teaching students how to identify propaganda, to discern whose purposes it serves, and to question how what it includes and what it excludes works toward those purposes.

INTRODUCTION

Within the past decade, several states across the nation have sought to shape and reshape American history and the way it is taught in schools in order to suit the social, political, religious, and economic ideology of a dominant group. In 2006, the state of Florida – in a move clearly opposed by academic historians across the country – declared by legislative fiat that

> American history shall be viewed as factual, not as constructed, shall be viewed as knowable, teachable, and testable, and shall be defined as the creation of a new nation based largely on the universal principles stated in the Declaration of Independence, (FL HB 7087E3, 2006, pp. 44; lines 1159-1163)

establishing by force of law a singular American narrative not subject to revision, dispute, or critique. Some few years later, Texas' State Board of Education explicitly rewrote its social studies and history standards to promote a factually untenable narrative which falsely attributed or grossly overstated the Founding Fathers' reverence for Christianity as a source of their political motivations and likewise eschewed slavery as a primary cause of the Civil War (19 TAC 113, 2010)

– earning among the harshest of criticisms from representatives of the Thomas B. Fordham Institute, a conservative educational think tank, for having produced "a politicized distortion of history ... [which] is both unwieldy and troubling, avoiding clear historical explanation while offering misrepresentations at every turn" (Stern & Stern, 2011, p. 141). Equally, within the last eighteen months, Georgia's State Senate proposed legislation entitled "The Teach Freedom Act" requiring American history to be taught in such a fashion as only to promote "a positive understanding of American history and government," using an originalist's lens of "the principles underlying the Declaration of Independence, the United States Constitution, and the Bill of Rights and key concepts from the Federalist Papers and Anti-Federalist Papers" (GA SB 426, 2012, pp. 1-2; lines 15-16, 33-35).

Taken together, these legislative actions demonstrate a concerted effort on the part of America's more socially conservative politicians to impose by force a narrative of American exceptionalism which promotes Christianity, unregulated free market capitalism, unrestricted gun ownership, and stringent limits on the powers of the federal government, all while serving as an apologia for the nation's past and present prejudices against racial, ethnic, linguistic, gender, and sexual minorities. In short they constitute a manner of sociocultural and sociopolitical propaganda reserving for themselves positions as being "above politics" while relegating all other historical interpretations as being politically motivated (Graff, 1993; Zimmerman, 2002). The issue is further exacerbated when classroom teachers who would promote alternative and critical interpretations of American history are accused of indoctrinating or brainwashing students (Chandler, 2006; Dahlgren, 2009; Dahlgren & Masyada, 2009) – even though one of the express purposes of a quality history education is preparing students to "demonstrate an understanding that different people may describe the same event or situation in diverse ways, citing reasons for the differences in views" (NCSS, 1994, p. 34). Social studies and English Language Arts teachers in fact have a responsibility to prepare their students to distinguish between fact and opinion, to determine an author's purpose in the production of text or media, and to evaluate such texts and media critically for both soundness and whether they are grounded in sufficient valid evidence (e.g., Georgia Department of Education, 2011, 2012) – all elements which are required in the critical evaluation of the manner of propaganda currently advanced in state legislation.

TEACHING WITH SCIENCE FICTION FOR CRITICAL ENDS

As a literary genre, science fiction has existed for quite some time and, in the last thirty years or so, gave rise to a field of science fiction studies which now "can boast its full quota of learned societies, journals, reference tools, annual conferences, and awards for scholarly achievement" (Parrinder, 2001, pp. 1-2). This field holds that through the sci-fi lens – be it worn by academics or the wider science fiction fan community – we can learn about our own culture and intimate what the future will look like, all while troubling and complicating the relationships we have with ourselves and with the Other (Bacon-Smith, 2000). Indeed, there exists a veritable wealth of discussion on the worth of science fiction in its teaching a wide variety of subjects – sociology (Laz, 1996), evolutionary biology (Bixler, 2007), physics (Dubeck et al., 1990), reading skills (Cullinan, 1987), and moral values (Prothero, 1990) to name but a few. In spite of its utility across a broad range of disciplines, however, "traditional academic discourses and discursive practices far too often dismiss science fiction as a legitimate genre of thought" (Anijar, Weaver, & Daspit, 2004, p. 3), forcing science fiction aficionados into positions in which their genre of choice must be "smuggled into the curriculum under the pretense of serving other, more easily sanctioned purposes" (Gunn, 1996, p. 377). While on the one hand we feel the science fiction genre should be taught because it has its own intrinsic worth, on the other hand – as former K-12 teachers and current teacher educators – we acknowledge the importance of satisfying the requirements of a disciplinary content-based and standards-driven curriculum. We thus position ourselves as educators who enjoy the intellectual stimulation science fiction provides in and of its own right, acknowledge its utilitarian value in resolving the divide between the curriculum of content coverage *and* the curriculum which promotes higher-order thinking (see Onosko, 1991) while using its utilitarian value as justification in promoting enjoyable teaching and learning experiences in the classroom.

Researchers have also argued that science fiction as a genre – perhaps because its futuristic, imagined, and fantastic features distances it from our immediate lived realities – also promotes a critical evaluation of systemically uneven power structures and institutionalised discrimination of the Other. EE Nunan and David Homer (1981) argued over thirty years ago that science fiction as a genre had tremendous potential to stand as a critique of the industrialisation and unequal distribution of wealth associated with free market capitalism. Sayyid (2010) argued more recently that science fiction novels such as Philip Dick's (1968/1996) *Do Androids Dream of Electric Sheep?* expose the lie of post-racial theory, arguing that superficial acceptance of the Other – a "splash of colour" in one's landscape – simply provides cover for ongoing systemic and hegemonic discrimination:

> The recruitment of ethnically marked representatives for decidedly xenophobic parties and platforms is no longer seen as extraordinary but a confirmation that diversity like democracy and developed economies is a hallmark of what it means to be European. (Sayyid, 2010, pp. 3, 4)

Carl Freedman (1987, 2000) argued that the science fiction genre as a whole aligns above all other genres with critical theory, problematising normative gender roles – particularly as portrayed between Rick Deckard, Iran Deckard, and Rachel Rosen in *Androids* (Dick, 1968/1996) – and their iterations in our lived world. Indeed, science fiction as a genre contains within itself the necessary elements to prompt deep and meaningful thinking on such themes as

> the foundation of new political orders, the endeavor to realize utopia, the exigencies underpinning tyranny, the relationship of a saintly politics to the

practice of *realpolitik*, and the potential and limitations of radical politics in the present age. (Paik, 2010, pp. 1-2)

Its power lies ultimately in prompting us to consider alternative social orders and realities which – although entirely imagined – hold within them the promise of a more just society. On these grounds, we also position ourselves as educators who value science fiction's potential in developing within our students critical thinking skills aimed at troubling social inequities in the pursuit of justice-oriented citizenship (Westheimer & Kahne, 2004).

SCIENCE FICTION, PROPAGANDA AWARENESS, AND *ENDER'S GAME*

In preparing the next generation of citizens to be well-informed, classroom teachers need to prepare their students to be critical consumers of information – rather than passive recipients who accept what they hear and see at face value. They need, as Bonnie Cramond (1993) suggests, to be taught "about *ethos*, speaker credibility; *logos*, logic of arguments; and *pathos*, psychological appeals" and that "teaching propaganda techniques and how they affect our opinions" (p 18). As George Bernstein (1992) holds additionally that "propaganda and critical thinking rest at polar opposites" (p. 14), teaching students how to sift through the constituting elements of propaganda in order to glean information useful to one's own purposes – rather than the purposes of those who produced it – is an essential enterprise. This is particularly important in an ostensibly democratic society; for, as power is supposed to reside ultimately in the hands of its citizens, and as "the use of propaganda is inevitably the exercise of power in some form" (p. 14), teaching students to identify propaganda and to interrogate its validity is to provide them the tools necessary to ensure they as citizens retain the ultimate power of the intelligent and well-informed vote. Given the highly political nature of propaganda and that the purpose of a social studies education properly formulated is to prepare young citizens for their lives as adult citizens (NCSS, 2010), teaching the two together continues to be a natural fit (Niensted, 1971).

Within the science fiction realm, there are innumerable examples of propaganda which are clearly discernible to the audience – none more obvious than the interactive recruitment videos for the United Citizen Federation in Paul Verhoeven's (1997) adaptation of Robert Heinlein's (1959/2006) *Starship Troopers*, featuring the constant refrain, "Would you like to know more?" Instances in which the characters themselves are aware of their indoctrination, with few notable exceptions – Suzanne Collins' (2008) *Hunger Games* trilogy among them – are few. And while these notable exceptions are useful in teaching students to identify propaganda, we contend that their usefulness in promoting a critical analysis of propaganda is limited – precisely *because* it is so easily identified, both by the audience and characters alike. None are surprised that Collins' (2008) protagonist Katniss Everdeen is disdainful of the Capitol's celebratory pageantry surrounding the reaping for the 74th Annual Hunger Games, specifically because the Capitol is commemorating the events which led to Katniss' district living in abject poverty. Instances in which characters and audience members alike transition from a state of obliviousness to one of painful awareness – whether gradually or jarringly – are, however, substantially more powerful instructional tools. Orson Scott Card's (1985/1994) *Ender's Game*, winner of the Young Adult Literature Service's 2008 Margaret A. Edwards Award, stands as one of the best.

In *Ender's Game*, we are introduced to an Earth in the distant future in which humankind finds itself pitted against an alien Other – a race known as the Buggers – in which officials from the International Fleet (IF), charged with humanity's defense, recruit child geniuses at a very young age to train as soldiers and to become Fleet commanders. The story's protagonist, Ender Wiggin, a child of only six years at the story's outset, is thought to be the saviour of the world in the upcoming Third Bugger Invasion, and is guilted by Colonel Graff into volunteering for Battle School:

> The Buggers may seem like a game to you now, Ender, but they damn near wiped us out last time. They had us cold, outnumbered and outweaponed. The only thing that saved us was that we had the most brilliant military commander we ever found. Call it fate, call it God, call it damnfool luck, but we had Mazer Rackham.
>
> We need the best we can get, and we need them fast. Maybe you're not going to work out for us, and maybe you are. Maybe you'll break down under the pressure, maybe it'll ruin your life, maybe you'll hate me for coming here to your house today. But if there's a chance that because you're with the fleet, mankind might survive and the Buggers might leave us alone forever – then I'm going to ask you to do it. To come with me. (pp. 24-25)

The manner in which people perceived the Buggers was no secret. Citizens had to watch annual videos of the Bugger Invasions produced by the government and the International Fleet, which in turn shaped their prejudices and predilections for supporting military action against the alien Other:

> [Ender] thought of the films of the Buggers that everyone had to see at least once a year. The Scathing of China. The Battle of the Belt. Death and suffering and terror. And Mazer Rackham and his brilliant maneuvers, destroying an enemy fleet twice his size and twice his firepower, using the little human ships that seemed so frail and weak. Like children fighting with grown-ups. And we won. (p. 25)

If the only way to save his sister Valentine's life – the one person whom he truly loved – was to participate in this conflict, to Ender there seemed little other option.

And so Ender went with Graff to Battle School and later again to Command School, finding himself perpetually friendless and purposefully isolated by the Schools' staffs, forever forced to fend for himself – enduring physical assaults, mental exhaustion, and psychological breaks. Questioning instead whether the teachers at the Schools were the enemy – and not the Buggers (pp. 110-111) – Ender made two defiant acts in order to end the suffering he was experiencing at the hands of the teachers at the Schools. First, while studying at the Battle School, after Colonel Graff consistently changed the rules of the combat simulation training exercises Ender led and endured as Commander of Dragon Army, Ender simply refused to continue playing the School's game:

> Everything they can do to beat me, thought Ender. Everything they can think of, change the rules, they don't care, just so they beat me. Well, I'm sick of the game. No game is worth Bonzo's blood pinking the water on the bathroom floor. Ice me, send me home, I don't want to play anymore. (pp. 214-215)

Second, while studying at the Command School, after his mentor at the Command School – Mazer Rackham, hero of the Second Invasion – strongly cautioned him against using a planet-killer weapon named the Molecular Detachment Device as it could invite reprisals (p. 290), Ender went ahead anyway in order to put an end to the physical, mental, and psychological exhaustion he was being forced to endure:

> It *was* funny. The adults taking all this so seriously, and the children playing along, playing along, believing it too until suddenly the adults went too far, tried too hard, and the children could see through their game. Forget it, Mazer. I don't care if I pass your test, I don't care if I follow your rules. If you can cheat, so can I. I won't let you beat me unfairly – I'll beat you unfairly first.
>
> In that final battle in Battle School, he had won by ignoring the enemy, ignoring his own losses; he had moved against the enemy's gate.
>
> And the enemy's gate was down.
>
> If I break this rule, they'll never let me be a commander. It would be too dangerous. I'll never have to play a game again. And *that* is victory. (p. 293)

By acting in extreme defiance of the wishes of those in control of the Command School, Ender sought to put an end not only to this conflict, but all the next conflicts he would experience – precisely the same reasoning which made him a suitable candidate for Battle School to begin with (pp. 18-19).

However, Ender did not experience the victory he sought. First as a tragedy for Ender and then as a farce for the readers (Žižek, 2009), we are shocked and horrified to find out that Ender's acts of defiance – done as desperate measures to exert some manner of self-control and to reclaim a sense of individual freedom – in fact accomplish precisely the ends toward which those at the Battle School and the Command School had been aiming all along. Having withheld crucial information from Ender on the Buggers' physiological and sociological nature, on the actual extent of the threat they posed to Earth, on the purpose of the games he played at both Battle School and Command School, and on the real purpose of the Third Invasion – stifling political unrest and maintaining an uneasy peace on Earth which existed so long as the Bugger threat persisted (pp. 110-111, 125-126) – Ender's acts of defiance caused him to commit genocide against an alien Other whom he came to love and with whom he identified more easily than the majority of his own species:

> "It came down to this: In the moment when I truly understand my enemy, understand him well enough to defeat him, then in that very moment I also love him. I think it's impossible to really understand somebody, what they want, what they believe, and not love them the way they love themselves. And then, in that very moment when I *love* them – "
>
> "You beat them." For a moment [Valentine] was not afraid of his understanding.
>
> "No, you don't understand. I *destroy* them. I make it impossible for them to ever hurt me again. I grind them and grind them until they don't *exist*." (pp. 238-239)

The tragedy of the Bugger xenocide was that it was not Ender's wish at all in this case; the only enemies he was seeking to grind into dust were those at the Battle School and Command Schools. He wanted to never have to play another game again, to seek an end to his suffering at the hands of those above him:

> Ender grabbed Mazer's uniform and hung onto it, pulling him down so they were face to face. "I didn't want to kill them all. I didn't want to kill anybody! I'm not a killer! You didn't want me, you bastards, you wanted Peter, but you made me do it, you tricked me into it!" He was crying. He was out of control.
>
> "Of course we tricked you into it. That's the whole point," said Graff. "It had to be a trick or you couldn't have done it. It's the bind we were in. We had to have a commander with so much empathy that he would think like the Buggers, understand them and anticipate them. So much compassion that he could win the love of his underlings and work with them like a perfect machine, as perfect as the Buggers. But somebody with that much compassion could never be the killer we needed. Could never go into battle willing to win at all costs. If you knew, you couldn't do it. If you were the kind of person who would do it even if you knew, you could never have understood the Buggers well enough." (pp. 297-298)

As Ender later comes to realise the Buggers posed no real threat to humanity at all, and that the Buggers experienced soul-crushing agony and remorse for the human deaths they had caused during the Second Invasion (pp. 320-321), one cannot help but question whether the xenocide was necessary and could have been avoided all together had the Hegemon's, the Polemarch's, and the Strategos' propaganda machine not kept from Ender the truth.

WHY WE FIGHT: TROUBLING WARTIME PROPAGANDA

The propaganda videos – referred to as "vids" – which portrayed the Buggers as an evil alien Other in Card's (1985/1994) *Ender's Game* threw real obstacles in Ender's path. His initial exposure to them prompted him to attend Battle School, placing him under the influence of the International Fleet; subsequent exposures frustrated him, keeping from Ender the information he needed to free himself from this influence. In one class period, we provide students the opportunity to explore some of the more significant passages in the novel relating to Ender's interactions with the propaganda vids, troubling their vids' content, how they presented information on the Bugger Wars to those who watched them, and the underlying purposes they truly served. In a second class period, we wanted students to make their science fiction learning experience more historically concrete – having them apply critical questioning skills to Frank Capra's (1942/2012a) *Prelude to War* – and to consider how the same media techniques which allowed the justifiable villainisation of the Nazis, the Italian fascists, and the Japanese imperialists improperly led to the xenocide of an alien race in *Ender's Game* (Card, 1985/1994).

The three passages we have selected from *Ender's Game* (Card, 1985/1994) cover Ender's exposure to International Fleet propaganda in a variety of ways. The first passage (see Appendix A) introduces us to the start of Ender's questioning the content of the IF propaganda videos. Dink, one of Ender's fellow students at Battle School, plants the seed of doubt in Ender's mind regarding the constructed nature of the vids' master narrative, and we too along as the audience begin to question the IF's motives. The second passage (see Appendix B) shows the progression of Ender's distrust, leaving both he and the audience with the sense that the vids are mostly useless and hinder the children's development rather than help it. The final passage (see Appendix C) leaves us with the knowledge that the uncensored did not teach Ender anything he had not all ready gleaned from interrogating the propaganda vids – showcasing the importance of critical literacy.

In reading these passages, we recommend using a modified version of the National School Reform Faculty's (2009) "Save the Last Word for Me" discussion protocol. In this discussion, groups of four students – one of whom doubles as a timekeeper – silently read and identify the parts of the passages they feel are most important. Students should have approximately eight to ten minutes for this stage. Once this stage is complete, one of the students will volunteer to start the discussion in s/he reads aloud the selected passage without commentary. Each of the other students in turn has one minute to comment on the passage selected: Why do *they* think it is interesting? What connections can they make across the text and to other things they have learned? After the other students have all had the chance to comment, the student who originally selected the passage explains why s/he chose the passage, why s/he considers it important, and comments using the same guiding questions – thus having had the "last word." The process repeats for the other three students, allowing each student the opportunity to have the "last word" in the discussion – ensuring for an equitable participation. This second stage should take approximately thirty minutes. Finally, the classroom teacher should bring the students back together for a ten-minute whole-class discussion, using a series of guiding questions (see Appendix D) to prompt discussion. All told, the whole process should take roughly fifty minutes – the length of a traditional class period, or approximately half of a block schedule period.

To move their understanding of propaganda beyond the science fiction world of *Ender's Game* (Card, 1985/1994) into the real world, in either the school's media lab or in your classroom with the aid of a laptop cart we recommend screening the first 15:30 of Frank Capra's (1942/2012a) *Prelude to War*, available either on DVD or for download free of charge from the US Government's Internet Archive. To ensure students remain intellectually engaged during the screening, we recommend using the included Visual Discovery Worksheet (see Appendix E). Prompt students to consider what similarities and differences exist between this US Army Special Services Division video and the vids described in *Ender's Game* (Card, 1985/1994). In the same groups as before, then have students select one of the episodes of Frank Capra's (1942/2012b) *Why We Fight* series, equally available from the US Government's Internet Archive (see Appendix F), and examine the first fifteen minutes. During the examination, have them consider the following list of questions:
– What do the first fifteen minutes of my group's chosen episode of Capra's (1942/2012b) *Why We Fight* series teach?
– What does the film purposefully include – and to what purpose?
– What would need to be added to the film in order to provide a full historical account, covering all sides?
– What manner of documents and primary sources would provide this additional information?
– Where would I look for these primary sources?

For the purposes of the summative assessment, students will spend the remaining portion of the class period – approximately twenty minutes – answering these questions, using internet search tools to provide a fuller picture of what was presented in their selected episode, and completing for homework a 750-900 word essay on the inclusion and exclusion of historical facts and perspectives from the construction of historical narratives, the motives of historical authors, and the responsibilities citizens have in interrogating historical narratives which seem misleading or incomplete.

This approach would allow students elements of choice in choosing an element of Capra's (1942/2012b) series they found personally engaging and of interest – not focused strictly on combat actions but also on the home front as well. This approach additionally has the benefit of highlighting the unidimensional nature of propagandistic grand narratives and of providing students the practical skills necessary to interrogate these constructed narratives – skills which are equally applicable to constructed history as it is presented in official school textbooks.

CONCLUSIONS

As in the case of *Ender's Game* (Card, 1985/1994), historical narratives constructed outside the realm of science fiction are as subject to propagandistic distortions driven by social, political, religious, and economic motives. Science fiction literature can serve as a safe and useful tool to introduce students to the contentious notion that history is neither simply a representation of what factually happened nor bias-free – in spite of what several state governments have made efforts to legislate ("FL HB 7087E3," 2006; "TN HB 229," 2011; "GA SB 426," 2012; "19 TAC 113," 2010). By drawing connections between science fiction literature such as *Ender's Game* (Card, 1985/1994) and actual propaganda – both past and present, both foreign and domestic – Social Studies and English Language Arts teachers are well-suited to discharge their responsibilities in promoting critical thinking skills and the redress of social inequities through the promotion of justice-oriented citizenship.

APPENDIX A

Card, O. S. (1994). Ender's Game (pp. 110-111). New York: Tor Books. (Originally published in 1985)

"Maybe you can be a commander and not be crazy. Maybe knowing about craziness means you don't have to fall for it."

"I'm not going to let the bastards run me, Ender. They've got you pegged, too, and they don't plan to treat you kindly. Look what they've done to you so far."

"They haven't done anything except promote me."

"And she make you life so easy, neh?"

Ender laughed and shook his head. "So maybe you're right."

"They think they got you on ice. Don't let them."

"But that's what I came for," Ender said. "For them to make me into a tool. To save the world.:

"I can't believe you still believe it."

"Believe what?"

"The Bugger menace. Save the world. Listen, Ender, if the Buggers were coming back to get us, they'd *be here*. They aren't invading. We beat them and they're gone."

"But the videos – "

"All from the First and Second Invasions. Your grandparents weren't born yet when Mazer Rackham wiped them out. You watch. It's all a fake. There *is* no war, and they're just screwing around with us."

"But why?"

"Because as long as people are afraid of the Buggers, the IF can stay in power, and as long as the IF is in power, certain countries can keep their hegemony. But keep watching the vids, Ender. People will catch onto this game pretty soon, and there'll be a civil war to end all wars. *That's* the menace, Ender, not the Buggers.

And in *that* war, when it comes, you and I won't be friends. Because you're American, just like our dear teachers. And *I* am not."

They went to the mess hall and ate, talking about other things. But Ender could not stop thinking about what Dink had said. The Battle School was so enclosed, the game so important in the minds of the children, that Ender had forgotten there was a world outside. Spanish honor. Civil war. Politics. The Battle School was really a very small place, wasn't it?

But Ender did not reach Dink's conclusions. The Buggers were real. The threat was real. The IF controlled a lot of things, but it didn't control the videos and the nets. Not where Ender had grown up. In Dink's home in the Netherlands, with three generations under Russian hegemony, perhaps it was all controlled, but Ender knew that lies could not last long in America. So he believed.

Believed, but the seed of doubt was there, and it stayed, and every now and then sent out a little root. It changed everything, to have that seed growing. It made Ender listen more carefully to what people meant, instead of what they said. It made him wise.

APPENDIX B

Card, O. S. (1994). Ender's Game (pp. 110-111). New York: Tor Books. (Originally published in 1985)

Ender was teaching them all about null gravity tactics. But where could Ender go to learn new things?

He began to use the video room, filled with propaganda vids about Mazer Rackham and other great commanders of the forces of humanity in the First and Second Invasion. Ender stopped the general practice an hour early, and allowed his toon leaders to conduct their own practice in his absence. Usually they staged skirmishes, toon against toon. Ender stayed long enough to see that things were going well, then left to watch the old battles.

Most of the vids were a waste of time. Heroic music, closeups of commanders and medal-winning soldiers, confused shots of marines invading Bugger installations. But here and there he found useful sequences: ships, like points of light, maneuvering in the dark of space, or, better still, the lights on shipboard plotting screens, showing the whole of a battle. It was hard, from the videos, to see all three dimensions, and the scenes were often short and unexplained. But Ender began to see how well the Buggers used seemingly random flight paths to create confusion, how they used decoys and false retreats to draw the IF ships into traps. Some battles had been cut into many scenes, which were scattered through the various videos; by watching them in sequence, Ender was able to reconstruct whole battles. He began to see things that the official commentators never mentioned. They were always trying to arouse pride in human accomplishments and loathing of Buggers, but Ender began to wonder how humanity had won at all. Human ships were sluggish; fleets responded to new circumstances unbearably slowly, while the Bugger fleet seemed to act in perfect unity, responding to each challenge instantly.

Of course, in the First Invasion the human ships were completely unsuited to fast combat, but then so were the Bugger ships; it was only in the Second Invasion that the ships and weapons were swift and deadly.

So it was from the Buggers, not the humans, that Ender learned strategy. He felt ashamed and afraid of learning from them, since they were the most terrible enemy, ugly and murderous and loathsome. But they were also very good at what they did. To a point. They always seemed to follow one basic strategy only – gather the greatest number of ships at the key point of conflict. They never did anything surprising, anything that seemed to show either brilliance or stupidity in a subordinate officer. Discipline was apparently very tight.

And there was one oddity. There was plenty of talk about Mazer Rackham but precious little video of his actual battle. Some scenes from early in the battle, Rackham's tiny force looking pathetic against the vast power of the main Bugger fleet. The Buggers had already beaten the main human fleet out in the comet shield, wiping out the earliest starships and making a mockery of human attempts at high strategy – that film was often shown, to arouse again and again the agony and terror of Bugger victory. Then, the fleet coming to Mazer Rackham's little force near Saturn, the helpless odds, and then –

Then one shot from Mazer Rackham's little cruiser, one enemy ship blowing up. That's all that was ever shown. Lots of film showing marines caring their way into Bugger ships. Lots of Bugger corpses lying around inside. But no film of Buggers killing in personal combat, unless it was spliced in from the First Invasion. It frustrated Ender that Mazer Rackham's victory was so obviously censored. Students in the Battle School had so much to learn from Mazer Rackham, and everything about his victory was concealed from view. The passion for secrecy was not very helpful to the children who had to learn to accomplish again what Mazer Rackham had done.

APPENDIX C

Card, O. S. (1994). Ender's Game (pp. 110-111). New York: Tor Books. (Originally published in 1985)

There were compensations. Mazer took Ender through the videos of the old battles from the First Invasion and the disastrous defeats of the IF in the Second Invasion. These were not pieced together from the censored public videos, but whole and continuous. Since many videos were working in the major battles, they studied Bugger tactics and strategies from many angles. For the first time in his life, a teacher was pointing out things that Ender had not already seen for himself. For the first time, Ender had found a living mind he could admire.

"Why aren't you dead?" Ender asked him. "You fought your battle seventy years ago. I don't think you're even sixty years old."

"The miracle of relativity," said Mazer. "They kept me here for twenty years after the battle, even though I begged them to let me command one of the starships they launched against the Bugger home planet and the Bugger colonies. Then they – came to understand some things about the way soldiers behave in the stress of battle."

"What things?"

"You've never been taught enough psychology to understand. Enough to say that they realized that even though I would never be able to command the fleet – I'd be dead before the fleet even arrived – I was still the only person able to understand the things I understood about the Buggers. I was, they realized, the only person who had ever defeated the Buggers by intelligence rather than luck. They needed me here to – teach the person who *would* command the fleet."

"So they sent you out in a starship, got you up to a relativistic speed – "

"And then I turned around and came back home. A very dull voyage, Ender. Fifty years in space. Officially, only eight years passed for me, but it felt like five hundred. All so I could teach the next commander everything I knew."

"Am I to be the commander, then?"

"Let's say that you're our best bet at present."

"There are others being prepared, too?"

"No."

"That makes me the only choice, then, doesn't it?"

Mazer shrugged.

"Except you. You're still alive, aren't you? Why not you?"

Mazer shook his head.

"Why not? You won before."

"I cannot be the commander for good and sufficient reasons."

"Show me how you beat the Buggers, Mazer."

Mazer's face went inscrutable.

"You've shown me every other battle seven times at least. I think I've seen ways to beat what the Buggers did before, but you've never shown me how you actually *did* beat them."

"The video is a very tightly kept secret, Ender."

"I know. I've pieced it together, partly. You, with your tiny reserve force, and their armada, those great big heavy-bellied starships launching their swarms of fighters. You dart in at one ship, fire at it, an explosion. That's where they always stop the clips. After that, it's just soldiers going into Bugger ships and already finding them dead inside."

Mazer grinned. "So much for tightly kept secrets. Come on, let's watch the video."

They were alone in the video room, and Ender palmed the door locked. "All right, let's watch."

The video showed exactly what Ender had pieced together. Mazer's suicidal plunge into the heart of the enemy formation, the single explosion, and then –

Nothing. Mazer's ship went on, dodged the shock wave, and wove his way among the other Bugger ships. They did not fire on him. They did not change course. Two of them crashed into each other and exploded – a needless collision that either pilot could have avoided. Neither made the slightest movement.

Mazer sped up the action. Skipped ahead. "We waited for three hours," he said. "Nobody could believe it." Then the IF ships began approaching the Bugger starships. Marines began their cutting and boarding operations. The videos showed the Buggers already dead at their posts.

"So you see," said Mazer, "you already knew all there was to see."

APPENDIX D

– How does propaganda influence people? Why is it often successful in influencing people?
– In what ways can propaganda be helpful? In what ways can it be harmful?
– In what ways does propaganda reveal the truth? In what ways does it conceal the truth?
– What connections can we make between these passages and other English Language Arts or Social Studies content we have seen before?

APPENDIX E

Gathering Evidence

– What do you see/hear in this image/video clip?
– What are some of the key details, or pieces of evidence, you see?
– How would you describe the scene and the people?

Interpreting Evidence

– What do you think is happening in this scene?
– What evidence do you use to base this interpretation?

Making Hypotheses from Evidence

– What do you think the people in the image/video clip were thinking or feeling?
– What *other* resources have we looked at that would corroborate your hypothesis?

Personal Connections

– What is *your* reaction to the image/video?
– Why do you react to this scene in this fashion?

APPENDIX F

Maj. Frank Capra's Why We Fight *Series by Instalment*

Instalment	Year Released	Running Time	Web Address
Prelude to War	1942	51:35	http://archive.org/details/PreludeToWar
The Nazis Strike	1943	40:20	http://archive.org/details/TheNazisStrike
Divide and Conquer	1943	56:00	http://archive.org/details/DivideAndConquer
The Battle of Britain	1943	51:30	http://archive.org/details/BattleOfBritain
The Battle of Russia	1943	76:07	http://archive.org/details/BattleOfRussiaI http://archive.org/details/BattleOfRussiaII
The Battle of China	1944	62:16	http://archive.org/details/BattleOfChina
War Comes to America	1945	64:20	http://archive.org/details/WarComesToAmerica

APPENDIX G

In 750-900 words, reflect on your learning experiences the past two days/this block schedule period. You are to answer the following questions in roughly 250-300 words each.

– How do the inclusion and exclusion of historical facts and perspectives shape the construction of a historical narrative?
– Why are those who construct historical narratives purposefully motivated to include and emphasise/omit and deemphasize certain historical facts and perspectives?
– As critical thinkers and active citizens, what steps can we take to interrogate historical narratives which may be misleading or incomplete? Why do we have a responsibility as critical thinkers and active citizens to do this?

Your submission will be evaluated based on the rubric below:

Criterion	Meets Expectations 5 Points	Needs Improvement 3 Points	Unacceptable 1 Point
On the Inclusion and Exclusion of Facts and Perspectives	The submission details how the inclusion and exclusion of historical facts and perspectives can shape the construction of a historical narrative, giving specific	The submission explains how the inclusion and exclusion of historical facts and perspectives can shape the construction of a historical narrative, giving some general	The submission provides an insufficient explanation as to how the inclusion and exclusion of historical facts and perspectives can shape the construction of a

	references to both *Ender's Game* and *Why We Fight*.	references to both *Ender's Game* and *Why We Fight*.	historical narrative, giving insufficient references to *Ender's Game* and *Why We Fight*.
On the Motives of Historical Authors	The submission details how historical authors' motives shape the choice of including certain facts and perspectives over others, giving specific references to both *Ender's Game* and *Why We Fight*.	The submission explains how historical authors' motives shape the choice of including certain facts and perspectives over others, giving some general references to both *Ender's Game* and *Why We Fight*.	The submission provides an insufficient explanation as to how historical authors' motives shape the choice of including certain facts and perspectives over others, giving insufficient references to *Ender's Game* and *Why We Fight*.
The Role of the Critically Thinking Citizen	The submission details *how* people can challenge historical narratives and *why* this is important, drawing on what we have learned so far this year on good citizenship.	The submission explains *how* people can challenge historical narratives and *why* this is important, though it does not connect to what we have learned so far this year on good citizenship.	The submission provides an insufficient explanation as to *how* people can challenge historical narratives and *why* this is important.
Style and Formatting	The submission is properly paragraphed and contains three or fewer grammar or spelling errors.	The submission is properly paragraphed and contains more than three but fewer than ten grammar or spelling errors.	The submission is either missing paragraphs or contains more than ten grammar or spelling errors.

REFERENCES

An act relating to education, HB 7087, Engrossed 3, Florida House of Representatives, 2006 Sess. (2006).

An act to amend Tennessee Code Annotated, Title 49, Chapter 6, Part 10, relative to education, HB 229, Tennessee General Assembly, 107th Regular Sess. (2011).

Anijar, K., Weaver, J. A., & Daspit, T. (2004). Introduction. In J. A. Weaver, K. Anijar, & T. Daspit (Eds.), *Science fiction curriculum, cyborg teachers, and youth culture*. New York, NY: Peter Lang.

Bacon-Smith, C. (2000). *Science fiction culture*. Philadelphia, PA: University of Pennsylvania Press.

Bernstein, G. (1992). Propaganda, politics and critical thinking. *Inquiry: Critical Thinking Across the Disciplines, 9*(2), 14-15.

A bill to be entitled "The Teach Freedom Act," SB 426, Georgia Senate, 2012 Sess. (2012).

Bixler, A. (2007). Teaching evolution with the aid of science fiction. *American Biology Teacher, 69*(6), 337-340.

Capra, F. R., Maj. (Director). (2012a). Prelude to war [DVD]. In F. R. Capra, Maj. (Producer), *Why we fight*. United States of America: Topics entertainment. (Originally released in 1942)

Capra, F. R., Maj. (Director). (2012b). Why we fight [DVD]. *United States: Topics entertainment*. (Originally released in 1942)

Card, O. S. (1994). *Ender's game*. New York, NY: Tor Books. (Originally published in 1985)

Chandler, P. T. (2006). Academic freedom: A teacher's struggle to include "Other" voices in history. *Social Education, 70*, 354-357.

Collins, S. (2008). *The hunger games*. New York, NY: Scholastic.

Cramond, B. (1993). Speaking and listening: Key components of a complete language arts program for the gifted. *Roeper Review, 16*(1), 44-48. doi: 10.1080/02783199309553534.

Cullinan, B. E. (Ed.). (1987). *Children's literature in the reading program*. Newark, DE: International Reading Association.

Dahlgren, R. L. (2009). Fahrenheit 9/11 in the classroom. *Teacher Education Quarterly, 36*(1), 25-42.

Dahlgren, R. L., & Masyada, S. (2009). Ideological dissonance: A comparison of the views of eight conservative students with the recruitment document from a southeastern college of education. *Social Studies Research and Practice, 4*(1), 1-11.

Dick, P. K. (1996). *Do androids dream of electric sheep?* New York, NY: Del Rey. (Originally published in 1968)

Dubeck, L. W., Bruce, M. H., Schmucker, J. S., Moshier, S. E., & Boss, J. E. (1990). Science fiction aids science teaching. *Physics Teacher, 28*(5), 316-318.

Freedman, C. (1987). Science fiction and critical theory. *Science Fiction Studies, 14*, 180-200.

Freedman, C. (2000). *Critical theory and science fiction*. Hanover, NH: University Press of New England.

Georgia Department of Education. (2011). *Georgia performance standards for social studies – Grade 8*. Retrieve July 10, 2013, from https://www.georgiastandards.org/Frameworks/GSO%20Frameworks/SS%20Gr%208%20Curriculum%20Map.pdf

Georgia Department of Education. (2012). *8th grade English language arts common core Georgia performance standards*. Retrieved July 10, 2013, from https://www.georgiastandards.org/Common-Core/Common%20Core%20Frameworks/CCGPS_ELA_Grade8_Standards.pdf

Graff, G. (1993). *Beyond the culture wars: How teaching the conflicts can revitalize American education*. New York, NY: W. W. Norton.

Gunn, J. (1996). Teaching science fiction. *Science Fiction Studies, 23*, 377-384.

Heinlein, R. A. (2006). *Starship troopers*. New York, NY: Ace Books. (Originally published in 1959)

Laz, C. (1996). Science fiction and introductory sociology: The handmaid in the classroom. *Teaching Sociology, 24*(1), 54-63.

National Council for the Social Studies. (1994). *Expectations of excellence: Curriculum standards for social studies*. Washington, DC: Author.

National Council for the Social Studies. (2010). *National curriculum standards for social studies: A framework for teaching, learning, and assessment*. Alexandria, VA: Author.

National School Reform Faculty. (2009). *Save the last word for me*. Retrieved July 24, 2013, from http://www.nsrfharmony.org/protocol/doc/save_last_word.pdf

Niensted, S. (1971). Reading in a thinking curriculum. *Reading Teacher, 24*(7), 659-662.

Nunan, E. E., & Homer, D. (1981). Science, science fiction, and a radical science education. *Science Fiction Studies, 8*(3), 311-330.

Onosko, J. J. (1991). Barriers to the promotion of higher order thinking in social studies. *Theory and Research in Social Education, 19*(4), 341-366.

Paik, P. Y. (2010). *From utopia to apocalypse: Science fiction and the politics of catastrophe*. Minneapolis, MN: University of Minnesota Press.

Parrinder, P. (Ed.). (2001). *Learning from other worlds: Estrangement, cognition, and the politics of science fiction and utopia*. Durham, NC: Duke University Press.

Prothero, J. (1990). Fantasy, science fiction, and the teaching of values. *English Journal, 79*(3), 32-34.

Sayyid, S. (2010). *Do post-racials dream of white sheep?* Coimbra, Portugal: Centro de Estudos Sociais. Retrieved July 12, 2013, from http://www.ces.uc.pt/projectos/tolerace/media/Working%20Paper%201/6%20CERS%20-%20Do%20Post-Racials%20Dream%20of%20White%20Sheep.pdf

Stern, S. M., & Stern, J. A. (2011). *The state of state US history standards, 2011*. Washington, DC: Thomas B. Fordham Institute.

Texas Essential Knowledge and Skills for Social Studies, 19 TAC 113 (2010).

Verhoeven, P. (Director). (1997). *Starship troopers* [DVD Movie]. USA: Columbia TriStar Home Entertainment.

Westheimer, J., & Kahne, J. (2004). What kind of citizen? The politics of educating for democracy. *American Educational Research Journal, 41*(2), 237-269.

Zimmerman, J. (2002). *Whose America?: Culture wars in the public schools*. Cambridge, MA: Harvard University Press.

Žižek, S. (2009). *First as tragedy, then as farce*. Brooklyn, NY: Verso.

KEVIN SMITH

14. CRITICAL HITS & CRITICAL SPACES

*Roleplaying Games and Their Potential in
Developing Critical Literacy and New Literacy Practices*

ABSTRACT

In Roleplaying games (RPGs), players perform characters in a game-world based on fictional or non-fictional elements. With the aid of a narrator/referee, players take part in a type of shared-storytelling, engaging in conflict resolution through roleplay, interaction and exploration. This type of playful performance can provide meaningful opportunities for players to examine and critique various texts and the narrative and tropes they contain. More important, they have the potential to aid players in developing their critical literacy, which in turn can inform their understanding of the world and provide new opportunities for social action that may bring about positive social change in their immediate circumstances and beyond. In this chapter, I draw on my experiences as a secondary school teacher and mobilise a critical performative pedagogy in theorizing the potential of roleplaying games as creative and transformative practices of a critical pedagogy that accommodates and encourages the development of students' political literacy.

INTRODUCTION

Pupils' lives include constant interaction with a multiplicity of texts. Film, novels, television and even various forms of gaming all provide opportunities for reflection, meaning-making and critique (Schwarz, 2010; Thomas, 2006). Roleplaying games (RPGs) offer players opportunities to interact with established settings, characters and plots from a variety of media and pop-culture sources. They also feature a cooperative, creative process where forms of expression, analysis and critique may take place within a collaborative and improvisational context. RPGs offer structures and frameworks for players to create and develop their own settings. Within these settings, players perform as agents in the narratives they co-construct and explore. As such, RPGs can allow players to create and interact in virtual worlds where they engage in, experiment upon, examine, analyse and critique various narratives and tropes not only found in literature, film and other cultural media, but also in their day-to-day social and political discourse (Shapiro & Leopold, 2012).

P. Paugh et al. (eds.), Teaching towards Democracy with Postmodern and Popular Culture Texts, 239–256.
© 2014 Sense Publishers. All rights reserved.

A typical role-playing game involves players creating and performing various personas, or "player characters" (PCs), who serve as the protagonists in a form of shared storytelling. Individual players create PCs that satisfy their personal preferences while taking into consideration the needs and expectations of the other players in the group. Once characters are created, the players then work together in negotiating the elements of the game world, with one player acting as a referee and guide, and the others serving as "members of the cast." The gaming world can be established upon existing fictional settings, such as *Star Wars*, *The Lord of the Rings*, and Marvel Comics, as well as settings created by game companies like Wizards of the Coast (WoTC) and their *The Forgotten Realms*, *Eberron* and *Greyhawk* settings. In each of these settings, players can follow the established narrative of a particular story or branch out into alternative narratives, and it is the potential of these alternative narratives that provide a potentially powerful opportunity for students to develop their critical literacy (Freire, 2006). While game settings are often set in fantastic or futuristic settings, they can also be based in the "real world," and may provide players with opportunities to participate in historical or contemporary storylines that can accommodate critical investigations of power, culture and social landscapes. Popular RPGs such as *Dungeons & Dragons* evolved from rules systems for wargames where conflict resolution was primarily conducted through simulated combat. However, as rules systems have grown in sophistication, and an emphasis on player collaboration over competition has emerged, alternative means of conflict resolution have been introduced. As such, RPGs demonstrate an elegant combination of structured rules-based-play that accommodates flexibility and broad interpretation, characteristics that can lend to their use in game-based pedagogy (Francis, 2006). The privileging of player collaboration lends to the creation of experimental and performative spaces in which players, while in character, engage with each other and elements of the game world.

In this chapter, I briefly discuss the recent rise in popularity and the norming of roleplaying games in popular culture and then utilize a performative studies perspective, and in particular, critical performance pedagogy (Boal, 1974; Denzin, 2003; Elliot, 2007; Harman & French, 2004; Harman & McClure, 2011) in theorizing the potential of roleplaying games and their elements as performative and potentially transformative practices in which students can collaboratively generate narratives for critical inquiry and reflection. In addition, I discuss lesson plan ideas for teachers who want to incorporate elements of RPGs in accommodating students' development and application of their critical literacy.

THE ORIGINS OF RPGS

Modern roleplaying games (RPGs) emerged in the mid-1960s, where a number of committed "wargamers" worked together in promoting their favorite hobby. Wargames typically involved two or more players who commanded armies of plastic or metal figures as they engaged in mock combat scenarios. These scenarios were often re-enactments of historic battles, and depending on the players, the scenes could even be played-out on miniaturized terrain meant to recreate that particular historical and military milieu. Gary Gygax and Dave Arneson were two wargaming enthusiasts who forever altered the landscape of wargaming by incorporating non-traditional game elements and methods of play into their own games. As the popularity of these changes resonated throughout their gaming communities, they eventually published rulebooks to support games incorporating these new, fantastic elements. Eventually, these publications grew in both sophistication and scope and not only laid the foundations for the roleplaying game *Dungeons & Dragons* (Wizards of the Coast, 2004), but also served as the inspiration for other "pen and pencil" and video-game based RPGs.

The introduction of fantastic elements into traditional wargaming was influenced by the explosive popularity of what is regarded by RPG players as "high fantasy" literature such as *The Lord of the Rings* and "pulp fantasy" or "sword & sorcery" literature such as Michael Moorcock's *Elric of Melniboné* series, H.P. Lovecraft's *The Call of Cthulu* and Jack Vance's *The Dying Earth*. High and pulp fantasy share common roots in that the authors create imaginary characters in fantastic settings that usually involve magic, monsters and the supernatural. However, where "high" and "pulp" fantasy differ might be in the scope of the stories being told and by their critical and commercial success. For example, Tolkien's *The Lord of the Rings* trilogy is an epic tale of world-changing events that is reminiscent of ancient Nordic sagas, while Moorcock's *Elric of Melniboné* series follows the exploits of a non-human, self-exiled monarch as he searches for a sense of purpose and meaning in life. Tolkien's *The Lord of the Rings* and *The Hobbit* have enjoyed enormous critical and economic success, and have shifted from somewhat marginal texts in the mid 1960s to fixtures of contemporary popular culture. The popularity of these stories and the classical narrative they employ have encouraged schools to embrace them as examples of classical literature and have allowed them to be included in reading lists alongside the works of Fitzgerald and Steinbeck, but works of "pulp fantasy," while often populating library shelves in the same schools, rarely become official elements of a school's curriculum.

It is the alternative distinctiveness of "pulp fantasy" that inspired traditional wargamers like Gygax and Arneson to modify and transform their hobby from a battle-simulation exercise into a performance-based, collective form of storytelling. Where traditional wargaming was governed by rules intended to support historical re-enactments of famous military conflicts, Gygax and Arneson developed rules to incorporate fantastical elements such as elves, dwarves and magic. As Gygax published and distributed his rules for these changes, another shift in how these games were played was taking place. Like the narratives of high fantasy novels, wargaming was typically broad in scope in that players commanded armies and executed play on a larger, somewhat impersonal scale. However, Arneson, inspired by the narratives in pulp fantasy that focused more closely on individuals and their perspective on their fantasy-world, approached Gygax with a set of rules for wargaming where players assumed the roles of individual characters. With this new approach, players no longer played as faceless generals in opposition controlling a mass of un-named soldiers, but rather, they directly interacted with each other and the elements of the game world designed and performed by the referee (also called the dungeon master – DM or game master – GM) as they adopt and perform the persona of their PCs.

Equally important to the performance aspect of this type of play, is the concept of collaboration and teamwork. Unlike the games prior to RPGs, player collaboration now takes precedence over player competition. In this new iteration of the game, players work together in facing the encounters presented to them in the game world by the referee. The challenges placed before players can include anything the DM/GM can create and is appropriate to the setting. For example, if a game setting is a typical, "high fantasy" setting, the challenges developed by the DM could be combat scenarios against orcs and goblins, puzzles and traps the PCs face as they infiltrate ancient ruins, or even a diplomatic negotiation between rival NPCs, or non-player characters, that the DM performs. The collaborative, improvisational, performance-based approach to storytelling is supported by a sophisticated system of structured yet flexible rules that encourage roleplaying through dialogue and player interaction. Roleplaying supports creative and alternative pathways for problem-solving, reflection and expression, and it is this amalgamation of playful performance, analysis and interaction that is the most distinctive feature of such games and is where the pedagogical potential of RPGs lies.

The work of Gygax, Arneson and others eventually coalesced into the game *Dungeons & Dragons,* the first commercially successful roleplaying game. Since its introduction in the early 1970s, the popularity of *Dungeons & Dragons* has inspired the creation of other RPGs such as *Pathfinder, GURPS* and *Mutants & Masterminds*. However, in spite of the popularity of these games, often negative, stereotypical connotations have been applied to RPG enthusiasts – with references in popular culture representing this community of gamers as "geeks," "nerds" and socially inept "loners." In the 1980s, opposition to RPGs grew in response to a perceived connection to the occult. Advocacy groups such as BADD (Bothered About Dungeons & Dragons) created by Patricia Pulling, and Chick Publications, an evangelical Christian organization specializing in publishing cartoon religious tracts, made claims connecting *Dungeons & Dragons* to occultism and witchcraft (http://www.chick.com/reading/tracts/0046/0046_01.ASP, 2013). Other allegations imposed against RPGs by Christian-based groups claimed RPGs encouraged drug use, violent behavior and suicide amongst players (Waldron, 2005). In the US, the fervor regarding roleplaying games and the occult made national headlines as it was promoted by news programs such as 60 Minutes, a news magazine broadcast on CBS (CBC Digital Archives, 2014). The allegations levied against RPGs contributed to the marginalization of RPG players, with long-lasting effects that continue to resonate in contemporary popular culture.

However, in spite of these accusations (and perhaps even in response to them), RPGs maintain a palpable presence through references in popular culture. For example, in the film *E.T. The Extraterrestrial* the character Elliot is shown playing an RPG with his brother and friends. The script for the film specifically mentions

Dungeons & Dragons, "Five boys are seated around a kitchen table. They are into the final hours of a late-night DUNGEONS AND DRAGONS (SIC) game" (Mathison, 1982, p. 7). Numerous episodes from a number of television programs including *The Simpsons, Dexter's Laboratory, Futurama, Spongebob Squarepants*, and *The Big Bang Theory* have made multiple references to RPGs. While the narratives and tropes surrounding these references often continue to cast the players of RPGs as abnormal misfits, a competing geek-chic counter-narrative also celebrates the "gamer persona." This is especially evident in the television sit-com *The Big Bang Theory* where the protagonists who are socially-awkward, intellectual gamers are presented as loveable, quirky "unlikely heroes."

A similar perspective is maintained in Episode 14 of the second season of the television program *Community* entitled *Advanced Dungeons & Dragons* (Guest, 2011). The main characters of this program are a group comprised of a variety of personality types, many of whom are not associated with being a "nerd" or "geek." However, in this episode, the characters play *Dungeons & Dragons* to befriend and improve the self-esteem of a character who is an RPG player and clearly an outsider. In this episode, one of the main characters, described as socially awkward and even slightly autistic, is the "Dungeon Master" who quickly masters the rules of the game, even creating pre-generated characters for the rest of the players. Throughout the episode, the "social outsider" trope is firmly reinforced through the characterization of the DM and RPG player the main characters try to help. At the same time, the narrative of the plot underscores the potential collaborative/ performative quality of RPGs as the group of characters play the game, understanding that their in-game decisions are performative, potential models for real-world actions that can have real and meaningful outcomes. At the same time, this sympathetic view of roleplayers exists in opposition to the stereotypical narrative that RPG players possess characteristics that keep them at the fringes of "normal" society.

CRITICAL PERFORMANCE PEDAGOGY

In the paragraphs above, I've referenced the terms "performative" and "performance" in discussing RPGs. In the following, I discuss these terms and how they relate to theorizing the use of RPGs in developing critical literacy practices. Critical performance pedagogy (CPP) draws from the social foundations of performance studies, and in particular, performance pedagogy and critical pedagogy, in creating conditions for students and teachers to actively examine the ever-present (but not always observable) social, political, cultural and economic factors of their lives. Performance pedagogy is an approach to teaching and learning that privileges "the doing" – the performativity of knowing and learning that is gained through performance. Burke (cited in Denzin, 2003, p. 189) describes a performance as an interpretive event involving "actors, purposes, scripts, stories, stages, and interactions." Langellier (cited in Denzin, 2003, p. 189) situates performance as an intervention "between experience and the story told" (2003, p.

189). It is a representation of an experience interpreted through the body and language (Carlson, 1996).

A performance is embedded in language in that the act of speaking creates conditions and accomplishes tasks (Denzin, 2003). This creation and action is performative. In other words, performativity does not describe the potential or capacity of an event to be performed, but rather, it addresses "the reiterative power of discourse to reproduce the phenomena that it regulates and constrains" (Butler, 1993, p. 2). In other words, the speech act produces the subject, with that production relying upon previous language and performances. This act of referencing, citing and then constructing a representation in our own performance means that every performance is an original and an imitation (Denzin, 2003). It also means that performativity references the doing – the construction of both identities and knowledge, and it is this doing – the constitutive engagement of action, creation and knowing that is sympathetic to a critical pedagogy and provides educators and students with the potential for a particularly powerful approach to critically-informed educational experiences.

As mentioned above, CPP draws from performance and critical theory studies, and at its foundation is an approach to learning and instruction that is primarily concerned with helping students (and teachers) to develop their critical literacy through a dialogical, kinesthetically-interactive, performance-based method of inquiry and expression. In describing the critical foundations of CPP, Pinaeu (2002) suggests that critical pedagogy is best understood as

> a network of convictions and commitments that draw a 'language of critique' from the Marxist social theories of the Frankfurt School and a corresponding 'language of possibility' from John Dewey's charge that schools should be public arenas that prepare citizens for active participation in a democratic society. (p. 42)

In this chapter, I situate the critical aspect of CPP specifically in reference to Freire's (1985) concept of conscientization, or critical consciousness, where people learn to "perceive social, political, and economic contradictions, and to take action against the oppressive elements of reality," with the goal of such action to recognize our reality exists not as a limited, fixed reality, but as a world "in the making" (Freire, 1985, p. 67). This transformative perspective allows students and teachers to engage in actions that challenge socially unjust practices that limit their agency and inclusion in the public sphere. Ultimately, the transformative goal of actions informed through a critical pedagogy is not simply "an excision of unjust practices and worldviews, but the creation of a reality in which these practices and perspectives cannot exist" (Smith, 2013). Paramount to this process of transformation through a critical interaction and interpretation of the world is Freire's (2006) concept of praxis, which "underscores the need to use action and reflection to challenge dominant educational practices" (Harman & McClure, 2011, p. 382). Action and reflection followed by a purposeful-doing enhanced through a critical awareness, is central to both critical and performance pedagogy and provides the robust theoretical landscape from which critical performance pedagogy has emerged. The concept of the performative in schools – specifically, educational action and speech that constructs and produces critical agents and perspectives through performance provides what (Giroux, 1997) describes as

> an articulating principle that signals the importance of translating theory into practice while reclaiming cultural texts as an important site in which theory is used to 'think' politics in the face of a pedagogy of representation that has implications for how to strategize and engage broader issues. (p. 2)

> Critical performance pedagogy offers a compelling and fascinating rethinking of critical pedagogy that recognizes the "complexity, contradictions and messiness of educational practice …" and situates critical pedagogy "as an aspirational practice akin to that of radical democracy." (Avis & Bathmaker, 2004, p. 42)

PERFORMANCE, PLAY AND CRITICAL LITERACY

Roleplaying games find their origins in literature that is rarely regarded as "high quality" and is typically not included in the "Western canon." For example, Appendix N entitled "Inspirational Reading" in the *Advanced Dungeons & Dragons Dungeon Master's Guide* (Gygax, 1979) lists over 20 texts generally considered as "sword & sorcery" literature, with no references to any of the great sagas or classical tales that comprise the typical body of literature students are required to study in school. With a significant portion of the gaming community being represented as abnormal, quirky – even subaltern, and with the tradition of RPGs stemming from non-classical, popular fiction, it seems fitting that RPGs can not only be an effective tool in exploring texts that exist outside of a school's curriculum, but they can also be used as vehicles for developing critical literacy skills and emphasizing the importance of varying voices, views and texts that are excluded from the standardized, "classical" literature regularly foisted upon students. The importance of drawing upon a variety of different texts – in different forms such as film, comic books and roleplaying games is underscored by Gee (2003) who suggests that children often feel that they don't belong, or can't relate, to the worlds described in their textbooks and other officially endorsed texts in a school's curriculum due to the depersonalized and abstract prose used to describe them. In other words, many of the texts schools use alienate students through the language employed, as well as the narratives produced, which is counterintuitive to creating an aesthetic and efficacious learning environment, particularly when educators are attempting to develop critical literacy practices as part of their pedagogy.

Roleplaying is not a new concept to teaching and learning. Shapiro and Leopold (2012) discuss the debate between opponents and proponents of roleplaying in education as they argue for the inclusion of roleplaying as a meaningful, aesthetically-charged component of the classroom that "resides in the middle ground between creative thought and real-world interaction" (p. 123). In their discussion, they elevate the status of roleplaying from an instructional method to a process of critical examination as they call for a "critical turn" in the use of roleplaying in school

> Critical role-play requires students to embody voices and perspectives that may be quite different from their own. It asks them to speak and write using discourse that may be unfamiliar. It encourages them to explore relationships among people, texts, and contexts. (Ibid.)

Roleplay, and in particular RPGs, accommodate such critical explorations because they encourage a combination of play, performance, collaboration and examination. In discussing play, Jenkins (2013) builds upon and expands the concept in an educational setting as not simply a potential motivator for good behavior and reward for non-play activities, but rather as an approach to learning,

> Through play, children try on roles, experiment with culturally central processes, manipulate core resources, and explore their immediate environments. (p. 22)

Play, as Jenkins (2013) suggests, and in particular games, can further accommodate a critical performance pedagogy in that they provide a context wherein play and performance are merged together within a system of rules and guidelines.

> Games construct compelling worlds that players move through. Players feel a part of those worlds and have some stake in the events unfolding. Games not only provide a rationale for learning: what players learn is put immediately to use to solve compelling problems with real consequences in the world of the game. (p. 23)

Furthermore, Jenkins (2013) emphasises that the incorporation of play/games into the classroom encourages a participatory culture that possesses

> ... relatively low barriers to artistic expression and civic engagement, strong support for creating and sharing one's creations, and some type of informal mentorship whereby what is known by the most experienced is passed along to novices. (p. 3)

Conquergood (1989) provides a complimentary, performative conception of play as pedagogy in stating that the

> metacognitive signal 'this is play' temporarily releases, but does not disconnect us, from workaday realities and responsibilities and opens up a privileged space for sheer deconstruction and reconstruction. (p. 83)

In discussing performative research, Pinaeu (2002) reiterates Conquergood's position and draws connections between performative research and performative pedagogy which enables not only a critically informed play pedagogy, but a critical performance pedagogy that includes play as a performative act

> As a performative act, play enables the kinetic and kinesthetic understanding of real and imagined lived experience, set apart from the responsibilities and culpabilities that normally attend such experimentation. (p. 27)

Both Conquergood (1985) and Pinaeu (2002, 2005) remind us that performative approaches to learning, whether through research or in schools, are deeply concerned with issues of power and authority, and more important, since

> performances are public events ..., they are a 'site of struggle where competing interests intersect, and different viewpoints and voices get articulated.' (Pinaeu, 2005, p. 33)

These public struggles exist in the performative redefinition of performers, the texts they use in constructing their performances and even the audiences who witness these events.

The literature regarding critical performance pedagogy outlines the theoretical foundations, motivations and goals of such an approach to education, but what can a critical performance pedagogy that incorporates aspects of roleplaying games in developing critical literacy practices look like in the classroom? As mentioned in the lesson plan idea below, the incorporation of RPGs into the classroom requires some preparation in that RPGs can be comprised of complex rules systems. Part of the complexity of these rules stems from the necessity to replicate real-world activities and task-resolution in a game setting. Another factor is that the publication of rule books is a major revenue stream for RPG companies. Thus, the more rules that are published, the more books that are sold and the more profit is produced. However, a "rules-light" approach to RPGs in the classroom can provide students and teachers with a basic understanding of the game, and as outlined below, there are a number of resources for students and teachers to use in gaining these basics. However, how that game is then interpreted into the curriculum is up to the teacher and students. For example, as opposed to providing students with a text to read and then analyze, an RPG influenced curriculum could have students develop and then participate in stories that take place in the settings they establish and involving characters they create and perform. As another example, students could be introduced to a text and then asked to recreate that text in an RPG setting. When I use the word text, I mean any narrative including books, films, television shows and even commercials. In addition to creating RPG versions of these texts, students can then also redefine them by producing alternative narratives that are then performed within their game setting. However, while these are somewhat unconventional approaches to learning, they aren't particularly critical learning experiences. In order to transform a performance based pedagogy into a critical performance pedagogy, students and teachers must adopt and develop critical literacy practices that assist them in identifying what Quantz (2009) describes as

> the contradictions that exist between the way people make meaning of their world and the way the world is materially organized through the structures and institutions and codes of social life. (p. 2)

This can be accomplished through performing existing, unaltered texts that are re-imagined through alternative narratives, or original texts developed by students. For example, a scene in Tolkien's *Return of the King* describes King Theoden and his army as they encounter the "wild men," who are described as squat, gnarled men dressed in grass skirts using poison darts and speaking in broken English. In the scene, Theoden attempts to establish the wild men as his allies against the evil forces of Sauron. The presentation of the wild men is a complicated representation of the "ennobled savage" – the chief, although speaking in broken English, is also stately, sophisticated and eventually berates Theoden for speaking down to him. In a critical roleplaying experience, students can perform the characters in this scene, paying particular attention to how they perform a "king" and a "chief." Students can be asked to reflect on how they felt in reading Tolkien's script as they performed their roles, as well as how they physically responded to being "in character," considering what the physical interpretation of their characters means in regard to representations of the civilized king and the barbaric chief. Students also might be asked to re-write the scene, providing their own dialogue and reinterpreting the scene in ways that challenge the performers' and audience's orientation to the discourses of the "civilized" and the "primitive."

Moreover, a critical roleplaying experience should allow for the inclusion of the students' actual lived experiences, adopting texts that they normally interact with in their daily lives, and should assist and encourage students to envision new possibilities and hopeful solutions to injustices presented to them in the text as a means of preparing them for further engagement of the injustices they face in the real world. Such an approach could include cues from Boal's (1974) *Theatre of the Oppressed*. A full discussion of *Theatre of the Oppressed* is outside of the scope of this chapter, but in the simplest of terms, *a Theatre of the Oppressed* experience includes spectators/actors (called Spec-actors) who perform a scene involving a form of conflict. As the scene progresses, audience members can stop the performance and propose more just alternatives to what they are witnessing. The experience is facilitated by a "Joker" who, as a neutral party, assists the spec-actors in crafting their narrative. Boal (1974) underscored the performative – the doing that is necessary for the transformative quality of roleplay to be engaged – by asking "Should actors and characters go on dominating the stage, their domain, while I sit still in the audience?" His response:

> I think not. We must invade. The audience mustn't just liberate its Critical Conscience (sic), but its body too. It needs to invade the stage and transform the images that are shown there. (p. xx)

A critical performance pedagogy incorporating RPG elements provides a sympathetic structure for students to engage in critical roleplay. The role of the DM/GM is a facilitator role that can easily adopt elements of Boal's "Joker." As participants in the game setting, the players are already spec-actors, viewing the performances of the DM and other players and responding to those performances and the setting with their own performance. In addition to the "gaming" of the curriculum, another element that can enhance a critical roleplaying experience is the element of chance. Dice are important tools for conflict resolution in RPGs and often indicate the level of success a player has in performing a task. In fact, the title of this paper is derived from games based on a 20-sided die. For example, when a player rolls a "natural 20," that signifies they have made a critical hit – it is the ultimate roll and most sought after result. Players and DMs role dice to determine how a number of tasks are resolved. For example, performing a skill-based task in an RPG can include roleplaying on behalf of the player and the DM, but it may also include a "skill check" wherein the player rolls a die. The result can be modified by the PC's training in that skill (represented by a numeric bonus the player can add to the die roll) and other statistical and circumstantial factors. With the inclusion of chance, the players in a critical roleplaying experience can perform the resolution of a task and then incorporate a die roll to determine the level of success. A successful check can provide players with an opportunity to discuss their solution and the possible outcomes, while a failure can cause players to regroup and re-evaluate their approach, stimulating dialogue and causing students to challenge themselves in thinking about and performing alternative solutions that may not have presented themselves in their first attempt.

Irrespective of the actual mechanics used in enacting an RPG based pedagogy, the overall goal is to encourage students to find opportunities to performatively investigate and engage in texts they find compelling, engaging and important with a critical perspective that brings into clarity factors that obfuscate how social, political, economic and cultural factors negotiate and possibly limit their inclusion in society. Before describing how RPG elements can assist in this undertaking, I refer to Boal (1974) again as he describes the performative/transformative potential of critically informed roleplay and how it can affect the individual, and hopefully, others as well

> By taking possession of the stage, the Spect-Actor is consciously performing a responsible act. The stage is a representation of the reality, a fiction. But the Spect-Actor is not fictional. He (sic) exists in the scene and outside of it, in a dual reality. By taking possession of the stage in the fiction of the theatre he acts: not just in the fiction, but also in his social reality. By transforming fiction, he is transformed into himself. (p. xxi)

INCORPORATING RPG ELEMENTS INTO THE CLASSROOM

In the following paragraphs I'll introduce an RPG-based idea for teachers to use in their work with students in developing critical literacy skills. The following is not a full-fledged lesson plan. As a teacher, I've come to appreciate a number of approaches to developing ways to teach students, and I don't believe there is a singular, "fool-proof" formula for creating effective lesson plans. Instead, I describe one of the RPG-based concepts I've used in my own experience as a middle-school and high school technology teacher that I believe provided my students and me with opportunities to critique and question aspects of curriculum, schooling and certain elements of our personal lived experiences.

While incorporating RPG elements into the classroom may seem most appropriate to an English or literary curriculum, they can also be used in history, social studies and even technology curricula. For example, I incorporated the "character sheet" concept described below into middle school and high school technology classes. I was able to address a number of curricular benchmarks for my middle school technology course, such as inserting tables, formatting text, managing pagination, and inserting pictures into a Word document, while at the same time creating spaces for my students and I to "resist" the limiting structure of the "official curriculum" as we examined, reflected-upon and discussed the choices we made in developing and performing the characters we created and re-created. In my high school technology courses, much of the "official" curriculum was concerned with conducting online research, how to locate and evaluate reliable information on the Internet, and developing the skill to effectively interpret and synthesize new information as students reported their findings. Both of the concepts I outline below not only helped us meet these curricular goals, but also provided us with rich, and often unexpected, opportunities to critically consider the subjects of our research.

Incorporating aspects of RPGs into the classroom may seem challenging, particularly if the teacher or students have little experience with playing RPGs. However, certain aspects of RPGs have crossed-over into other forms of media and as a result, may feel more accessible to teachers and students. For example, the "character sheet" – a simple synopsis of a player character's game statistics and personal story or background originated in pen and pencil RPGs like *Dungeons & Dragons*, but the popularity of video-game based RPGs, such as *The Legend of Zelda* (Nintendo) and *Skyrim* (Xbox) – games heavily influenced by pen and pencil RPGs – situate the concept of the character sheet as central to the overall gaming experience. The prevalence of the character sheet concept and its importance in video-game based RPGs has elevated it from the relative obscurity of pen and pencil gaming and has situated it as one of the most important and recognizable aspects of video-game based RPGs. In my experience, many students – even those who don't play pen and pencil or video-game based RPGs, quickly grasp the concept and seemed comfortable with its use in the classroom.

For roleplayers, the character sheet is not only a type of quick reference crib-sheet; it is also a physical representation of their virtual character in the real-world. In video games like those mentioned above, the character sheet is usually found in an in-game menu where the player views the PC's health status, abilities and inventory. However, in pen & pencil RPGs, the character sheet is more than a static representation of abilities and resources; it can also contain information about the PC's personal history, background and alliances. In many cases, players record non-player characters (NPCs) their PCs come in contact with during the course of the game. They record the names of these NPCs, the location where they were first introduced into the game, their relationship to the PC and their connection to other parties in the game setting. Essentially, the character sheet provides a point of origin for a player's orientation to the gaming world. It represents the introduction of the character into the setting, the character's origins, motivations and overall goals. It can document the PC's accomplishments and relationships to other PCs and NPCs. Most important, however, is it provides a personal description of the PC that represents the entirety of that character. It is the summation of the PC's physical, mental and social capabilities – and even his or her moral and ethical alignment in the game world – and provides players with the essential, performative foundation from which they interpret and perform that character.

The idea behind using a character sheet in class is to provide students with an opportunity to construct, examine and discuss a representation of a character or characters – either fictional or actual characters, and in some cases I've asked the students to complete their own character sheet representing themselves. A considerable portion of this section is spent on describing the elements of an RPG character sheet, with a less-significant portion on how I used this concept in class. I've done this intentionally because I feel that a more thorough treatment of the concept will allow the reader to understand how to incorporate this idea into their lesson plans on "their own terms." Introducing new elements to the classroom requires some careful preparation. Obviously, the teacher must be familiar enough with the idea to be able to describe it to the students. A helpful resource for learning more about RPGs can be online community forums such as those hosted by Wizards of the Coast, a subsidiary of Hasbro and owners of the *Dungeons & Dragons* license (community.wizards.com/) and Paizo, who publish the *Pathfinder* RPG (http://paizo.com/paizo/messageboards). Another resource is the System Reference Document (SRD), a set of roleplaying content created and distributed in open-license format by Wizards of the Coast. RPG enthusiasts have created a number of sites using the SRD (www.d20srd.org, dndsrd.net) as they modify their existing, and create new, RPGs. A basic understanding of RPGs and how they are played is important in ensuring that the inclusion of RPG elements in the classroom are relevant, appropriate and create opportunities for meaningful, educational experiences.

The character sheets I gave my students were comprised of five sections: Character description, Abilities, Skills, Feats and Background. I chose these sections because these are the typical categories found in most RPG character sheets and because I thought they would provide an interesting way for students to examine and think about real-world figures or construct fictional characters.

Abilities

The following are the six abilities typically used in RPGs:
– Strength: Physical power
– Dexterity: Agility, reflexes and balance
– Constitution: Health and stamina
– Intelligence: Capacity for learning and reason
– Wisdom: Willpower, common-sense and intuition
– Charisma: Force of personality – leadership, persuasiveness and possibly physical attractiveness

Initially, I relied on my experience in playing pen and pencil RPGs in setting parameters for the students. For example, traditionally *Dungeons & Dragons* has used a range of 3 – 18 (numbers usually generated by rolling sets of 6-sided dice) to establish a character's ability scores and I used these rules as a foundation for character creation with my students. However, we did not randomly roll dice to set the ability scores. Rather, students assigned their own ability scores on their sheet.

Skills

Skills represent a player character's ability to complete a task or resolve conflict without necessarily resorting to combat. The introduction and subsequent emphasis on skills is one of the most notable shifts in the design of RPGs. Typical skills that are relevant to using a character sheet in the classroom might include Diplomacy, Sense Motive, Knowledge (which includes a number of categories such as history, religion, etc.) and Profession. In game, the level of skill a character might possess is determined by a PC's relevant ability score, experience level and training. However, for the classroom, I found it useful to use categories such as Beginner, Intermediate, Advanced and Expert. My students and I also worked together in creating new skills categories that were appropriate to our setting. For example, when creating their own character sheets, my students and I included skills such as "cooking," "computers," and "sports (including a number of categories such as football, cheerleading, etc.)."

Feats

In RPGs, feats typically represent a special quality a character possesses or an enhanced ability to complete a task. A feat is typically associated with combat or skill resolution. However, in the classroom, I used this as an opportunity for students to either discuss special achievements or qualities their character might possess. For example, in completing a character sheet for Dr. Martin Luther King, a student might create a feat called "mighty orator" to represent Dr. King's talent for inspiring others. Feats also provide opportunities for students to express what they believe are special qualities they possess. In completing their own sheets, some of my students chose feats such as "critical thinker" and "resilient spirit." They also included accomplishments, some light-hearted and some more serious, such as "trampoline master" from a student who was a gymnast and "toughness" from a student who was battling cancer.

Background

This section includes a historical synopsis of a real-world figure (including the student) or a fictional character and includes an origin story, important accomplishments, strengths and weaknesses, motivating factors and possibly even a discussion of the moral/ethical orientation of the character.

CONSTRUCTION, DECONSTRUCTION AND PERFORMANCE

As a teacher, I asked students to create their own character sheets where they would recreate themselves using the guidelines I mentioned above. Reading these character sheets enabled me to learn more about my students and who they were outside of the classroom. Later that semester, my students were asked to read Steinbeck's *Of Mice and Men* in their English class. Many of the students mentioned their assignments in class and were frustrated by being "forced" to read the book. They also complained regularly about writing chapter synopses and worksheets. I used the character sheet from my class in helping students to deconstruct the characters in the text and then reconstruct them. Once the character sheets were developed, I suggested the student then perform the characters in scenes found in the book. The critical dimension came into play when the students and I incorporated practices that examined elements such as power, institutions and representations in the text and reflected on how such elements exist in the "real world." Apart from the actual formatting of the character sheets, as the technology teacher, the interpretation and portrayal of these characters was not part of my curriculum. However, the experience was rewarding as, through roleplaying *Of Mice and Men*, the students tried to investigate the economic conditions, social interactions and representations and expressions of identity of the characters in the text. Although our experience with performing these texts was limited, I echo Pinaeu's (2005) affirmation that

> When engaging literary texts, performance methodology combines literary criticism with dramatic characterisation ... to the performance practitioner it is a rigorous and systematic exploration-through-enactment of actual and possible lived experiences. (p. 30)

This was my first attempt transitioning from simply creating character sheets to performing the personas described in those documents, which eventually led to including performance as a significant part of my curriculum. Later on, I would ask my students to create character sheets of figures they encountered in their research projects. The students would create character sheets for political figures such as Dr. Martin Luther King and Elizabeth Cady Stanton, as well as celebrities such as Lady Gaga and fictional characters such as Darth Vader from Star Wars and Eric Cartman from South Park. After the students constructed representations of these figures, we would discuss them in class, deconstructing the creation of the characters and asking questions about the choices made in assigning ability scores, skill ranks, feats and the characters' background information. From this exercise, students were given time to consider the variations and contradictions that exist in the presentation of historical and popular figures and how to begin to question the discourses that arrange and promote such presentations.

These were the first steps in our investigation of an RPG-based critical performance pedagogy that involved texts students selected, and I encourage teachers who enjoy incorporating play, performance and critical perspectives into their classroom to consider an approach to education that Pinaeu (2005) describes as

> inherently, and exhilaratingly, countercultural at both the pedagogical and theoretical levels. The common practices of performance studies classrooms are often exemplars of critical pedagogy (p. 30)

as they experiment and expand on the suggestions listed above in developing effective and emancipative learning environments and critical literacy practices for them and their students.

CONCLUSION

An RPG-based critical performance pedagogy is an attempt to create opportunities for critical inquiry and the development of critical literacy skills through the interpretation and analysis of texts, including the "great books" of the Western canon, as well as popular texts erupting from the everyday lives of students, through a performative, performance-based model of inquiry. The goal is to enable students and teachers to develop the critical, analytical aplomb necessary to inform and infuse their action as agents of positive, social change in the world. The method through which this goal is achieved can be described as playful, and sometimes the performers are even described as "jokers" or "tricksters." However, as Conquergood(1989) reminds us, these should be characteristics should be understood as empowering and liberating terms in that in

> playing with the social order, unsettling certainties, the trickster intensifies awareness of the vulnerability of our institutions. The trickster's playful impulse promotes a radical self-questioning critique that yields a deeper self-knowledge, the first step toward transformation. (p. 85)

Although the method is playful, the purpose and goals of a critical performance pedagogy are seriously committed to enabling students and teachers to act as empowered agents who strive to authentically know, interpret and act upon the positive transformation of the conditions of their everyday lived experiences.

REFERENCES

Avis, J. & Bathmaker, A. (2004). Critical pedagogy, performativity and a politics of hope: Trainee further education lecturer practice. *Research in Post-Compulsory Education, 9*(2), 301-316.
Boal, A. (1974). *Theatre of the oppressed*. London, UK: Pluto.
Butler, J. (1939). *Bodies that matter: On the discursive limits of sex*. New York, NY: Routledge.
Carlson, M. (1996). *Performance: A critical introduction*. London,UK: Routledge.
CBC Digital Archives. (2014). *Is Dungeons & Dragons dangerous?* 60 Minutes. New York. Columbia Broadcasting System. Retrieved from http://www.cbc.ca/archives/categories/lifestyle/leisure/leisure-general/is-dungeons-and-dragons-dangerous.html

Chick, J. (2013). *Dark dungeons.* Retrieved from http://www.chick.com/reading/tracts/0046/0046_01.ASP

Conquergood, D. (1985). Performing as a moral act: Ethical dimensions of ethnography of performance. *Literature in Performance, 5,* 1-13.

Conquergood, D. (1989). Poetics, play, process and power: The performance turn in anthropology. *Text and Performance Quarterly, 9,* 82-88.

Denzin, N.K. (2003). *Performance ethnography: Critical pedagogy and the politics of culture.* Thousand Oaks, CA: Sage.

Elliott, D. (2007). Puerto Rico: A site of critical performative pedagogy. *Action, Criticism, and Theory for Music Education, 6*(1). Retrieved from http://www.maydaygroup.org/ACT/v6n1/Elliott6_1.pdf

Francis, R. (2006). *Towards a theory of a games based pedagogy.* Paper presented at Innovating E-learning 2006: Transforming Learning Experiences. JISC online. Retrieved from http://www.academia.edu /428776/Towards_Theory_of_a_Games-Based_Pedagogy

Freire, P. (1985). *The politics of education: Culture, power, and liberation* (D. Macedo, Trans.). South Hadley, MA: Bergin & Garvey.

Freire, P. (2006). *Pedagogy of the oppressed: The thirtieth anniversary edition.* New York, NY: The Continuum International Publishing Group Inc.

Gee, J. P. (2003). *What video games can teach us about literacy and learning.* New York, NY: Palgrave-McMillan.

Giroux, H., & Shannon, P. (Eds). (1997). *Education and cultural studies: Toward a performative practice.* New York, NY: Routledge.

Guest, A. (Writer), & Russo, J. (Director). (2011). Advanced dungeons & dragons. In D. Harmon (Producer), *Community.* Los Angeles, CA: National Broadcasting Corporation.

Gygax, G. (1979). *Advanced dungeons & dragons dungeon masters guide.* Lake Geneva, WI: TSR Inc.

Harman, R., & French, K. (2004). Critical performative pedagogy: A feasible praxis for teacher education. In J. O'Donnell, M. Pruyn, & C. Chávez (Eds.), *Social justice in these times* (pp. 97-115). Charlotte, NC: Information Age Publishing.

Harman, R., & McClure, G. (2011). All the school's a stage: Critical performative pedagogy in urban teacher education. *Equity & Excellence in Education, 44*(3), 379-402.

Jenkins, H. (2013). *Confronting the challenges of participatory culture: Media education for the 21st century.* White paper manuscript, New Media Literacies, University of Southern California, University of Southern California, Los Angeles, CA, Retrieved from http://digitallearning.macfound.org/atf/cf/{7E45C7E0-A3E0-4B89-AC9C-E807E1B0AE4E}/JENKINS_WHITE_PAPER.PDF

Lorre, C., Kaplan, K., & Holland, S. (Writers), Cendrowski, M. (Director). (2012). The Santa simulation. In C. Lorre & B. Prady (Producers), *The big bang theory.* Los Angeles, CA: Columbia Broadcasting System.

Mathison, M. (1982). *E.T. The extra-terrestrial.* Retrieved from http://screenplayexplorer.com/wp-content/scripts/E.T.pdf.

Pineau, E. (2002). Critical performative pedagogy. In N. Stucky & C. Wimmer (Eds.), *Teaching performance studies* (pp. 41-54). Carbondale, IL: Southern Illinois University Press.

Pineau, E. (2005). Teaching is performance: Reconceptualizing a problematic metaphor. In B. Alexander, G. Anderson, & B. Gallegos (Eds.), *Performance theories in education: Power, pedagogy and the politics of identity* (pp. 15-40). London: Lawrence Erlbaum Associates Publishing.

Quantz, R. (2009). *Interpretive discourses.* Unpublished essay.

Schwarz, G. (2010). Graphic novels. *Curriculum and Teaching Dialogue, 12,* 53.

Shapiro, S. and Leopold, L. (2012) A critical role for role-playing pedagogy. *TESL Canada Journal. 29*(2), 121-130.

Smith, K. (2013). Covert critique: Critical pedagogy 'under the radar' in a suburban middle school. *International Journal of Critical Pedagogy, 4*(2), 127-146.

Thomas, A. A. (2006). Fan Fiction online: Engagement, critical response and affective play through writing. *Australian Journal of Language and Literacy, 29*(3), 226-239.

Waldron, D. (2005). *Role-playing games and the Christian right: Community formation in response to a moral panic*. Retrieved from http://ptgptb.org/0025/moral.html

Wizards of the Coast. (2004). *30 years of adventure: Celebrating Dungeons & Dragons*. Renton, WA: Wizards of the Coast.

ABOUT THE CONTRIBUTORS

Tim Barko is a Doctoral Candidate at the School of Teaching and Learning at the University of Florida, Gainesville, FL.

Tobie Bass is a Doctoral Student in the Department of Language and Literacy Education at The University of Georgia, Athens, GA.

Christopher Andrew Brkich is an Educational Consultant and former Instructor in the Department of Teaching and Learning at Georgia Southern University, Statesboro, GA.

Katie Lynn Brkich is an Assistant Professor in the Department of Teaching and Learning at Georgia Southern University, Statesboro, GA.

Cara Crandall is a Doctoral Candidate at the University of Massachusetts Amherst, Amherst, MA.

Matt Hicks is an English Teacher at Cedar Shoals High School, Athens, GA.

Denise Ives is an Associate Professor of Language, Literacy, and Culture at the University of Massachusetts Amherst, Amherst, MA.

Lindy L. Johnson is an Assistant Professor in the School of Education at The College of William and Mary, Williamsburg, VA.

Tricia M. Kress is an Associate Professor in the Leadership in Education Program, College of Education and Human Development at the University of Massachusetts Boston, Boston, MA.

Robert Lake is an Associate Professor at Georgia Southern University in Statesboro, GA.

Megan C. Marshall is a Doctoral Candidate in the College of Education at the University of Wyoming, Laramie, WY.

Heather Matthews is a Master's Student in the Department of Education at the State University of New York at Binghamton, Binghamton, NY.

Justin Patch is an Instructor, in the Music Department at Vassar College, Poughkeepsie, NY.

Patricia Patrissy is a Librarian at St. Jean Baptiste High School, New York, NY.

ABOUT THE CONTRIBUTORS

Patricia Paugh is an Associate Professor in the Department of Curriculum & Instruction, College of Education and Human Development at the University of Massachusetts Boston, Boston, MA.

Tonya B. Perry is the Project Director and PI of the UAB Red Mountain Writing Project, Birmingham, AL and an Associate Professor in the School of Education at the University of Alabama at Birmingham, Birmingham, AL.

William M. Reynolds teaches Foundations and Curriculum Studies at Georgia Southern University, Statesboro, GA.

Laura Rychly is an Assistant Professor at Georgia Regents University in Augusta, GA.

Kevin Smith is a Research Associate with The Wales Institute for Social and Economic Research, Data & Methods (WISERD) at Cardiff University, Cardiff, Wales, UK.

Amber M. Simmons is a High School Teacher in Gwinnett County, Georgia and an Adjunct Professor at Mercer University, Macon GA.

P.L. Thomas is an Associate Professor of Education and Faculty Director of First Year Seminars at Furman University, Greenville, SC.

Kjersti VanSlyke-Briggs is an Associate Professor of Secondary Education at State University of New York Oneonta, Oneonta, NY.

CPSIA information can be obtained at www.ICGtesting.com
Printed in the USA
BVOW02s1912091114

374375BV00001B/10/P

9 789462 098732